Publication of this book was sponsored by the American Association for State and Local History, Madison, Wisconsin, under its continuing program to promote a better understanding of our national heritage at a local level.

IMMIGRANT CITY
Lawrence, Massachusetts, 1845-1921

by

DONALD B. COLE

Chapel Hill

THE UNIVERSITY OF NORTH CAROLINA PRESS

For

Tootie

Foreword

Lack of space has forced general accounts of American history to ignore most cities and mention the others only in connection with some specific event. Generations of Americans, therefore, have grown up thinking of cities in terms of labels and inaccurate stereotypes. Hartford is inevitably the site of the Hartford Convention, but readers are rarely aware of its more durable role as the insurance center of America. Although writers invariably connect Atlanta with Sherman's march to the sea, they almost never explain its great contribution to the rise of the new south after the Civil War. New Bedford is portrayed as a whaling city, while its vital part in American industrial and immigration history is neglected.

So it has been with Lawrence, which appears only because it was the scene of the I.W.W. textile strike of 1912. Terms such as immigrant, labor union, and radicalism have established the image of Lawrence as a slum-ridden city filled with poor immigrant revolutionaries. And since Lawrence is often one of the few immigrant cities that are even mentioned, the reader's mind soon leaps to the more dangerous assumption that all immigrants were poverty-stricken and un-American. This work proposes to find the truth about Lawrence and in the process to discover much about the immigrant in urban America.

Until recently, immigrant studies approached the subject principally from the point of view of this country. As early as the American Revolution, Hector St. John de Crèvecoeur was describing the effect of the melting pot on the formation of American nationality. Countless authors followed with glowing accounts of the opportunities that America offered to the poor of Europe. Even when writers began to describe the terrible living conditions of the immigrants in eastern cities, they were more concerned with the impact of these slums on the United States than on what they meant to the new arrival. The work of Marcus Hansen and Oscar Handlin shifted the attention from this country to the immigrant and introduced the problem of immigrant acculturation. But while there have been some recent studies of immigrant cities, none has been carried on down through the great middle period of American immigration history from the Irish potato famine in 1846 to the quota law of 1921. Lawrence has proved an ideal city for such a project. Founded in 1845 as a textile city, its population was so heavily foreign-born that, by 1910, 90 per cent of its people were either first- or second-generation Americans, representing almost every country in the world.

Immigrant City begins with an account of the city as it appeared to most native Americans during the strike of 1912—a notorious, penniless, un-American slum. Then follows a narrative of the city's history from 1845 to 1912, which puts the strike in its proper perspective. Throughout this narrative one theme keeps recurring—the immigrant's constant search for security in the new world—and consequently the next section is devoted to finding whether the immigrant, from his own point of view, was able to find security. Only after these steps have been taken, does the book return to 1912, and by that time the true meaning of the strike and the city is clear. In sum, *Immigrant City* attempts to determine whether or not the immigrant found the security for which he was looking and whether he was able to become an American. If he succeeded in these two quests, then life for the foreign-born in America was not as grim as some authors have suggested.

Originally the work was a doctoral dissertation at Harvard under Professor Handlin, but since then it has been completely revised and the documentation drastically reduced. Anyone interested in more tables and more statistics may consult the dissertation copy in the archives of the Harvard College Library. The first two chapters of the dissertation appeared in the October, 1956, issue of the *Essex Institute Historical Collections*.

The study proved to the author's satisfaction that no immigrant was on his own in America and his research convinced him that no writer does anything alone either. I owe a debt to many, especially Phillips E. Wilson, John B. Heath, and David Tyack, who read portions of the manuscript, George Abdo, who translated issues for three years of an Arabic newspaper, and Edwin Fenton, who was more than generous with materials from Italian newspapers and interviews on the Lawrence strike. Two leaves of absence from the Phillips Exeter Academy made the research and writing possible. The librarians at Widener, Baker, and Littauer libraries at Harvard, the Massachusetts State Library, the Massachusetts Historical Society, the Boston Public Library, the Essex Institute, and the Lawrence Public Library were unstinting in their aid. Publication of this book was assisted by a grant from the American Association for State and Local History, under the terms of its annual manuscript competition. I am much indebted to the staff of The University of North Carolina Press for its careful work in publishing the book. Like so many scholars in the field of immigration the author received most of his inspiration and guidance from Oscar Handlin.

The book is dedicated to my wife Tootie, who did the more important job of bringing up a growing family while the research and writing went on.

DONALD B. COLE

Exeter, New Hampshire
December, 1962

Contents

Maps

IMMIGRANT CITY
Lawrence, Massachusetts, 1845-1921

CHAPTER I

The Notorious City, 1912

"Victory is in sight. The working class will back you up to a finish in your fight against peonage and starvation. The slave pens of Lawrence, . . . are a disgrace to American manhood." So wrote Eugene Debs as he sought to encourage the leaders of the Lawrence textile strike in the winter of 1912. "The civilization of the Old Bay State is on trial," contended the *Brooklyn Eagle.* Bill Haywood, leader of the Industrial Workers of the World, who barely had been acquitted from implication in the murder of Governor Steunenberg of Idaho, came to take over the strike. Lincoln Steffens, Samuel Gompers, and Victor Berger watched closely from the sidelines, for "peaceful Lawrence" was "now riot-ridden." For two months the story of the Lawrence strike dominated the front page of *The New York Times* and all the Boston newspapers. When the I.W.W. newspaper *Solidarity* offered a special edition devoted to Lawrence, the public bought a record-breaking 12,000 copies. Faneuil Hall, long familiar with revolutionary gatherings, and Carnegie Hall both echoed to the shouts of strident meetings called to raise money for the Lawrence strikers. At Carnegie Hall, Haywood broke into a debate between the anarchist Emma Goldman and the socialist Sol Fieldman to plead for funds. The audience, deeply moved, hurled a torrent of coins and bills onto the floor of the stage. And after the strike was over, interest continued. When the United States Labor Commission issued a report on the strike, copies were so much in demand that they were soon "hard to come by."[1]

1. "The Lawrence Strike: A Poll of the Press," *The Outlook,* C (1912), 357; *The New York Times,* Jan. 13-Mar. 31, 1912; *Boston Evening Transcript,* Jan. 12-Mar. 8, 1912, especially Jan. 12, Feb. 3, 13, 1912; *Solidarity,* Mar. 9, 1912;

The Lawrence strike of January and February, 1912, took 30,000 workers away from their jobs in the cotton and woolen mills. Since Lawrence was the largest worsted center in the world and the headquarters of the enormous American Woolen Company, the strike was bound to affect the entire textile industry of the United States. The public saw it as a clash between the radical forces of labor and the reactionary agents of big business. Bill Haywood and Joe Ettor, the latter a board member of the I.W.W. and the original leader of the Lawrence strike, typified the labor agitators; Billy Wood, President of the American Woolen Company, stood for the robber barons. The press confirmed these attitudes with lurid stories of the workers' brutal violence and descriptions of the horrible living conditions thrust on them by the mill owners. The *Times* deplored the destruction of mill equipment in a lead editorial titled "Smash the Machinery," but it sympathized with the pitiful life of the poor in an article called "High Rents behind Lawrence Strike." While the radical press defended the "exploited mill workers" and said "Soldiers Bayonet Hungry Strikers," the conservative publications called the "reign of terror" of the I.W.W. "our country's greatest danger."[2]

When Ettor and the socialist poet Arturo Giovannitti were indicted for murder, the story of Lawrence carried even across the sea. Italian newspapers gave it complete coverage. Italian socialists, led by Giovannitti's brother, Aristide, considered a general strike and sent a telegram to President Taft. After *La Scintilla* of Ferrara took up the case and meetings were held in Cerveteri and Spezia, the Italian Chamber of Deputies felt obliged to discuss it. All major cities had sections of the Ettor-Giovannitti Defense Committee, and special assemblies met in Florence and Rome. Demonstrations took place also in Trafalgar Square, Budapest, and Berne.[3]

Charles P. Neill, *Report on Strike of Textile Workers in Lawrence, Mass. in 1912,* 62 Congress, 2 Session, Senate Doc. 870 (Washington, 1912).

2. *Times,* Jan. 26, 30, Feb. 1, 1912; *The New York Call,* Jan. 13, 16, 1912; Robert W. Beers, *Our Country's Greatest Danger* (Lawrence, 1912); Citizens' Association, Lawrence, Mass., *A Reign of Terror in an American City* (Lawrence, 1912).

3. *L'Araldo Italiano,* May 31, June 20, July 20, Sept. 12, Oct. 1-2, Dec. 8, 14, 30, 1912, kindness of Edwin Fenton. Professor Fenton has written his doctoral dissertation on Italian immigrants in American labor organizations in northeastern United States for Harvard.

Coming at the height of the Progressive movement, the strike attracted all types of social workers, who came "by the carload" to see at first hand the conditions in the Lawrence tenements. While some merely looked, others raised money and set up soup kitchens, and many wrote and spoke. Among the clergy there was much disagreement. Harry Emerson Fosdick said the workers were treated like "dumb cattle" and lived in tenements "vile beyond description," while T. C. Cleveland, an Episcopal rector from Boston, condemned the great wealth of the owners. At the same time, two other Boston ministers preached sermons supporting the owners, and the Boston Ministers Association would not even vote on a resolution favoring the workers. But Reverend Adolf Berle of Tufts College summarized the attitude of most when he declaimed, "Somebody is doing a satanic wrong."[4]

Among the muckraking magazines *The Survey* and *The Outlook* were the most thorough and objective. Mary Heaton Vorse in *Harper's Weekly* pictured halls filled with garbage. Al Priddy in *The Outlook* compared the workers with harmless children. "Imagine," he said, "a group of children—who love pageantry and martial noise. . . . They shouted as children would shout and sang. . . . It was just the outflow of children's spirits bent on nothing more than an afternoon's recreation—a parade."[5] One day alone brought four prominent liberals from Boston: Max Mitchell, President of Jewish Charities; Dudley Holman, secretary to Governor Foss; Vernon Briggs of the commission for alien insane; and Frank Carter, a banker. The arrival of Mrs. William Howard Taft and Mrs. Gifford Pinchot symbolized the hold the Lawrence strike had on those prominent in the Progressive era.[6]

But the conservatives did not sympathize with the workers. "Never in any American City," said John N. Cole, former Speaker of the Massachusetts House of Representatives, "have I seen a better

4. Harry E. Fosdick, "After the Strike—in Lawrence," *The Outlook*, CI (1912), 343-44; *Boston Evening Transcript*, Jan. 22-23, Feb. 5, 1912.
5. Mary Heaton Vorse, "The Trouble in Lawrence," *Harper's Weekly*, LVI (1912), 10; Richard Child, "Who's Violent?" *Collier's Weekly*, XLIX (1912), 12-13; Al Priddy, "Controlling the Passions of Men—in Lawrence," *The Outlook*, CII (1912), 343; *The Survey*, XXVII (1912), 1, 771-72, 774; XXVIII (1912), 72-80, 693-94; *The Outlook*, C (1912), 151-52, 309-12, 356-58, 385-86, 405-6, 531-36; CI (1912), 340-46; CII (1912), 343-45; CIV (1913), 351-52.
6. *Boston Evening Transcript*, Jan. 17, Feb. 26, 1912.

dressed gathering of operatives, men and women, than will be found in . . . Lawrence." Even if the laborers' pay "was many times what it is they unquestionably would prefer to live as they do," announced another defender of the owners. William Wood and William Whitman, President of the Arlington Mill, asserted that they paid as much as they could—more than other industries —and that the immutable law of supply and demand decided such matters anyway. Winthrop L. Marvin expressed what the others thought when he denounced the strike as socialist-inspired. Such arguments were but a prelude to those uttered during the summer and fall by the candidates of the "New Freedom," the "New Nationalism," and the "Old Guard," in the presidential campaign.[7]

Equally intense was the fighting between the two major labor unions in Lawrence. After years of trying to organize the textile workers of the city, the American Federation of Labor was furious to see a strike led by its bitter rival, the Industrial Workers of the World. After some indecision, John Golden, President of the A.F.L. United Textile Workers of America, finally intervened in the strike, but only to bring about a compromise. Lincoln Steffens, who defended Golden, called him the "bête noire" of the I.W.W. In a flamboyant article entitled "Strawberries and Spaghetti," the A.F.L. journal *The Textile Worker* attacked Ettor and Giovannitti for eating better than the strikers and running up a bill of $42 for a dinner at Boehm's Cafe. Unaware that the I.W.W. was but a momentary phase in the American labor scene, the A.F.L. believed it was facing a serious challenge to its leadership among the workers.[8]

The I.W.W., equally shortsighted, considered the Lawrence strike an important step toward its eventual control of American labor. Haywood prompted the Industrial Workers of the World to abolish the wage system and build industrial unionism in the United States. The "Wobblies" for a time included socialists such as Eugene Debs, members of the Socialist Labor party of

7. John N. Cole, "The Issue at Lawrence," *The Outlook,* C (1912), 405; Walter M. Pratt, "The Lawrence Revolution," *New England Magazine,* XLVI (1912), 8; *Boston Evening Transcript,* Jan. 20, Feb. 1, 1912; William Whitman and others, "Why Are Wages Not Higher in the Textile Industries?" *Boston Sunday Globe,* Jan. 28, 1912.

8. *Boston Evening Transcript,* Jan. 16, Feb. 5-8, 1912; *Solidarity,* Mar. 30, 1912; "Strawberries and Spaghetti," *The Textile Worker,* I (1912), 17-18.

Daniel DeLeon, and anarchists like Emma Goldman. Many feared that Haywood, having thrown the western mines into a turmoil, would now upset the textile world. No one realized that the Lawrence and Paterson strikes of 1912 would be his high water mark and that violence in these strikes would prompt the Socialist Executive Board to leave the I.W.W.

When a group of Italian workers sent for Joseph Ettor to head the Lawrence strike, it meant that the I.W.W. would not have to force its way into the city. It had been invited. During the strike the I.W.W. brought its case before the American people. Even though its weekly newspaper, *Solidarity,* circulated mostly among an already sympathetic audience, it did at least put the I.W.W. side of the strike in print. It accused the A.F.L. textile union, led by the "Golden Clique," of encouraging men not to strike and of engaging in "craft union scabbery." The workers' children, in this unorganized city, said *Solidarity,* were born undernourished. Mary K. O'Sullivan, who gave bail for Ettor and Giovannitti, brought the attack on the A.F.L. to a wider audience through her article in *The Survey.* Only a few months after the strike was over, Justus Ebert wrote the definitive I.W.W. account of the strike called *The Trial of a New Society.*[9]

Although the socialists cooperated with the I.W.W., they had different motives. Instead of trying to control the workers in an industry, they were intent on showing the failure of private ownership. In Lawrence, pale, courteous, trembling Arturo Giovannitti, poet-editor of the New York Italian Socialist newspaper *Il Proletario* and National Secretary of the Italian Socialist Federation, spread the doctrines of socialism in both Italian and English; while in New York, *The Weekly People* said the evil capitalists of Lawrence were using state troops to try to break up the strike. Selected for particular scorn were John Golden, "The militia-of-Christer strike-breaker"; Colonel Sweetser, "would-be dictator" of the state troops; and William Wood. Even more lurid was *The New York Call,* which proclaimed that the owners were "howling for more troops to shoot down hungry workers," in what *Il Proletario* labeled

9. *Solidarity,* Jan.-April, Sept.-Oct., 1912; Mary K. O'Sullivan, "The Labor War at Lawrence," *The Survey,* XXVIII (1912), 72-74; Justus Ebert, *The Trial of a New Society* (Cleveland, 1913).

"Another Great Working Class Revolution." Also in New York, Walter E. Weyl, soon to be associate editor of the *New Republic*, called the owners' wage cut a "ruthless ill-advised proceeding" because wages were already "indecently low." Victor Berger, the first Socialist Congressman, demanded a federal investigation of the strike as well as executive action from President Taft. And Lena Morrow Lewis, national organizer of the Socialist party, came all the way from San Francisco to see the troubles of capitalism first hand. Such Socialist vigor presaged the great success of Eugene Debs in November.[10]

The Democratic party also planned to turn the Lawrence strike to its advantage, not by attacking capitalists, but by condemning the lavish tariff protection granted them by the Republican party. Whitman, Wood, and Marvin were all protectionists. Whitman wrote the section of the Payne-Aldrich Tariff dealing with textiles, and Marvin maintained that wage increases depended upon higher tariffs. The Democrats, consequently, used the strike to show that the tariff might have fattened stockholders but had not raised the standard of living of the Lawrence workers. Aware of the tariff dispute within the Republican ranks, they were delighted when Progressive Republican Senator Poindexter of Washington pointed out the "fallacy of an excessive tariff" after visiting the slums of Lawrence. Democratic Governor Foss of Massachusetts, eager for his party's presidential nomination, called for investigation of the strike to determine how much protection the workers received from tariff laws "designed, and only justified, on the ground that they protect[ed] and elevate[d] American labor." When John Martin of the New York City Board of Education came away from Lawrence, he said: "Truly, anybody who has seen the underfed, ill-clad stunted masses in Lawrence must laugh aloud at the argument that a high tariff protects labor in America against the pauper labor of Europe." The Lawrence strike helped lead

10. *Boston Evening Transcript*, Jan. 19, 26, 1912; "The Social Significance of Arturo Giovannitti," *Current Opinion*, LIV (1913), 24-26; *The Weekly People* (New York), Jan. 27, Feb. 3, 10, 17, 24, Mar. 2, 1912; *The New York Call*, Jan. 20, 27, 1912; *Il Proletario*, Jan. 19, 1912, kindness of Professor Fenton; Walter E. Weyl, "The Strikers in Lawrence," *The Outlook*, C (1912), 309; *The Strike at Lawrence, Mass. Hearings before the Committee on Rules of the House of Representatives . . . 1912*, 62 Congress, 2 Session, House Doc. 671 (Washington, 1912).

America from Payne-Aldrich protection in 1910 to Underwood-Simmons reduction in 1913.[11]

The strike was instrumental also in the adoption of the literacy test for restricting immigration. For many years the Immigration Restriction League, dominated by Brahmin Bostonians, had fought for a change in American immigration policy. Fearful that the United States could no longer assimilate the poor illiterates of southeastern Europe, the League urged severe restrictions. In 1907 it succeeded in getting Theodore Roosevelt to appoint an Immigration Commission to study the condition of immigrants in America. Since the commission included Senators Henry Cabot Lodge and William Paul Dillingham and industrial expert Jeremiah Jencks, all ardent restrictionists, the eventual tenor of the report was predictable. Dillingham went on from the commission to introduce the quota law of 1921. Jencks was the author of the forty-one-volume report of the Commission in 1911. Although it failed to prove that southeastern Europeans were any more criminal or impoverished than other immigrants, the report assumed their inferiority and resorted to racist terminology. It ended by advocating the literacy test. Jencks and Jett Lauck, who was in charge of the investigation of immigrants in industry for the commission, wrote a popular version of the report entitled *The Immigration Problem*, which further spread the ideas of the Immigration Restriction League.[12]

The squalor of the Lawrence slums, the violence of the Italians, and the anarchistic leadership of the strike only a few months after the report naturally helped the league. Every time an immigrant threw ice at windows, displayed a dirk, or denounced capitalism, restriction was closer. Ironically enough, Lawrence had already done its part because it had been the worsted goods city studied for the report. Lauck himself in the *North American Review* tied the strike to the restriction movement. Since the American mill workers, according to Lauck, faced unfair competition from the

11. Whitman and others, "Why Are Wages Not Higher?"; "The Lawrence Strike Children," *The Literary Digest*, XLIV (1912), 472; *Boston Evening Transcript*, Jan. 25, Feb. 14, 1912; John Martin, "The Industrial Revolt at Lawrence," *The Independent*, LXXII (1912), 491-95; *Harper's Weekly*, Feb. 10, 1912, p. 4.
12. Barbara Solomon, *Ancestors and Immigrants* (Cambridge, Mass., 1956), pp. 197-202; Immigration Commission, *Reports*, 41 vols., 61 Congress, 2 Session, Doc. 633 (Washington, 1911).

"dumb, easily led, illiterate" southeastern Europeans, the government should keep the Europeans out. "We pauperize American labor," said D. M. Holman, secretary to Governor Foss, "by forcing it to work down to the level of the incompetent pauper labor which we bring in from Europe. . . ." Even men who had long stood for free immigration were scared by the strike, men such as John Graham Brooks, who asked: "What have we done that a pack of ignorant foreigners should hold us by the throat?" Only John N. Cole, staunch supporter of the American Woolen Company and close friend of Billy Wood, defended immigration. He argued that the woolen industry needed the labor and that assimilation was easy. It was ironic that Cole, representing nine generations in Essex County, should have favored immigration.[13]

As the close of the strike faded into World War I, prejudice ran even higher. Madison Grant in 1914 published the classic *Passing of the Great Race,* which denied that southeastern Europeans could be assimilated. A year later Jeremiah Jencks said that employers would never raise wages as long as immigrants with low living standards flooded into the country. By 1917 the combination of forces succeeded in securing the literacy test. Four years later the quota law froze American society. The Lawrence strike contributed to both laws.[14]

The restrictionists were particularly interested in Lawrence because it was almost a completely immigrant city. Unlike so many New England mill cities with their colonial backgrounds, Lawrence did not exist before the great immigrant invasions. Established in 1845 by the Essex Company on the sylvan banks of the Merrimack, its population rose by 1855 to 16,000, two-fifths of whom were born abroad, mostly in Ireland. By 1910 the population was 86,000, almost all of whom were either first- or second-generation Americans. Within one mile of the mills there were immigrants

13. Immigration Commission, "Woolen and Worsted Goods in Representative Community A," *Immigrants in Industries, Part 4: Woolen and Worsted Goods Manufacturing,* II, Immigration Commission, *Reports,* X (Washington, 1911); W. Jett Lauck, "The Lesson from Lawrence," *North American Review,* CXCV, Pt. 2 (1912), 665-72; Lorin F. Deland, "The Lawrence Strike: A Study," *Atlantic Monthly,* CIX (1912), 698; *Boston Evening Transcript,* Jan. 25, 31, Feb. 17, Mar. 8, 1912; Solomon, *Ancestors,* 199.

14. *Ibid.,* pp. 200-1.

representing fifty-one countries and speaking forty-five languages.[15]

The immigrants came in three groups. Before the Civil War, Irish fleeing famine at home settled along the Merrimack to form the city. They continued to come after the war and were joined by French Canadians, English, and Germans. Between 1890 and 1912 the earlier immigration slowed as Italians, Austrians, Lithuanians, Poles, and Syrians brought a new flavor to the city. Although they usually lived by themselves, the new immigrants were close enough to the old to permit the exchange of ideas and the growth of friction. Tipperary Irish in the heart of the city mixed with Mount Lebanon Syrians and Sicilian Italians; to the east, Galician Poles and Lithuanians adjoined Silesian or Saxon Germans; while to the west, Vermonters mingled with arrivals from Quebec or Lancashire. Smaller groups such as Scots, Armenians, Portuguese, Franco-Belgians, and Chinese rounded out the immigrant society of Lawrence during the strike.

The proportion of foreign-born to total residents in Lawrence, hovering steadily at the 45 percent mark, was so high that no more than three cities in the United States exceeded it between 1880 and 1900. In Massachusetts, Lawrence was second to Fall River or Holyoke until 1905 and from then on it led the state. The large Irish immigration doubled the population between 1850 and 1855. Invasions after the Civil War raised it by a third again by 1870. The influx of southeastern Europeans added 15,000 between 1905 and 1910.[16] Immigration almost completely controlled the history of the city.

15. In 1910, 74,000 were either first- or second-generation Americans. See Table I. Maurice Dorgan, *History of Lawrence, Mass., with War Records* (Cambridge, Mass., 1924), pp. 11-14, 44, 174; Francis DeWitt, *Abstract of the Census of . . . Massachusetts . . . 1855 . . .* (Boston, 1857), pp. 105, 206; United States Census Bureau, *Thirteenth Census of the United States . . . 1910: Abstract of the Census . . . with Supplement for Massachusetts . . .* (Washington, 1913), pp. 596, 609; *Boston Evening Transcript*, Jan. 12, 1912.

16. See Tables I, II, IV. Lawrence was third of fifty cities in the United States in 1880, fourth of 124 in 1890, third of 161 in 1900. United States Census Office, *Tenth Census of the United States . . . 1880*, I (Washington, 1883), 538; United States Census Office, *Eleventh Census of the United States: 1890*, I (Washington, 1895), cxxvii-cxxviii; United States Census Office, *Twelfth Census of the United States . . . 1900*, I (Washington, 1901), cix, cx. Holyoke was first in Massachusetts (except for 1875) until 1890 and then Fall River until 1905. Lawrence was always second or third. Chief of the Bureau of Statistics of Labor, *Census of . . . Massachusetts 1905* (Boston, 1909), pp. xliii, 678.

To the American immigrant, Lawrence was a prominent city. It was the leading Irish center north of Boston and a thousand Hibernians met there in 1890. That same year over a quarter of the foreign-born in the city were from England and only one city in the United States exceeded that percentage. The French Canadians were so numerous that a convention of Canadian societies from as far away as Chicago and Montreal took place in Lawrence in 1887. Next to Boston it was the largest German city in the state. It had more Syrians than any city in the nation except New York. All over the world hungry people looked to Lawrence with hope.[17]

But to America in 1912 Lawrence was a symbol of notoriety. Not only the indictments of the press but the reports of two federal surveys and one local study painted an unfavorable picture of the city. The Russell Sage Foundation sponsored a study of the city's living conditions in 1911. The report, filled with extremely accurate diagrams of crowded homes and blocks and illustrated by pictures of squalid slums, confirmed the journalists' descriptions. The strike hearings before the House Rules Committee included the lurid testimony of selected immigrants as well as the contrived questions and statements of Victor Berger. And Labor Commissioner Charles Neill, already familiar with Lawrence as a member of the Immigration Commission, corroborated all the other descriptions with his report. Even more damaging was the image of a lawless un-American Lawrence that emerged in the testimony at the Ettor-Giovannitti-Caruso trial after the strike. Although the state failed to prove that Caruso murdered Annie LoPezzi after being incited by Ettor and Giovannitti, the trial severely damaged the reputation of the city and its immigrants.[18] And if this immigrant city were as slum-ridden, diseased, poverty-stricken, lawless, and un-American as people said, then were not all immigrant cities? If the picture of Lawrence in 1912 was accurate, then the

17. *The Evening Tribune*, June 20, 1894; *Eleventh Census . . . 1890*, I, clii; *Sunday Sun*, June 14, 1908; W. Jett Lauck, "The Significance of the Situation at Lawrence: The Condition of the New England Woolen Mill Operative," *The Survey*, XXVII (1912), 1773; *Census of Mass., 1905*, I, 109.

18. Robert E. Todd and Frank B. Sanborn, *The Report of the Lawrence Survey* (Lawrence, 1912); *Strike at Lawrence;* Neill, *Report;* Transcript of the Trial of *Commonwealth* vs. *Joseph Caruso, Joseph J. Ettor, Arturo Giovannitti, alias*, Superior Court, Essex County, Massachusetts, Sept.-Oct., 1912.

millions of immigrants who came to America after 1845 had failed to find any semblance of security and had failed to become Americans.

But the immigrants themselves did not see it that way. Many of the oldtimers could look back half a century or more to the beginnings of Lawrence, when they themselves had met with an unfavorable reception. They realized that as other immigrants came to the city, their own position had improved until now they were tacitly accepted by the natives and had become Americans. The coming of successive waves of immigrants to Lawrence, which we shall call the immigrant cycle, made life easier for those that came first. While prejudice continued, and it was never stronger than in 1912, it was directed against different nationalities. The same oldtimer smiled when he heard the lurid descriptions of life in Lawrence, for he realized that there was more to security in a new world than housing and health alone. After six or seven decades in this immigrant city, he could explain, if he were asked, how the newcomers found security amid the squalor of Lawrence. No native could understand Lawrence in 1912, and no one using his point of view could understand the city even today. But if we imagine ourselves immigrants and transport ourselves back, not to 1912, but to the founding of the city in 1845, then we discover the truth about Lawrence and immigrant life in America. First we shall trace the story of Lawrence down through the years to 1912, unravelling the results of the immigrant cycle. Then we shall explore from the vantage point of the immigrant the many ways in which he found security. Only when we have completed these steps, shall we return to the Lawrence strike of 1912, but when we do, we shall be able to understand its true meaning.

Part One

Model Town to Immigrant City, 1845-1912

CHAPTER II

Model Town, 1845-1850

At the beginning of the nineteenth century a traveller leaving Boston for Concord, New Hampshire, would walk north on the Essex Turnpike, and after an all day journey would cross low hills into the Merrimack Valley and reach Andover Square. Here he could stay at Locke's Tavern, stop at a private home, or camp out. The three-mile walk to the Merrimack the next morning would be easy because it was downhill and pleasant, following the meandering Shawsheen River. The turnpike crossed the Merrimack near Deer Jump Falls, where the river moved swiftly and powerfully, dropping twenty-six feet in a short distance. Since the bridge was frequently washed away, the traveller often went up or downstream a few hundred yards to a ford. Once across he soon passed an old county road connecting Lowell with Haverhill and then the tiny Spicket (originally "Spigot") River, which emptied several lakes into the Merrimack. Beyond was Methuen and the New Hampshire line, where the Londonderry Pike carried the walker to Concord. Only a few farmers tilled the sandy banks on either side of Deer Jump Falls. Here, halfway between Lowell and Haverhill, a group of Boston merchants in 1845 decided to build Lawrence.

Two of the merchants, Patrick Jackson and Nathan Appleton, had brought the spinning and weaving functions of the American cotton industry together for the first time in Waltham in 1814. The wonderful success of this venture led them eight years later to establish the Merrimack Manufacturing Company in Lowell, which by 1837 had 25 per cent of the cotton spindles in the state. In 1830 they sold stock to several merchants including Abbott Lawrence, who had risen from an obscure farm boy in Groton to one

Map I

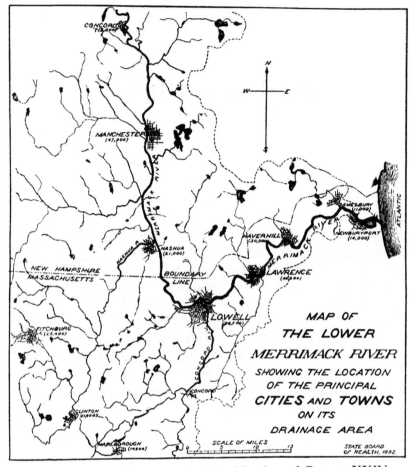

Source: Massachusetts Board of Health, *Annual Report,* XXIV,
Mass. Pub. Doc. 34, p. 668

of the richest businessmen in Boston.   After listening to Daniel
Saunders, who first thought of a dam at Deer Jump Falls, the
triumvirate of Jackson, Appleton, and Lawrence brought in Charles
Storrow, an engineer from Boston, and formed the Essex Company.
Lawrence, president and principal owner, and Storrow, treasurer,
took actual charge of the construction during the next few years.[1]

1. J. F. C. Hayes, *History of the City of Lawrence, Mass.* (Lawrence, 1868),
pp. 9-17.

The mills and dam rose rapidly. "On every side . . . up and down the river . . . [were] piled masses of granite and huge piles of brick, lumber, etc. Dirics [derricks] . . . rose along the river . . . in such profusion as to give the shore the appearance of a small seaport and its swarm of masts." The pride of the new town was its dam, which Charles Bigelow, a former army engineer, completed by 1848. Unlike its counterpart at Holyoke, which collapsed the day it was unveiled, Bigelow's dam stood up under the pounding of water that rushed down at it from the White Mountains and a century later is still an impressive sight. The longest dam on the Merrimack, it was for years one of the longest in the world. As the construction went on, the founders referred to the town as "New Settlement," "Andover Bridge," and "Merrimac"; the public, skeptical of the venture, dubbed it "Saunders' Folly."[2] But when the General Court came to chartering the new town in 1847, it named it for Abbott Lawrence. It was a reasonable decision because the many-sided Lawrence continued to invest money and time in the town that bore his name.

The court formed Lawrence by taking three and a half square miles out of Methuen and two and a half from Andover.[3] South of the Merrimack, Lawrence was a sandy plain with no particular landmarks save the Shawsheen River which made its eastern boundary. To the north, however, a crescent-shaped series of hills sloping down to the sluggish Spicket made half a circle about the marshy plain between the Spicket and the Merrimack. This flat rectangular area with Tower Hill to the west and Prospect Hill to the east was the heart of Lawrence from 1847 to 1912. Here were the mills, the stores, the government, the churches, and the Common, and within this core lived most of the residents, particularly the immigrants. The digging of a canal north of the river turned the southern section of this rectangle into an island covered by mills. North of the canal were several parallel

2. *The Merrimack Courier,* Oct. 17, 1846; F. Morton Smith, *The Essex Company on the Merrimack at Lawrence* (New York, 1947), p. 17; George H. Young, "The City of Lawrence, Massachusetts," *New England Magazine,* New Series, XVII (1897-98), 582-83; United States Worsted Company, *Romance of USWO CO* (New York, 1912).

3. "An Act to Incorporate the Town of Lawrence," MS, Massachusetts Archives, Acts 1847, Ch. 190, House Doc. 136, passed by House, April 9, 1847, and Senate, April 15, 1847.

streets running east and west: Canal and Methuen Streets with
the corporation boarding houses and then Essex and Common
Streets with the early stores. The Lawrence Common came next
and north of that was Haverhill Street, formerly the old county
road, and the Spicket River.

Early pictures show that Lawrence was originally a pleasant
town with trees, grass, wandering animals, and children at play.
Nor were these charms present by mere chance, since the founders
had great interest in the physical appearance of their project. Like
the early Puritans these Boston Brahmins took their responsibilities
seriously and did not want observers to think they had done a poor
job. They planted elms, laid out broad streets, and set aside
many acres for a common and parks.

It never occurred to the founders or observers that anything
unclean could come out of Lawrence. The *Boston Daily Advertiser* was thrilled with "the apparition of the new city of Lawrence,
rising suddenly amidst the most quiet, rural scenery." Because
of this "delightful" location "in the midst of a fertile and highly
cultivated country," the *Merrimack Courier* believed Lawrence
"designed by nature for the lovliest [sic] city in the world." Even
in 1869 a book on the Merrimack closed with this note about
Lawrence: "The desert waste grew green, active busy life dispelled
the unpleasant silence, and the solitary place forthwith resounded
with the cheerful rattle of machinery, the ring of the anvil, the
vigorous strokes of the artisan and mechanic, the whirl and bustle
of trade, and the constant rush of steadily augmenting throngs
where once the few hardy fishermen . . . captured the . . . sal-
mon. . . ." Boston Brahmins were proud that some of their number
put money into such laudable enterprises. William Prescott wrote:
"Under these auspices towns and villages grew up along the borders
of the Merrimac and its numerous tributaries; and the spots which
had once been little better than barren wastes of sand, where the
silence was broken only by the moaning of the wind through the
melancholy pines, became speedily alive with the cheerful hum
of labor."[4]

4. *The Lawrence Courier,* Aug. 21, 1847; *The Merrimack Courier,* Oct. 17,
1846; J. W. Meader, *The Merrimack River* (Boston, 1869); William H. Prescott,
Memoir of the Honorable Abbott Lawrence (N.p., 1856), p. 16.

And as the town grew into a city, it retained its half-rural characteristics. The first immigrants found trips to Crawford House, Profile House, and Flume House in the White Mountains advertised in the *American*. They caught trout a few miles outside the city, gathered wildflowers, picked grapes on Tower Hill, and attended cattle shows. Even after the Civil War the bucolic flavor remained. Excursion trains ran out from Boston on Sunday so that the tired workers of the big city could enjoy the river, dam, and rural pleasures of the small city. Butchers dressed their own steers while farmers planted crops, raised poultry, and milked cows. A bear got loose in 1876, and in 1885 some one shot a muskrat in the Spicket. Here was an environment more rural than in a large city and more urban than on the frontier.

Since the founders planned a model town in these pleasant surroundings, they kept close watch over most of the early homes. Haverhill Street could have only one house per lot and one family per dwelling for the first twenty years. Essex Street was restricted to brick and stone construction with a maximum of three stories and roofs of slate or metal. In addition to the brick boarding houses there were many wooden frame houses between the mills and the Common. East and north of the Common the first settlers built small, well-constructed homes with gardens. The wooden two-family houses on the "plains," an area bounded by the Spicket River and Haverhill, Jackson, and Hampshire Streets, had large slate mansard attics and dry stone cellars. The more affluent owned substantial homes on Haverhill Street or mansions on Prospect and Tower Hills.[5]

Most workers, though, stayed at the corporation boarding houses along Canal and Methuen Streets just north of the mills and river. The four brick blocks of the Bay State Mills were typical of the other boarding houses. Three stories high, each was divided into eight sections. On the first floor there was an office for the mistress, two dining rooms, and a kitchen; while above, the section contained a parlor, a sick room, and fourteen sleeping chambers

5. Smith, *Essex Company*, pp. 18-23; [Lemuel Shattuck], *Sanitary Survey of the Town of Lawrence* (Boston, 1850), p. 5; Young, "City of Lawrence," p. 584; Robert E. Todd and Frank B. Sanborn, *The Report of the Lawrence Survey* (Lawrence, 1912), p. 32; *The Lawrence Sentinel*, May 8, 1869; *Lawrence American*, Dec. 10, 1864.

for thirty-six boarders. Wood shed, privy, and well were in the backyard. The solid brick and slate construction, the ample yards, and the hundred square feet per person made the Bay State Company boarding houses much in demand. They were as good as decent Boston homes and superior to those found in the villages of New Hampshire and Maine. The girls ordinarily took their meals at the boarding houses for $1.25 a week, but the men often preferred to eat out rather than pay the $1.50 or $2.00 rate. Lemuel Shattuck, who surveyed the town for the State Sanitary Commission in 1850, maintained that the mills set up the boarding houses to supervise the employees, not for any profit.[6]

The city's founders and mill owners certainly felt responsible for the moral, mental, and physical welfare of their workers. For the unmarried girl, whether from Kennebunk or Dublin, the Bay State boarding-house rules provided security. The landlady had to inform the mill agent whether her boarders went to church. Doors closed at 10 P.M. and no one could have company at "unseasonable" hours. All had to be vaccinated, free of charge. Ashes were to be cared for so as to prevent fires. Equally paternalistic was the Pacific Mill, which could discharge a man for "lack of capacity and neatness," for "unfaithfulness," for "intemperance," for "profanity," and for "improper" treatment of overseers. The Pacific Corporation also required its workers to attend church and join its library association. Upon the library the operative looked with mixed sentiments. For the dubious privilege of borrowing some of its 7,000 books, the immigrant, who frequently could not read, contributed one cent a week, a not insignificant sum at the time. The library balance, furthermore, was $1,000 to $2,000 that the mill could use interest free. Two cents a week contributed to the relief fund entitled the employee to thirty weeks of benefits when sick or injured.[7] While the workers gained from these paternalistic arrangements, they also lost considerable freedom.

6. [Shattuck], *Sanitary Survey,* pp. 9-20; *Lawrence Journal,* Jan. 25, 1879.
7. [Shattuck], *Sanitary Survey,* pp. 11-12; Pacific Mills, *General Regulations* (N.p., N.d.); Letter from W. C. Chapin to Samuel Austin, Lawrence, July 1, 1856, MS, Essex Institute; Pacific Mills, *Statement Presented to the Special Jury of the Paris Exposition of 1867* (Lawrence, 1868), pp. 12-13 and notes; Pacific Mills Relief Society, *Regulations, 1854* (Lawrence, 1854); *ibid.,* 1868; *Journal,* Aug. 23, 1884.

The petition to the legislature asking for the incorporation of Lawrence revealed the founders' concern for their people's welfare. It complained that there was a "great increasing want of school houses," and said that a police force was "absolutely necessary . . . because of the peculiar and mixed character of the population." The petition also wanted "suitable accommodations for the reception and relief of the poor and sick and those disabled by accidents or sudden illness. . . ." In order to cope with disease the founders attracted a dozen doctors to Lawrence within the first year. When Charles Storrow wrote Horace Mann about education in the new town, he commented that the population had doubled and numbered 6,000. "They have come here mostly from New England homes," he said, "and therefore have New England wants among which schools are first." He wanted Mann to help him set up a high school and to establish a state normal school in Lawrence. "Where else," he commented, "can you find as here the elements of society ready to be moulded into a good or an evil shape: nothing to pull down, all to build up: a whole town composed of young people to influence and train as you would a school."[8]

Though the normal school never materialized, the public school system flourished at once. Mirrored in the reports of the School Committee were the aspirations and ideals of early Lawrence. The first report stressed the importance of education and the apathy shown it in Massachusetts. In a straightforward way it told teachers they must "assiduously teach their pupils to avoid idleness, truancy, falsehood, deceit, thieving, obscenity, profanity, and every other wicked and disgraceful practise. . . ."[9] As early as 1850 there were eleven schools, all on land donated by the Essex Company.

As in most communities a public library had to wait until after the Civil War, but Lawrence soon had six private collections, one with over 11,000 volumes. The preamble to the Franklin Library

8. Petition to Establish the Town of Lawrence, MS, Massachusetts Archives, Acts, 1847, Ch. 190; *The Evening Tribune,* Centennial Edition, 1953; Letter from Charles S. Storrow, Lawrence, Mass., to Horace Mann, Feb. 8, 1848, MS, Horace Mann Letters, Massachusetts Historical Society Library.

9. School Committee of . . . Lawrence, *Annual Report, 1847-1848* (Lawrence, 1848); School Committee of . . . Lawrence, *Rules and Regulations . . .* (Lawrence, 1856), p. 10; School Committee, *Rules, 1858,* p. 7; [Shattuck], *Sanitary Survey,* pp. 5, 11-12.

Association Charter in 1847 declared that "the welfare of every community was closely dependent upon the diffusion of general knowledge. . . ." When Abbott Lawrence gave $1,000 to the Franklin Association for books, he said the books should be the sort that would "tend to create mechanics, good Christians, and patriots." "Let the standard be high," he added, "in Religion, Moral and Intellectual Culture, and there can be no well grounded fear of the results. There will soon gather around you a large number of Mechanics, and others, who will desire to obtain a knowledge of the higher Mechanic Arts. . . . If you possess a well furnished library . . . you will . . . send forth into the community a class of well educated Machinists, whose labors and influences will be felt throughout our country. . . ." Nathaniel White had a similar concern for the welfare of the mechanics when he left money for the first public library and for a series of "edifying" public lectures. Both Herman Melville and Ralph Waldo Emerson spoke in the city before the Civil War.[10]

The workers for whom the founders showed such concern came first from New England or Ireland: by 1848 there were 3,750 Americans and 2,100 Irish in Lawrence. Farm boys and girls were drawn from all over New England, the 1870 figures showing 10,000 from Massachusetts, 4,600 from New Hampshire and Maine, and 1,200 from Vermont, Connecticut, Rhode Island, and New York. *The Lawrence Courier's* concern for New Hampshire politics demonstrated how close Lawrence was to rural New England. Since its editor Jonathan Hayes was opposed to slavery, there were feature editorials in 1846 rejoicing in the election of New Hampshire Free Soilers, Amos Tuck and John P. Hale, to the House and Senate. Another Lawrence newspaper, the *Messenger,* was shifted to the town from Exeter, New Hampshire.[11]

10. *Lawrence American,* Feb. 1, 1862, Dec. 3, 1864, Dec. 15, 1865; *The Essex Eagle,* Dec. 27, 1873; Franklin Library Association, *The Act of Incorporation . . .* (Lawrence, 1847); *The Evening Tribune,* Centennial Edition, 1953; *The Lawrence Courier,* July 17, 1847; *The Lawrence Sentinel,* Dec. 10, 1864; Francis V. Lloyd, Jr., "Melville's First Lectures," *American Literature,* XIII, No. 4 (Jan., 1942), 391-94; *Municipal Records and Memoranda 1856-1859,* II.

11. *The Lawrence Courier,* Nov. 11, Dec. 5, 1846, Jan. 6, Feb. 13, 27, Feb. Extra, Mar. 20, April 3, July 31, Aug. 7, 1847; Maurice Dorgan, *History of Lawrence, Mass., with War Records* (Cambridge, Mass., 1924), pp. 44, 174; United States Census Office, *Ninth Census of the United States . . . 1870,* I (Washington, 1872), 380-81.

Map II
STREETS AND IMMIGRANT CENTERS IN LAWRENCE

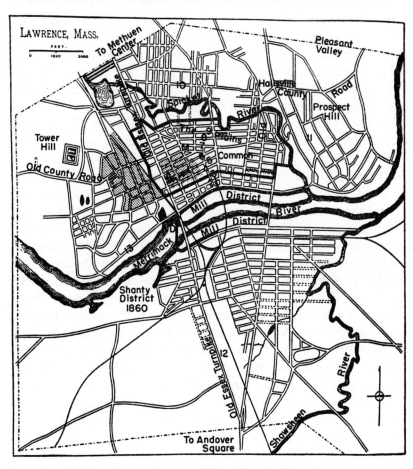

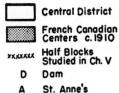

		STREETS	
	Central District		
	French Canadian Centers c.1910	1. Canal	7. Haverhill
		2. Methuen	8. Oak
xx,xxxxx	Half Blocks Studied in Ch. V	3. Essex	9. Elm
D	Dam	4. Common	10. Park
A	St. Anne's	5. Valley	11. Prospect
M	St. Mary's	6. Lowell	12. Broadway
		13. Water	

The model town had great respect for these American working-men and never treated them with the scorn later shown in 1912. "The majority of the female operatives," said one observer, "were good, wholesome farmers' daughters, often working to clear their fathers' farms or to send their brothers through college." "The Iron Workmen of this country," said the *Courier,* "stand much higher than any other class of laboring men. . . . We have seldom found a man more truly independent, OPENHEARTED and MANLY than these workmen. . . . It is the laboring class . . . who are ultimately to prove the destruction or the salvation of our country. . . . Let the industrious working man, whether he be mechanic or farmer, whether he reside in . . . Lawrence . . . [or] Vermont . . . understand his own importance." Such statements were typical of the mid-nineteenth-century appreciation of factory "mechanics."[12]

But the admiration for native-born "mechanics" did not apply to the "menial" Irish "laborers" who had flocked to Lawrence to escape the horrors of the Irish potato famine of 1846. Sneering references to the intemperate Irish appeared at an early date. The *Courier,* furthermore, refused to believe that four hundred natives were living with the Irish in the shanty district near the dam. Segregation was practiced at the very beginning as the natives took the best parts of town. As more and more Irish came, the native-born moved to Prospect and Tower Hills and South Lawrence, all on the outskirts of Lawrence. Both physically and socially the Irish and natives were miles apart in the model town.[13]

Between 1845 and 1850 and for a few years thereafter Lawrence was a model town. Conceived, built, and directed by Boston Brahmins, it was designed to produce cottons and woolens, but to do it in an environment that was physically and morally sound. To Lawrence would come sturdy mechanics to do the city's work and be uplifted in the process. This was the way the founders looked on Lawrence. As more and more immigrants came, however, the model town soon changed to an immigrant city.

12. Bureau of Statistics of Labor, "Fall River, Lowell, and Lawrence," *Thirteenth Annual Report . . . 1882,* Mass. Pub. Doc. 15, p. 380; *The Lawrence Courier,* May 8, 1847.

13. *Ibid.,* Feb. Extra, 1847. See Tables I and V.

CHAPTER III

The Shanty Irish, 1850-1865

The Irish potato famine coincided with the founding of Lawrence: a simple fact that was to shape for all time the history of the city. Gaunt and wasted by the famine, Irish families from southern counties such as Cork sold their furniture and made their way to Dublin or Liverpool, England, in the late 1840's and early 1850's. There recently emptied ships from Canada and the United States lay waiting to load emigrants for the return trip. For many the sea was a final resting place, for filth, over-crowding, and inadequate food and water made the voyage to America long and menacing. Massed on the decks, the survivors looked hopefully on the new world as the ship entered Quebec or Boston. Those landing at Quebec found new horrors as unemployment drove them to the long foot journey down through Canada to New England. After months of agony Irish men, women, and children trickled into the mill cities of the Merrimack Valley, one of them Lawrence. The Boston arrivals found the walk or train ride to Lawrence relatively simple. The Irish moved into the city so rapidly that by 1875 there were over 8,000. Though the total was never again this high, it was greater than that of any other foreign-born group until 1900. Once in the city the Irish flocked to Wards Two and Three, which were soon the most densely populated areas. South of the Common they lived in the mill boarding houses and to the north they settled on the "plains." Many also inhabited a shanty village along the river near the dam.[1]

1. Irish-born in Lawrence—1865: 6047; 1875: 8232; 1885: 7643; 1895: 7487; 1905: 6557. Oliver Warner, *Abstract of the Census of Massachusetts,—1865* . . . (Boston, 1867), p. 63; Carroll D. Wright, *Census of Massachusetts 1875,* I (Boston, 1876), 291; Carroll D. Wright, *Census of Massachusetts: 1885*

As early as 1846 a priest held services, and after a few years of temporary meeting places, the Irish built the Immaculate Conception Church in 1853 and Saint Mary's between 1866 and 1871. The Irish Benevolent Society and the Ancient Order of Hibernians, both founded in 1863, were their first official clubs, but the Irish held meetings from the very moment they arrived. In 1853, for example, the Irish patriot T. F. Meagher, who had escaped from exile to Tasmania, lectured to them about the evils of British rule in the old country. Out of such meetings came the first Irish political leader, O'Hea Cantillon. But the first Irishman to capture the respect of the natives was William O'Sullivan, who became the captain of an Irish regiment in the Civil War and died for his new country.[2]

The wooden huts above the dam were responsible for the label "shanty" Irish. These were shacks of slabs and unfinished lumber with over-lapping boards for the roofs. Above each roof rose a stovepipe chimney and piled high around the walls was sod for insulation. Strangely like the sod houses of the western plains later in the century, these "underground mud huts of the 'city of Cork' " did not vanish until 1898. Other Irish pushed out onto the "plains" above Haverhill Street, where they built more wooden shanties. A *Lawrence American* reporter described what he saw there during a Democratic torchlight procession: ". . . in various localities a lone, solitary candle was observable in some attic

I, Part 1 (Boston, 1887), 507; Horace G. Wadlin, *Census of . . . Massachusetts: 1895*, II (Boston, 1897), 607; Chief of the Bureau of Statistics of Labor, *Census of . . . Massachusetts 1905*, I (Boston, 1909), 109, lxxvii. See Table III. Alice W. O'Connor, "A Study of the Immigration Problem in Lawrence, Massachusetts" (unpublished social workers' thesis, Lawrence, Mass., 1914), p. 10. An analysis of twenty Irish priests and politicians showed that most were from southern Ireland. *The Lawrence Sentinel*, Aug. 28, 1869, Feb. 26, 1870, Jan. 6, April 6, 1872, Jan. 3, 1874; *The Essex Eagle*, Jan. 2, May 29, 1875; *Lawrence Journal*, Jan. 5, 12, Dec. 7, 1878, Dec. 31, 1881, Feb. 16, 1884; *Lawrence American*, Jan. 11, 1884; *The Evening Tribune*, Jan. 16, 1892; Marcus Lee Hansen, *The Immigrant in American History* (Cambridge, Mass., 1940), pp. 158-60; *The Lawrence Courier*, Sept. 28, 1855; United States Census Bureau, *Thirteenth Census of the United States . . . 1910: Abstract of the Census . . . with Supplement for Massachusetts . . .* (Washington, 1913), p. 609. See map, p. 25, for streets and immigrant centers.

2. *The Lawrence Sentinel*, April 4, 1868; *Lawrence American*, Aug. 24, 1866; Katherine O'Keefe, *A Sketch of Catholicity in Lawrence and Vicinity* (Lawrence, 1882), p. 61; *The Lawrence Courier*, Mar. 4, 1848, Feb. 24, 1849, Nov. 25, 1853; *The Lawrence Sentinel*, May 11, Aug. 3, Dec. 14, 1861, Nov. 14, 1863.

window, with sometimes a half dozen in a cellar window, set in
holes dug in potatoes, showing dimly through smoky glass . . .
total depravity. . . ." The huts often burned, and the destruction
of a large one near the reservoir in 1875 laid bare their shabbiness.
In this shack, measuring a hundred feet by twenty and divided in
the middle, lived a family, seventy-seven boarders, and two girl
cooks. The fire started at 1:30 A.M. in a cubicle usually occupied
by the two cooks but empty at the moment because they were
sleeping on the floor of the main room to escape bed bugs.[3]

When the Massachusetts Sanitary Commission investigated
Lawrence in 1850, it warned that the poor housing, particularly
the "habitations, habits, and peculiar modes of living of the Irish
laborers," menaced the health of all. The commission also feared
the "unwholesome exhalations" and exposure that threatened those
digging the canal.[4] Whatever the reason, it was a fortunate Irish
immigrant who did not fall prey to disease. Lawrence suffered
the most serious typhoid fever epidemic in the state's history in the
winter of 1850 and almost half of the deaths in the town before
1850 were from either typhoid fever or consumption. It was no
better in the next decade and a half as Lawrence ranked fourth in
the state in death rate and averaged over twenty-nine deaths an-
nually per thousand population.[5]

Water and food were partly to blame. The Merrimack was
full of sewage brought down from Lowell, and the outhouses polluted the wells. Poverty meant poor food for most and starvation
for some. As always there were exceptions. A grocer's ledger
revealed that Michael Carney, an Irish laborer with a wife and at

3. The first quotation is from the *Lawrence American*, Nov. 15, 1856, included in *Municipal Records and Memoranda 1856-1859*, I; Robert E. Todd and
Frank B. Sanborn, *The Report of the Lawrence Survey* (Lawrence, 1912), p.
32. The second quotation is from *Municipal Records*, I. *The Essex Eagle*,
July 17, 24, 1875; *Lawrence American*, Mar. 4, 1864.

4. [Lemuel Shattuck], *Sanitary Survey of the Town of Lawrence* (Boston,
1850), pp. 9-10, 20-21.

5. *Report . . . relating to the Registry and Return of Births, Marriages, and
Deaths . . .* , XIV (1855), Mass. Pub. Doc. 1, p. 45; XVII (1858), 66; XIX
(1860) xlvi; XXIV (1865), cxxvii; XXV (1866), cxix. From 1847 to 1849,
41 per cent of all deaths and over 50 per cent of Irish deaths were caused by
typhoid fever and consumption. Essex Institute, *Vital Records of Lawrence,
Massachusetts, to the End of the Year 1849* (Salem, Mass., 1926). The exact
death rate averaged 29.4 per thousand population for the years 1855, 1860, and
1865.

least two children, purchased the following during a four-month period:

Potatoes—six pecks	Eggs—53
Rice and meal—eight pounds	Crackers—one barrel
	Cheese and butter—80 pounds
Flour—three barrels and 54 pounds	Molasses—nine gallons
	Sugar—62 pounds
Beef—15 pounds	Oil—5 pounds
Pork—6 pounds	Tea and coffee—17 pounds
Fish—41 pounds	Vinegar—four pints

A censensus of six boarding-house menus showed equally heavy food:

Breakfast—Hot biscuit, butter, meat, bread, pie, doughnuts, tea

Dinner—Meat, potatoes, pudding, bread, butter, tea, vegetables

Supper—Bread, butter, tea, cold meat, sauce, cake

But Carney may have taken in boarders, and boarding-house keepers always exaggerated the amount of food they offered. Most Lawrence workers ate poorly.[6]

In spite of the unfavorable conditions the Irish went about their work building the towering dam, the mile-long canal, and the giant factories. By 1849 the Bay State Mills and Atlantic Mills were in production; three years later the Pacific joined them, making three million-dollar corporations in the city. Bay State shawls, Atlantic sheets and shirts, and Pacific cashmeres soon became household names throughout the United States. Altogether Irish and Yankee muscle built six cotton mills and five woolen mills by 1855, enough to give the city 10 per cent of the cotton spindles and 15 per cent of the sets of woolen machinery in Massachusetts. The model town had already become a prominent textile city.[7]

6. William D. Joplin, Ledger, 1847, MS at the Essex Institute, Salem, Mass., pp. 89-90, 139-40; Bureau of Statistics of Labor, Sixth Annual Report . . . 1875, Mass. Pub. Doc. 31, pp. 419-20.

7. A. W. Doe, Statistics of Lawrence (Mass.) Manufactures. January . . . 1861 (Manchester, N.H., 1861); William Filmer, The Directory of the Town of Lawrence (Lawrence, 1848); John A. Goodwin, The Lawrence Directory (Lawrence, 1853); George Adams, The Lawrence Directory (Lawrence, 1857);

The mills were not an unmixed blessing to the Irish. Although wages were supposedly $.25 to $.50 a week higher than anywhere else, they were low; certainly less than $1.00 a day. Working hours were long. In spite of mass protests reformers failed to get either a ten-hour day or a full hour off at noon. Irishmen leaving their shanties on the "plains" at six in the morning were lucky if they arrived home a dozen hours later. And they were fortunate also if they avoided injury. The *Courier* faithfully recorded the steady series of mutilations and deaths occurring in the mills,[8] but it remained for the Pemberton disaster to demonstrate the dangers of mill work.

The Pemberton Mill, five stories high with solid six-inch oak floors, wide windows, and handsome exterior, was the model mill in the model city. Here seven hundred workers eagerly awaited the close of a cold winter's day on January 10, 1860. A foreman pulled out his large key-winding watch, which read 4:45 P.M. A young girl leaned from an upstairs window of the Duck Mill and spoke to her lover in the Pemberton. Doctor Lamb looked out of his window in an office building close by. And then it happened. The pillars supporting the center of the building at the south end of the top floor began to buckle, bringing down the walls and roof. As the heavy flooring gave way, it fell through to the floor below setting off a rhythmical movement that ran through the factory from south to north bringing it to the ground within sixty seconds. The foreman never looked at his watch again. The girl in the Duck Mill screamed as she saw her sweetheart fall from the window to his death below. Doctor Lamb witnessed the entire collapse and then ran to bring aid to those still living. John Tatterson had just

---

C. A. Dockham, *A Directory of the City of Lawrence* (Lawrence, 1860); Horace Wadsworth, *History of Lawrence, Mass., with Portraits and Biographical Sketches of Ex-Mayors up to 1880* . . . (Lawrence, 1879), p. 93; Maurice Dorgan, *History of Lawrence, Mass., with War Records* (Cambridge, Mass., 1924), pp. 42-43; Francis DeWitt, *Statistical Information Relating to . . . Industry in Massachusetts . . . 1855* (Boston, 1856). Lawrence was incorporated as a city in 1853. Dorgan, *History*, p. 45.

8. *The Lawrence Courier*, Jan. 16, 1847, Jan. 15, 1848, Aug. 4, 1849, Sept. 6, 1851, Aug. 20, 1852. The average monthly pay of male laborers in Massachusetts in 1850 was $22.92 per month or $.88 a day. Laborers in Lawrence earned $.84 to $1.00 a day. *The Lawrence Courier*, April 10, 1855; Dorgan, *History*, p. 39. The noon hour was only forty-five minutes and workers found it difficult to get home to the "plains" and back in that time. *The Lawrence Courier*, April 27, 1857.

entered the north end of the building when he felt the start of its destruction. With great presence of mind he darted to a corner and calmly rode down with the floor to the ground. While most of the employees rode safely with him, dozens were killed and hundreds injured. Many more were trapped in the ruins and the entire city set about rescuing them. The biting cold of the January night, the flickering light of the huge bonfire built to light the work, the smell of oil and death, and the sounds of the crushed and dying brought intense terror to all. The pale faces of those staggering from the remains added to the horror. And then at eleven o'clock one of the rescuers happened to drive a pick through a lantern, dashing its flame onto the inflammable cotton and oily waste. Now the moans of pain became screams of panic as the fire raced through the ruins destroying those who were still caught. An overseer, Maurice Palmer, slashed his throat as the flames approached, but happily was rescued still alive and survived.

In the weeks that followed, thousands of dollars flowed into the city as the entire nation learned of the tragedy. Eighty-eight had died; 116 had been seriously injured, many maimed for life; 159 had received minor wounds; 307 had escaped with only memories. The country watched with interest as the jury met to fix the blame, for future mill construction would hinge on its findings. The too wide windows and the too heavy floors had made the rows of iron pillars running the length of the building on each floor the key to the structure. The jury found that these pillars on the top floor were defective. When they buckled, they had brought the entire mill down. The jury discovered also that several of the pillars had collapsed in 1854 causing one floor to settle, but no one then had heeded the warning.[9]

Poor homes, disease, and death were only some of the problems faced by the early Irish in Lawrence; ill will between them and the natives also contributed to their insecurity. An early example was the "Black House" riot in April, 1847, which started when Maria Sullivan, an Irish prostitute, spread the rumor that she had

9. J. F. C. Hayes, *History of the City of Lawrence, Mass.* (Lawrence, 1868), pp. 99-127; *The Lawrence Courier,* Jan. 14, 21, 28, 1860; *An Authentic History of the Lawrence Calamity* . . . (Boston, 1860); *The Evening Tribune,* Centennial Edition, 1953; *The Lawrence Courier,* Sept. 26, 1854; Donald B. Cole, "The Collapse of the Pemberton Mill," *Essex Institute Historical Collections* (January, 1960), pp. 47-55.

seen a man murdered and thrown into the river. When the very man appeared a few days later, an anti-Irish crowd gathered and ruined the brothel, popularly known as the "Black House," where she lived.[10]

Religious antagonism between the native Protestants and the Irish Catholics gave the impetus to the nativist movement. While the native *Courier* carried articles both for and against Catholics, its tone was always offensively patronizing. When Cantillon stated that a temperance oath was meaningless unless given before a priest, a letter to the *Courier* attacked him and accused all Catholics of being clannish. Later the *Courier* itself assailed the Catholics all over the country who would not join in the acclaim for Louis Kossuth, the Protestant Hungarian patriot, who visited America in 1851. Half of the people attending church in Lawrence were Catholics, a percentage that the natives considered ominous.[11]

Social distinctions also separated the Irish from the native-born. Since most of the Irish children worked in the mills, only six of them regularly attended school. Many of their parents were also illiterates. While at first the *Courier* tried to be fair about Irish drunkenness, by 1848 it was warning the immigrants about intemperance. At the same time the *Courier* was blaming an increase in crime on what it called the "most vicious population of Europe." Crime and disorder did seem to occur most frequently in such immigrant areas as Common Street and the "plains," where prostitution and gambling prevailed. The Irish attacked the police, brawled on Sunday, and defaced trees. The resulting court lists seemed entirely Irish. While the Irish nature was hardly as vicious as the newspapers portrayed it, a mixture of religious and social distinctions made the immigrants a group apart.[12]

But such differences did not cause an organized nativist movement until the Irish began to compete politically and economically with the native-born. Before 1850 the number of Irish voters was negligible, but by 1852 the vote was large enough to attract both parties. The Democrats, for example, tried to show that the Whig administration was doing nothing to help a group of Irishmen exiled from their homeland. They then nominated O'Hea Cantillon for

10. *The Lawrence Courier*, May 1, 1847.
11. *Ibid.*, Mar. 4, 1848, Sept. 8, 1849, Dec. 6, 13, 27, 1851, Feb. 4, 1858.
12. *Ibid.*, Nov. 21, 1846, July 31, Aug. 7, 12, 1847, Mar. 4, Oct. 7, 1848, Dec. 24, 1852, Jan. 15, April 24, 27, July 31, 1855.

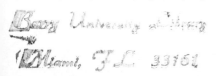

the state House of Representatives, but enough natives scratched his name from the ballot to defeat him. When the Democrats won the city election of 1852, the Whigs blamed it on the Irish vote. The native Whigs were then ready to join a nativist party.[13]

The local depression of 1854 and 1855 transformed the anti-Irish resentment into a political movement. At first there were plenty of jobs in Lawrence, but as soon as the dam was completed in 1848, the *Courier* warned the Irish that they would have a hard time finding any more work in the town. Even with the mill construction, the competition for jobs was so fierce that the *Courier* in 1850 was urging the Irish to move on west. By 1851 the *Courier* attributed unemployment to low tariffs and dependence on southern cotton. After good times in 1852 and 1853 the depression returned in 1854 and caused mass unemployment at the Bay State Mill in 1855.[14]

It was little wonder that the anti-Catholic, anti-immigrant Know-Nothing party rose rapidly in Lawrence in 1854. More surprising was the extent of the political revolution in the city and in the state. Lawrence lay in the Whig stronghold of Essex County, which was basically agrarian and conservative. In 1846, for example, the county cast over 6,000 ballots for the Whig candidate for governor and only 3,500 for the Democratic candidate. The model town of Lawrence conformed to the pattern. In the first three years, when Lawrence voted with Methuen, the Whigs carried the combined towns in each election, and even after Lawrence began to vote separately, the trend continued. Between 1850 and 1853 the Whigs got about half of the Lawrence vote, the Democrats 35 per cent, and the Free Soilers 15 per cent. At the state level the Democrats captured the governor's seat in 1850 and 1851 by uniting with the Free Soilers, but when this marriage ended, the Whigs won in 1852 and 1853.[15]

The *Courier* first referred to the Know-Nothings in May of 1853, when it argued that both a native American party and the immigrants were a threat to American institutions. Two months

13. *Ibid.*, Mar. 6, 1847, Feb. 7, Oct. 22, 1852, April 12, Nov. 25, Dec. 9, 1853.
14. *Ibid.*, April 8, 1848, June 1, Aug. 31, 1850, Jan. 11, Sept. 27, 1851, Jan. 3, 1852, Jan. 1, 8, 1855.
15. *Ibid.*, Nov. 14, 1846, Nov. 13, 1847, Nov. 18, 1848, Nov. 17, 1849, Nov. 16, 1850, Nov. 15, 1851, Nov. 9, 1852, Nov. 16, 1853.

later it denounced both President Pierce's appointment of foreigners to office and the rising menace of Know-Nothingism. Socially anti-Irish, the *Courier,* nonetheless, feared the political impact of a nativist party. When the Know-Nothing party first appeared in Lawrence, in the spring of 1854, its secrecy and ritual attracted many supporters. The first gatherings took place in a "wigwam" near the railroad bridge between Valley and Common Streets in the heart of the city.[16]

The summer of 1854 removed the secrecy from the Know-Nothing party and widened the Irish-native split. The case of Bridget Hogan, who came to Lawrence from Ireland in the late 1840's with her mother and two sisters, showed how intense the struggle had become. After her mother's death, Bridget went to live with the Bensons, a wealthy Protestant family, where she abandoned Catholicism. One Sunday in June her sisters met her on the way to church and tried to force her into the Catholic Church. Failing that, they went to court to bring her back home. When Mrs. Benson succeeded in keeping the girl, a fight nearly broke out then between the Irish and the Yankees.[17]

The tension reached the breaking point on the hot summer afternoon of July 1, 1854. Who started the riot is not certain. Some one, either a Nova Scotian derelict who had been promised a quart of rum by an Irishman or a Know-Nothing out to start trouble, raised an American flag upside down with a cross above it on the "plains." When the police removed the flag and cross unopposed, the affair might have ended, but the hot summer night brought a crowd of natives out on the streets of the "plains." Soon they formed a parade behind the Lawrence Brass Band and marched two thousand strong down to another Irish center on Common Street. The nativist *Courier* later called it an orderly group of "mechanics, traders, and business men"; while the opposition *Sentinel* said it consisted of bums and boys seeking trouble. The marchers waved banners, shouted defiance, and filled their pockets with stones. When they reached the home of an unpopular Irishman, they stopped and began to throw their stones, badly damaging his house. Whether the natives started it or whether

16. *Ibid.,* May 27, Aug. 5, 23, 1853, Mar. 28, April 18, 1854.
17. *Ibid.,* June 9, 13, 20, 1854.

they were first "assailed with stones, brick bats, and one or two shots . . . fired from the houses" is not clear; but the natives did most of the damage. Back they went to the engine house on Oak Street, gave three cheers for the flag, and dispersed.

Here again it might have stopped, but a small group returned home by way of Common Street and once more engaged the Irish with brick bats and gun shots. Only the timely arrival of the mayor, who read the riot act and called out the Lawrence Light Infantry, succeeded in breaking up the mob. Though nothing more happened, news of the riot spread throughout the United States. Even two years later the Michigan *Paw Paw Free Press* compared it with the "border ruffian" raid on Lawrence, Kansas. And by this time the story had grown, for the newspaper referred to a "band of twelve hundred 'Massachusetts freemen,' who assaulted at midnight the humble tenements and cabins inhabited by free white laborers" and "leveled forty of those dwellings of the poor."[18]

In the fall of 1854 the Know-Nothing party turned first the state and then the city party structure upside down as it annihilated the Whigs and Free Soilers and paved the way for the rise of the Republicans. Henry Gardner, its candidate for governor, carried 317 towns and cities, securing over 80,000 of the 127,000 votes. All state senators and 347 of the 355 state representatives were Know-Nothings. A month later Albert Warren of the Know-Nothing party won the first of two smashing victories in the race for the mayor's seat.

What the Know-Nothing party did to Lawrence politics is best seen in a study of the Lawrence vote in the state elections between 1853 and 1857. The Know-Nothing party apparently served as a halfway station for those leaving the Whig and Democratic parties and joining the Republican party. Listed below is each party's percentage of the votes cast for governor:

18. *The Lawrence Courier* and J. F. C. Hayes both denied that the flag and cross were raised to create trouble. *Ibid.,* July 11, 1854; Hayes, *History,* pp. 66-67. An old Irish settler reported in 1879 that the Know-Nothing Party started the affair. *Lawrence Journal,* Feb. 22, 1879. *The Lawrence Courier* was probably the most reliable. The *Paw Paw* article was quoted in the *Chicago Times,* requoted in a Lawrence newspaper, and inserted in *Municipal Records,* I.

	1853	1854	1855	1856	1857
Know-Nothing	0%	78%	59%	8%	29%
Republican	0%	2%	15%	66%	46%
Democratic	55%	12%	21%	25%	25%
Whig	30%	8%	5%	0%	0%
Free Soil	15%	0%	0%	0%	0%

A comparison of the actual votes cast in 1853 with those in 1854 reveals the source of the Know-Nothing strength:

	1853	1854
Know-Nothing	0	1126
Republican	0	30
Democratic	456	172
Whig	585	117
Free Soil	174	0

Former Whig votes made up 41 per cent of the Know-Nothing total; Democratic losses contributed 25 per cent; Free Soil losses 13 per cent; and new votes 20 per cent.[19]

The "conscience Whigs" and Free Soilers of Lawrence, who later became Republicans, went to the Know-Nothing Party first because it included many social reformers who were opposed to slavery. This dichotomy of interests, pro-reform and anti-immigrant, split the party. Since the reform elements would not endorse severe anti-immigrant measures in Boston, the Know-Nothing legislature passed few nativist laws. When it did disband several Irish military companies, the *Courier,* caught in the split, questioned the constitutionality of the move. And the activity of the state Hiss Committee, which was investigating nunneries, drew so much scorn that all Know-Nothings were dubbed "Hissites." The anti-slavery Know-Nothings of Lawrence and all New England could hardly agree with their unionist brothers in New York or their pro-slavery associates in the South.[20]

19. *The Lawrence Courier,* Nov. 14, 1854, for the state result. For the Lawrence vote, *ibid.,* Nov. 15, 1853; Record of Elections in the City of Lawrence, MSS, City Clerk's Office, Lawrence, Mass., I (1853-80), 19, 31, 43, 57.
20. There are references to the plight of the Know-Nothing Party in Oscar Handlin, *Boston's Immigrants* (Boston, 1941), pp. 209-11. A workmen's compensation law and a railway crossing law were two typical reforms. *The Lawrence Courier,* Sept. 7, 1855.

While these differences accounted in part for the decline of Know-Nothing strength in Lawrence in 1855, the granting of patronage in Lawrence to outsiders was even more important. As a result, many Know-Nothings either went back to the Democratic party or on to the Republican. The political confusion of the time appeared in the case of Josiah Osgood, who within twelve months was a Whig, a Know-Nothing, and a Republican. The movement from the Know-Nothing to the Republican Party accelerated during the next year. Even the *Courier,* now lukewarm in its opposition to slavery and reluctant to abandon Whiggism, came out strongly for the Republican John Fremont for president. When the bolting Know-Nothings in Massachusetts merged with the Republicans in renominating popular Governor Gardner, the combination swept both Lawrence and the state in November. In the city election in December all was confusion. The American party, made up of Whigs, Know-Nothings, and Republicans, defeated a Citizens party comprised of Whigs, Know-Nothings, and Democrats. The Irish voted on both sides.[21]

While this was the end of the Know-Nothing party in Massachusetts and throughout the United States, it held on in Lawrence because of the virulence of the anti-Irish feeling and because Lawrence textile men, who accepted nativism, were angry at the Republican failure to support a higher tariff. As a result the Know-Nothing party recovered for the year 1857 some of the strength it had lost to the Republican party. A nativist tinge, in the form of an "American" party lingered on almost until the Civil War in the city elections. Not until the Republicans adopted economic planks in 1860 did the native-born voters of Lawrence abandon Know-Nothingism.[22]

The Democratic party and the Irish, who were the joint targets of the Know-Nothing-Republican drive, banded together, meanwhile, to avoid annihilation. Their combined efforts were so successful that by 1859 the Democracy won 40 per cent of the gubernatorial vote in Lawrence and carried the city election in December. Because they were so essential, the Irish were able to seize

21. *Ibid.,* June 5, July 20, Oct. 18, 30, 1855, Dec. 11, 1856; Record of Elections, I, 31.
22. Record of Elections, I, 57; *Municipal Records,* II, V.

many of the top positions in the party. Terence Brady, next to Cantillon the outstanding Irish politician of the 1850's, dominated the Democratic city caucus of 1859. Since the Irish were poor, the Democratic politicians tended to be economically lower on the scale than the Republicans. By correlating the occupations of the foremost politicians in the two parties, it is possible to make the following comparison:

	Democratic 1848-1853	Republican 1854-1860
Mill executives	3%	14%
Bank and other business executives	6%	7%
Doctors, dentists, lawyers	21%	29%
Overseers and skilled craftsmen	26%	25%
Laborers and farmers	44%	25%

Half of the Republican leaders, as compared with only 30 per cent of the Democratic, were in the three top categories. The difference between the years for the Democratic and Republican figures is unimportant because the Democratic politicians did not change much between 1854 and 1860 even though their share of the votes fell off.[23]

The Irish, however, were not always perfectly loyal to the Democrats. In 1857, for example, the Republicans carried Ward Three, and in 1858 Father O'Donnel urged his parish to vote American-Republican rather than Democratic. Then in 1860 the Republicans abandoned nativism completely and gained sufficient Irish support to halt the Democratic gains of 1859. Their candidate for governor, John Andrew, carried the city handily.[24]

While the Know-Nothing movement was reshaping Lawrence

23. *The Lawrence Courier,* Sept. 15, 1859; *The Lawrence Sentinel,* Sept. 21, 1861. The sources of the Democratic lists: *The Lawrence Courier,* Nov. 10, 1849, Mar. 8, Aug. 23, 1851, Feb. 28, 1852, Sept. 16, 1853. The leadership of the party stayed about the same throughout the decade. *Ibid.,* Sept. 15, 1859, Sept. 21, 1861. For occupations see Filmer, *Directory;* Goodwin, *Directory;* Adams, *Directory.* For Republican lists: *The Lawrence Courier,* Sept. 5, 1854, Oct. 7, 1856, Mar. 22, 1860. Occupations of Republicans from Adams, *Directory.* Seven of twenty-two Lawrence delegates to the Democratic State Convention of 1861 were Irish; so were six of seventeen members of the City Committee.

24. Record of Elections, I, 31, 43, 57, 98; *Municipal Records,* V; *The Lawrence Courier,* June 8, 1857, Sept. 29, Dec. 8, 1859, June 7, 1860.

politics after the riot of 1854, tension between the natives and immigrants continued. The Irish contributed to it by raising arms to
defend themselves against further attacks. Then the School Committee made it worse by a policy of not recognizing the Catholic
school or the certificates the school issued to students seeking work
in the mills. According to the committee it was "a school . . . under Romanist influence, . . . at the head of which was an Irishman,
of manners and habits so gross and degraded" that had it not
closed, the police would have shut it down. An Irish brawl one
spring Sunday in 1855 led Americans to scorn them even more.
A year later it was no better as "a handful of drunken Irishmen
defied the whole police on Pine Street, and successfully, too."
After another group tripped up members of the Syphon Engine
Company on its way to a fire, the company came back and mauled
its assailants.[25]

A newspaper row meanwhile developed between the Know-
Nothing *Lawrence American* and the Democratic *Lawrence Sentinel*. The anti-Irish-Catholic attitude of the *American* was evident in its description of a Democratic parade in November of
1856:

A procession composed of the most noisy Irish rabble . . . com-
prising some 500 ragged, dirty-faced, filthy urchins culled and dragged
forth from the rum-holes, grog cellars and shanties of "the plains," with
a goodly delegation from the underground mud huts of the "City of
Cork," upon the South side . . . started directly for the Irish settlements of Oak and Elm Streets, making the night hideous with their
yells and outcries, while the robust form of the "great Bohea" [Can-
tillon] was seen here and there, shouting lustily in his "rich Irish
brogue," "three cheers for Buch-anan," . . . "three cheers for the
Pope," . . . no one we say, who witnessed these doings . . . will ever
need to read another lesson in Americanism. . . .

Calling the *American* "a bigoted Know-Nothing sheet," the *Sentinel*
accused it of wanting to "exterminate all Catholics and foreigners."
The *American* had previously referred to the *Sentinel* editor as a
"Roman Catholic Foreigner." When the *American* protested because the Catholic Library Society had put announcements of a

25. *Municipal Records*, I; *The Lawrence Courier*, Oct. 13, 1854, April 24,
1855; School Committee of . . . Lawrence, *Annual Report*, VI (1852-53), 7;
VIII (1854), 10; IX (1855), 7-8. There were other riots in July, 1856, and
April, 1857. *The Lawrence Sentinel*, May 10, July 1, 1856, April 22, 1857.

member's death in all other newspapers, the *Courier* responded that it was because the *American* had "treated all the foreign population in . . . a very abusive manner."[26]

The intensification of the slavery issue made an end to the Know-Nothing party and quieted the nativist struggle. The pro-immigrant planks of the Republican party in its 1860 victory muted it even more. The Civil War quelled it entirely. The Irish contributed so many men through their special brigade that they were able to demand and get additional rights. When sixty Lawrence immigrants enrolled at a meeting of naturalized citizens in April of 1861, the *Sentinel* remarked: "There can be no question of the devotion of our adopted citizens to our government and free institutions." A letter to the *Sentinel* said there was no reason to be surprised at the loyalty of the immigrant and added that we could not afford to "let England laugh and say we have failed in the experiment of self-government." When similar letters followed, the newspaper called on the government to give all soldiers their citizenship.[27]

By the end of the Civil War the Irish had passed through the first phase of their migration to Lawrence. The 1850's was one of the worst decades in the history of the city, a decade notorious for its disease, its tragedies, and its attacks on the immigrants. But for the Irish the worst was over. Already they had gained political importance in the Democratic party. Some of the Irish had already left the "plains" and the shanty district for better homes on Tower and Prospect Hills. The decline of the nativist movement during the Civil War and the building of the Arlington Mill in 1865 brought social and economic security much closer. Most important for the Irish, however, would be the influx of new nationalities after the war. The immigrant cycle was beginning to operate as new groups appeared at the bottom of the ladder and the Irish began to rise. Better years lay ahead.

26. *Lawrence American*, Nov. 15, 1856, in *Municipal Records*, I; *The Lawrence Courier*, Sept. 1, 1859; *Municipal Records*, II, VI.

27. *The Lawrence Sentinel*, April 27, May 4, Aug. 10, Nov. 23, Dec. 14, Jan. 25, 1862.

CHAPTER IV

Decades of Promise, 1865-1890

In Lawrence the spring of 1865 brought the end of the Civil War, the opening of the Arlington Mill, and the start of the Fenian movement. Each event in its own way marked the beginning of a new era in the history of the city. The revival of shipping after the war and the demand for workers at the Arlington soon attracted large crowds of Canadians, Englishmen, and Germans, as well as more Irishmen, to the city. As the poor Canadian *habitants* arrived to take their places in the Arlington Mill, the scene was similar to that in 1846 when poor Irishmen had started in on the dam and the early mills. But in the two intervening decades the Irishmen had won a place in the city which the Fenian adventures would soon strengthen. The immigrant cycle was operating.

Pushed out of the Saint Lawrence Valley by poor crops and overpopulation, the *habitants* trickled down into New England on the railroads that followed the Connecticut River or Lake Champlain or went along the trail blazed by the Irish immigrants of the 1840's and 1850's in Maine. In Lawrence they multiplied more rapidly than any group except the Irish. Only a handful at the time of Appomattox, the Canadians numbered 8,500 by 1900. One-fifth of the immigrants living in Lawrence in 1890 were French Canadians. Saint Anne's Church, whose school was the second largest in the Archdiocese of Boston, was built by 1873 in the heart of the French-Canadian district south and west of the "plains." In addition to the church and school the Canadians established a branch of the Saint John de Baptiste Society and several newspapers. From these organizations came men such as

Charles Roy and Charles Lacaillade, who were spokesmen for their fellow countrymen.[1]

Living close to the Irish and Canadians after the Civil War were a number of English textile operatives who deserted the north shires of York, Lancashire, and Cheshire to seek work in the Arlington Mill. They had an easier time than the other immigrants because they had had experience in the mills and because there were English immigrants in Lawrence who had arrived before the Civil War to help them. The English total was as large as the Canadian until the 1890's when the Canadians moved far ahead. Although they lived near the Irish and Canadians, the English occupied better areas. About half of the English lived on the old Essex Turnpike, which had been renamed Broadway, where they were close to the Arlington. The English did not quickly establish societies because they encountered no linguistic or religious conflicts with the natives. They set up the Albion Club in 1886 to get better representation in the city government, but the English Social Club was not founded until 1900. Nonetheless, a state British-American convention met in Lawrence in 1891 and a Daughters of

1. Carroll D. Wright, *Census of Massachusetts: 1875*, I (Boston, 1876), 301; Carroll D. Wright, *Census of Massachusetts: 1880* . . . (Boston, 1883), p. 50; Carroll D. Wright, *Census of Massachusetts: 1885*, I, Part 1 (Boston, 1887), 507; United States Census Office, *Eleventh Census of the United States: 1890*, I (Washington, 1895), clii, 670; Horace G. Wadlin, *Census of . . . Massachusetts: 1895*, II (Boston, 1897), 607; United States Census Office, *Twelfth Census of the United States . . . 1900*, II (Washington, 1901), 796; J. L. K. LaFlamme, David E. Lavigne, J. Arthur Favreau, "French Catholics in the United States," *The Catholic Encyclopedia* (1909), VI, 276. The leading French-Canadian Ward was as follows: 1865, Ward Three (38 per cent of all Canadians); 1875, Ward Four (38 per cent); 1880, Ward Four (45 per cent), 1910, Ward Five (42 per cent). Oliver Warner, *Abstract of the Census of Massachusetts,—1865* . . . (Boston, 1867), p. 63; *Census of Mass., 1875*, I, 301; *Census of Mass., 1880*, p. 50; United States Census Bureau, *Thirteenth Census of the United States . . . 1910. Abstract of the Census . . . with Supplement for Massachusetts . . .* (Washington, 1913), p. 609. *Lawrence American*, Feb. 27, 1864; *The Essex Eagle*, Nov. 15, 1873; W. J. Lauck, "The Significance of the Situation at Lawrence: The Condition of the New England Woolen Mill Operative," *The Survey*, XXVII (1911-12), 1772. Concerning the newspapers: *Le Drapeau* lasted only a short time and ended in September, 1874; in 1881 the *Methuen Enterprise* added a French column; then came the short-lived *Alliance* of 1886 and *Le Echo* 1890; *Le Progres*, 1890, and *Le Courrier de Lawrence*, 1899, were the first to give extensive coverage to French activities. *The Lawrence Sentinel*, Sept. 26, 1874; *The Essex Eagle*, June 18, 1874; *Lawrence Journal*, Mar. 12, 1881, Nov. 20, 1886, Mar. 4, 1887; *The Evening Tribune*, Oct. 31, 1890; *Le Progrès*, Dec. 30, 1898; *Le Courrier de Lawrence*, June 1, 1911. For the Saint Jean de Baptiste Society see *The Evening Tribune*, May 16, 1901.

Saint George meeting took place in 1902. The leading Englishmen down to 1900 were the politician James Derbyshire and the travel agent Duncan Wood.[2]

Like the British the Germans came from textile districts, in this case Saxony, Bavaria, and Silesia. Starting in 1854 they began to settle in a place they called Hallsville just above the Spicket River near the base of Prospect Hill. Here a thriving German community developed after the Civil War. It included a large number of societies ranging from the Turnverein with its gymnastics and radical political discussions to the Lyra Singing Society. When the Lyra dedicated its new hall in 1891, German glee clubs came from as far away as South Boston, Worcester, and Manchester, N.H. A school, a newspaper, and three churches supplemented the work of the societies and also helped provide leaders. While August Reichwagen, treasurer of the school, and Hugo E. Dick, editor of the *Anzeiger und Post,* vied for power in the 1870's and 1880's, August Stiegler was even better known in the 1890's. When he was finally defeated for office, the *Evening Tribune* simply stated, "Howgoost got it in the neck" and everyone knew what it meant.[3]

2. For the pre-Civil War immigrant population of Lawrence, Francis DeWitt, *Abstract of the Census of . . . Massachusetts . . . 1855 . . .* (Boston, 1857), pp. 105, 206. Lauck, "Significance," p. 1772. British authors referred to Lawrence as the "Bradford of America." James Burnley, *Two Sides of the Atlantic* (London, 1880), pp. 62-66; William Smith, *A Yorkshireman's Trip to the United States and Canada* (London, 1892), pp. 130-32; both sources cited in Rowland T. Berthoff, *British Immigrants in Industrial America 1790-1950* (Cambridge, Mass., 1953), pp. 38-39, 224. English-born in Lawrence—1855: 1132; 1865: 1892; 1875: 3353; 1885: 3928. *Census of Mass., 1855,* p. 105; *Census of Mass., 1865,* p. 63; *Census of Mass., 1875,* I, 288; *Census of Mass., 1885,* I, Part 1, 507; *Eleventh Census of . . . 1890,* I, clii. In 1875 and again in 1910 about 40 per cent of the English were in Ward Five. Those near Broadway worked at the Arlington Mill. Others lived on Tower Hill. *Census of Mass., 1875,* I, 288; *Thirteenth Census . . . Supplement for Mass.,* p. 609. Concerning clubs see *Lawrence Journal,* Dec. 19, 1885; *The Evening Tribune,* Feb. 9, 1891, May 20, 1901; *Lawrence Daily Eagle,* Oct. 1, 1902.

3. *The Evening Tribune,* Dec. 9, 1891; Lauck, "Significance," p. 1773. German-born population—1865: 151; 1875: 963; 1885: 1499; 1895: 2402; 1910: 2301. *Census of Mass., 1865,* p. 63; *Census of Mass., 1875,* I, 295, 311; *Census of Mass., 1885,* I, Part 1, 507; *Census of Mass., 1895,* II, 607; *Thirteenth Census . . . Supplement for Mass.,* p. 609. For the German origins see Lauck, "Significance," p. 1773; *The Lawrence Sentinel,* Jan. 3, 1874; *The Essex Eagle,* Jan. 10, 1874; *Lawrence Journal,* Dec. 31, 1881; *Lawrence American,* Jan. 11, 1884, supplement; *The Evening Tribune,* April 4, 1891, Oct. 9, 1896, June 28, 1904. For German locations in Lawrence see *Census of Mass., 1875,* I, 311; *Thirteenth Census . . . Supplement for Mass.,* p. 609. Additional references to German resi-

The simple Lawrence society of the 1850's, Yankees at the top and Irish at the bottom, soon vanished beneath the impact of the newer groups. Revelling in a newly-found seniority, the Irish were now able to look down upon many of the recent arrivals, particularly the French Canadians. They soon found, however, that the English and Germans, experienced in textile work, were often their equals. In the twenty years after the Civil War the Irish steadily improved their position in the city until it was finally clear that they had "arrived." Sometimes they advanced through positive accomplishments of their own, sometimes merely at the expense of others.

By the end of the first decade after the Civil War they had grown both ways. Their most praiseworthy achievement was the Fenian movement. Irish immigrants, angry at British failure to do anything about the famine, were so opposed to the union of Ireland and England that they held half a dozen repeal meetings before 1850. T. F. Meagher's lecture in 1853 helped keep the sentiment alive until the Fenian movement at the end of the Civil War. The Fenians, who wanted to capture Canada and use it as a hostage for British concessions in Ireland, first arrived in Lawrence on Saint Patrick's Day, 1865. Then on the Fourth of July, Fenians marched in the city parade and a month later paraded independently on their way to an excursion. Already they numbered three hundred, seventy-five of them in uniform with green caps, white shirts, and black leather pants. By September a Fenian Hall on the "plains" and a Fenian Sisterhood reflected the vigor of the new society.

The high point came in the spring of 1866 with a conflict between the Sweeney group, which favored the diversionary attack on Canada, and the Stephens wing, which preferred a revolt in Ireland. In spite of a speech by Colonel John O'Mahoney, Lawrence supported General Sweeney and named its circle for him. Posters appeared in the streets and the Fenians raised $5,200 and a hundred stands of arms for the Canadian attack. Suddenly

dences in Donald B. Cole, "Lawrence, Massachusetts: Immigrant City, 1845-1912" (Doctoral dissertation, Harvard University, 1956); see map at the beginning of Chapter III. The churches were the Evangelical Lutheran, Methodist, and Catholic. *The Evening Tribune,* Jan. 6, 1896; *Anzeiger und Post,* Feb. 4, 1899; *The Essex Eagle,* Dec. 25, 1875; *Lawrence Journal,* Dec. 17, 1881, Aug. 22, Dec. 19, 1885, Oct. 1, 15, 1887; *The Evening Tribune,* Sept. 18, 1890, July 2, Nov. 23, 1891, June 11, 1892, Sept. 3, 1905.

Sweeney was at the Canadian border and with great rapidity the Fenian excitement reached a climax. Immediately they collected $1,600 more and thousands crowded the railroad station to see the first hundred off to Canada. A few days later, however, they and the hundred who followed were back. General Sweeney was under arrest. The attack was off.

The utter failure and the arrival in Lawrence of James Stephens, the opponent of a Canadian invasion, should have ended the affair, but the Sweeney Fenians were determined. A parade in 1867 showed seventy-five men remaining in uniform, and in 1870, 172 left for another invasion of Canada. By the end of a week they also had returned from another farce. The *Sentinel,* heretofore sympathetic, called this the "Fenian Fiasco" and Fenianism in any form was dead in Lawrence.

In spite of its ludicrous qualities the movement was so important to the Lawrence Irish that "Irishmen who were not Fenians were not very plentiful." Since it raised the issue of loyalty to Ireland against loyalty to the United States, the Democratic politician James Tarbox urged the Irish to support the Fenians but not to be "imprudent." The Fenians stressed their devotion to the United States by intermixing Irish and American flags in their parades and by boasting of the Irish contributions to American independence. The movement added spice to the monotonous routine of the mill city, but at a price the Irish could ill afford. The $7,500 collected did not include individual assessments of $20.00 from all Fenians, tickets to a ball at $1.25 a couple, and the $10.00 bonds of the government of Ireland. Nor did it count the money spent on arms, food, and uniforms, or the time lost from work. Perhaps, though, it was worth it because Fenianism made the Irish proud that they were both Irishmen and Americans.[4]

Even with the end of Fenianism, Lawrence maintained its interest in Irish independence. In 1880 a "sober"-talking Charles Stewart Parnell raised over $1,000 from a crowd that jammed

4. *The Lawrence Courier,* Dec. 4, 11, 1847, Dec. 18, 1847-Feb. 12, 1848, April 15, Aug. 26, 1848; *Lawrence Watchman and Haverhill Chronicle,* Jan. 22, 1853. They paraded down Hampshire and Essex Streets on the way to the excursion train. *The Lawrence Sentinel,* July 8, 1865; *Lawrence American,* Mar. 4, Aug. 25, Sept. 8, 30, Oct. 20, 1865, Feb. 16, Mar. 2, 9, 16, April 6, 13, June 8, July 20, 30, 1866; *The Lawrence Sentinel,* Oct. 21, 1865, June 9, Oct. 13, 1866, April 14, June 29, 1867, May 28, June 4, 1870; *The Essex Eagle,* June 29, 1867.

city hall. Following him came Frank Byrnes, one of those who murdered two British officials in Phoenix Park, Dublin, and Michael Davitt, the originator of the Irish Land League, which was trying to secure land for tenants in Ireland. Backed heavily by the Irish owned *Lawrence Journal,* the Land League attracted many supporters in Lawrence. While some joined because they wanted to help the folks back home, liberals supported the league because of its reform program. E. T. Burke, for example, attacked its opponents as selfish conservatives and said he backed it for the same reasons that he had backed abolition. Burke compared himself with Wendell Phillips, another abolitionist turned Land Leaguer. In order to attract Germans the league showed an interest in their fight to gain concessions in Germany. Judging, however, from the number of politicians and society leaders who led the league, many joined for purely practical reasons. And some immigrants may have joined in order to keep future immigration down by improving conditions in Ireland. While the Land League Convention of 1883, which represented closely the viewpoint of the Lawrence Irish, pledged support to Parnell and urged an American boycott of English goods, it saw no reason why the United States government should support Irish paupers. An effort to settle an Irish colony in Lawrence failed. Even though the league had a thousand members in Lawrence in 1881, it collapsed in 1884 and left Lawrence apathetic about continued agitation. After a brief flurry over the Home Rule Bill in 1886, the Parnell trial of 1890 caused an irreparable breach in the ranks of the Irish. First *The Evening Tribune* accused the *Journal* of being anti-Parnell, but then admitted that no one in Lawrence was "interested in private quarrels" in Great Britain.[5]

While the Irish could be proud of these positive steps toward maturity, they were still open to occasional criticism. The Irish-Orange Riot in July, 1875, followed a picnic celebrating the Battle of the Boyne held by seventy-five members of the Loyal

5. *Lawrence Journal,* Jan. 24, June 26, 1880, May 14, 1881; *The Essex Eagle,* Aug. 29, 1884. The Land League Convention was in 1883, three years before the alliance of Parnell and Gladstone in support of the Home Rule Bill. *Lawrence Journal,* May 5, 1883, Mar. 15, 1884, April 23, May 7, 1887; *The Evening Tribune,* Mar. 18, April 1, 4, May 5, 1891, Aug. 3, 1895, June 16, 1902. For more details on Lawrence and Irish home rule see Cole, "Lawrence," pp. 130-36.

Lodge of Orangemen from the Protestant north of Ireland. After a day at Laurel Grove on the Merrimack the Orangemen, clad in their bright regalia, returned by steamboat only to find a thousand persons at the dock who stoned them and forced them to take refuge in the police station. When they tried to get to Prospect Hill under the protection of the mayor, the crowd followed and fired shots that wounded about twenty. Most Boston newspapers other than the Catholic *Pilot* said the Irish were at fault. In the city, the *Sentinel* and the Catholic priests denied that the church was involved. But it was generally assumed in Lawrence that the crowd was made up mostly of Irishmen. When the Orangemen paraded a year later, plain-clothesmen and priests forestalled trouble by circulating through the crowd.[6]

The growing Irish strength, evident long before the Orange Riot, brought a revival of Know-Nothingism. It started with a letter to the *American* in 1865 that accused mill workers of stealing and demanded restrictions on immigration. The *Sentinel* replied that if foreigners were kept out of the mills, Lawrence would be deserted. Alert to ferret out nativism, it carried a front-page story in 1869 saying that a branch of the American Protestant Association, whose members would vote only for old-time natives for office, was in the city. The *Sentinel* added that the American Order of Phoenix, a resurrected Know-Nothing club, also had a branch in Lawrence and was supporting Republicans. The anti-immigrant *American* taunted: "The Naturalized citizens,—we will try . . . not to say Irish democrats,— . . . will perhaps someday learn the difference between their solid vote for American Democratic candidates, and the serious defection of the latter whenever the foreign element is given representation." Apparently the English as well as the natives showed prejudice against the Irish because in 1870 the Irish voted for the Englishman Bower for one office, but the English, in spite of promises, would not support Sweeney for another. It happened because of the rumor that the "Micks" were "cutting" Bower and revealed deep distrust between the groups. Such considerations certainly influenced John

6. *The Essex Eagle,* July 17, 24, 1875, *The New York Times,* July 13, 1875, cited in Berthoff, *British Immigrants,* p. 193; *The Lawrence Sentinel,* July 17, Dec. 4, 1875, July 15, 1876. Orange meetings of 1896 and 1906 were uneventful. *The Evening Tribune,* Nov. 10, 1896; *Sunday Sun,* April 1, 1906.

Sweeney, editor of the Irish *Journal,* when he backed Ben Butler for governor in 1878 because Butler had once denounced Know-Nothingism.[7]

The most flagrant example of prejudice against the Irish occurred in 1875, when the city government shifted the boundaries of two wards. The six wards in Lawrence each elected three members to the City Council and the Republicans hoped to cut Democratic strength to three by gerrymandering most of the Irish into one ward. To accomplish this, a reform-Republican party under Mayor Tewksbury shifted parts of the "plains" and land north of the Spicket from Ward Four into Ward Three, which already had a large number of Irish voters. Here is what happened to the population:

	Before Gerrymander (1875 Census)		After Gerrymander (1880 Census)	
	Total	Irish	Total	Irish
Ward Three	5,366	1,815	8,184	2,358
Ward Four	8,404	2,359	7,214	1,190

Here is what happened in the vote for governor:

	1874		1876	
	Republican	Democratic	Republican	Democratic
Ward Three	203	367	250	659
Ward Four	346	529	474	428

Not only did the Republicans carry Ward Four in 1876, but they carried it in five of the next six elections studied down through 1888.[8] And after losing the mayor's office four out of five years through 1876, they suddenly won it four consecutive years from 1877 to 1880.

While control of Lawrence wavered between the two major parties from 1870 to 1880, the Irish vote was frequently decisive. John K. Tarbox won several elections by appealing to the Irish.

7. *The Lawrence Sentinel,* April 8, 1865, Feb. 6, 27, 1869, Oct. 28, 1876; *Lawrence American,* Nov. 9, 1877; *The Essex Eagle,* Nov. 12, 1870.

8. *The Essex Eagle,* June 19, 1875; *The Evening Tribune,* Nov. 30, 1894; Record of Elections in the City of Lawrence, MSS, City Clerk's Office, Lawrence, Mass., I (1853-80), II (1880-1923); *Census of Mass., 1875,* I, 291; *Census of Mass., 1880,* p. 50. See Map III.

Map III
LAWRENCE WARDS AND GERRYMANDERING

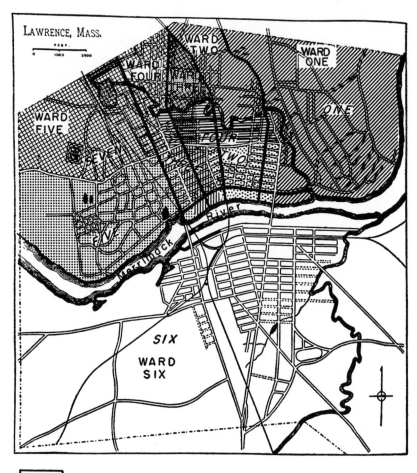

WARD BOUNDARIES 1853 on
One exception  –Part of
WARD FOUR before 1875
gerrymander (an Irish section).
Essex Eagle, June 19, 1875.

WARD BOUNDARIES and
NUMBERS proposed by
Bell Plan 1885. Journal,
October 24, 1885.

ONE   FOUR
TWO   FIVE
THREE   SIX
SEVEN

"The emigrant-ship freighted with stalwart muscle," he said, "is more valuable to our country than the vessel that comes laden with golden treasure, from the precious mines of Australia or California." To get the Irish vote Republicans "buttonholed" them "on every street corner," "cajoled and flattered" them, and just before the election of 1880 vigorously prosecuted a farmer charged with killing an Irish boy. The Democratic *Campaign Budget* commented upon the change in the Republicans' attitude: "Not a word of abuse for them today, there are no slurs, no talk about voters who can neither read nor write. . . . They want the votes hence they let up."[9]

But the Republicans were doomed to failure as the regime of John Breen began in 1882. The December election of 1881 was extremely bitter because Breen loomed as the first Irish Catholic mayor in Lawrence. After it was over, the *American* maintained that Breen won because "he was of Irish birth" and then began a series of attacks on the alleged abuses of the new regime. John Tarbox, on the other hand, rejoiced that Breen was "an Irish-American and a Roman Catholic" because he despised "that bigotry and prejudice which would deny to all men equal rights." Since there was no excitement when a Protestant immigrant was elected mayor in the 1870's, religion must have been more important than birthplace. Some believed that if a Catholic won, he would replace the eagle on the dome of city hall with a cross.

Although the eagle remained atop the hall, a new type of leader sat at the mayor's desk below. While Lawrence had many keen politicians, men such as Duncan Wood, Amedée Cloutier, and Emil Stiegler, its greatest party boss down to the great strike was John Breen. Born in Tipperary, he came to America as a youth and, after a short stay at Villanova College, became a bookkeeper in Boston. Moving to Lawrence he went into the undertaking business, married, and had two children. To his contemporaries he was "a genial and kindly appearing intelligent gentleman."

The techniques used by Breen to gain and hold office would make a textbook of machine politics. By exploiting his undertaking

9. *The Lawrence Sentinel,* July 12, 1862, July 16, 1864, Mar. 6, Dec. 25, 1869; *Lawrence Journal,* Aug. 21, 1880, Mar. 19, 1881; *The Campaign Budget,* Dec. 4, 1882.

business and his membership in the Washington Fire Steamer Company, he made friends and was soon on the City Council. When the *Campaign Budget* ran what it called a "Popular Catechism" in support of Breen, the questions and answers stressed one of his most effective devices:

"Q. Whose is the ready ear and helping hand to the poor and suffering?

"A. Breen's. . . .

"Q. Whose efforts any laboring man cannot honestly say were ever idle in securing him employment when at all possible?

"A. Breen's."

The city police, who influenced voters at the polls, were the heart of the machine, ably supported by the Health and Street Departments which provided patronage. The "big boss's mouthpieces" attacked the opposition in speeches and ward heelers used their fists. Some of Breen's men broke up a Lowell Democratic convention, while others assaulted Councilman O'Neill. Financial support poured in from the "Common Street [vice and liquor] dens," which had "grown fat" under his salutary neglect. More came from the illegal jobs that he and his henchmen performed for the city. Breen, Dixie Hannegan, Jim Shepard, John Ford, and Jim Joyce formed a ring comparable to the Tweed Ring in the city of New York.[10]

During Breen's three years in office several events severely tested the new maturity and power of the Irish. The first was the Pacific Mills strike of 1882. Before 1882 there had been no major strike in Lawrence, partly because there were not enough English agitators in the city to foment the sort of trouble they had stirred up in Fall River. The accessible countryside made unemployment more endurable by offering the unemployed useful occupations such as hunting, fishing, and berry picking. The City Missionary cited sound relief work, easy credit at the stores, and ample worker savings as other reasons for the absence of strikes. Whatever the cause, many considered Lawrence a "model cotton and woolen city" with a "superior and thrifty" labor force. It came, therefore,

10. *Lawrence American*, Dec. 9, 1881, Jan. 13, 26, 1882, Oct. 10, 19, Nov. 2, 9, 1883, Dec. 5, 1884, July 21, Nov. 13, 1885, Jan. 15, 1886; *Lawrence Journal*, Dec. 10, 17, 1881, May 24, Oct. 11, Nov. 15, 1884; *Campaign Budget*, Dec. 4, 1882.

as a great shock when a wage reduction brought on a strike on March 14, 1882. After a short lockout, the company promised to raise wages and let every one go back to work, but not until late in May did most of the operatives return. Employers, meanwhile, came from as far away as Paterson, New Jersey, to hire choice craftsmen and aid for the strikers poured in from many cities. Careful coverage in *The New York Times* gave it national importance.

The Irish showed that they could identify themselves with more than just the interests of the workers. In the 1850's they had acted only as workers and in the 1912 strike they supported the owners, but in 1882 they were on both sides. After first inciting the strikers, Peter McCorey, who edited the *Catholic Herald,* told them to go back to work because they were not well enough organized. While John Breen was always for the strikers, urging them to go west rather than return to their jobs, Father D. D. Regan helped the owners by calling for an end to the strike. Maggie Duffy first named those who abandoned the strike "slaves and scabs," but later accused the labor leaders of misusing funds. The Irish certainly seemed to see both sides of the issue.

Other nationalities, in Lawrence for a briefer time, were less fickle. Among the British, John Ogilvie, president of the Weavers Union, the Ford brothers, who helped the unemployed with food and money, and Duncan Wood, who denounced the use of strike-breaking detectives, fought to the end. The German weavers were the most important single group in the strike and they talked many German organizations into providing relief money. It was typical of the immigrant cycle that the more recent immigrants were most in favor of the strike. The French Canadians were an exception.[11]

The arrival of the Salvation Army in the city a year later gave the Irish another chance to demonstrate their maturity. At first neither they nor the natives did much of which to be proud. When the Salvation Army first appeared on the streets, it was attacked by a mob of five thousand. And it was immediately the target of both the Irish and native newspapers, which called it a

11. Bureau of Statistics of Labor, "Fall River, Lowell, and Lawrence," *Thirteenth Annual Report . . . 1882,* Mass. Pub. Doc. 31, p. 415; Lawrence City Mission, *Annual Report,* XXXVII (1896), 11-13; *The New York Times,* Mar. 14-April 18, 1882; *Lawrence Journal,* Mar. 25-June 3, 1882.

"travesty on religion" and a "roving band of itinerants." The city marshal, at first, would not let the Army parade. He denied that freedom of worship applied because "it was doubtful if worshipping God consisted of beating drums and tambourines and cymbals and parading in the streets." A letter to the *Lawrence Morning News* accused Catholics of causing a serious disturbance at a Salvation Army meeting. But both the Irish Mayor, John Breen, and the nativist *American* soon changed their positions. They agreed that as long as the Salvation Army did not disturb the peace, it might march and hold services. In spite of all attacks the Salvationists gained strength, numbering 150 by July and 200 at their first anniversary in December, 1884. When they held a parade without being attacked in May, 1885, and in August received praise from the *Journal,* they had won a position in the city. And the surprisingly liberal stand taken by Mayor Breen and eventually by the city showed that the Irish had grown up.[12]

At the same time the Irish faced a more serious test over the collapse of the Augustinian Fathers' bank. The Irish had never trusted banks. In 1878, for example, only a state stay law had been able to stop a run on the Essex and Lawrence banks. A tradition had grown consequently for Lawrence Catholics to deposite money with their Augustinian priests, who issued deposit books, paid interest, and had thousands of dollars under their control. As early as 1874 there were hints of trouble when Ann Doherty sued the fathers for $100. As depositors had difficulty withdrawing money, new attachments followed between 1880 and 1882. But in spite of these portents the Lawrence Irish community was stunned when the fathers announced in 1883 that all the money was gone and that the church had debts of $600,000.

While the fathers blamed poor investments, high interest rates, and a heavy building program, the Irish Catholic *Journal,* edited by the anti-clerical Sweeneys, believed that much had been siphoned off to less prosperous parishes. Nor was the *Journal* satisfied with the priests' financial statement which showed 703 deposits totalling about $400,000. Where, it asked, was the additional half million dollars the church had collected at services

12. *Lawrence Journal,* Dec. 15, 1883, April 19, July 19, Oct. 4, Dec. 13, 1884, May 23, Aug. 1, 1885; *Lawrence American,* April 18, 1884; *Lawrence Morning News,* April 17, 21, 24, May 7, 1884.

over the past nineteen years? When the *Journal* demanded lay control of church funds and ran articles attacking the priests, it split the parish into two camps. "Absolute power naturally tends to abuse," thundered the *Journal*; "few men are strong enough to resist its demoralizing tendency." When the Lawrence *Catholic Herald* told the editors to be silent because they were Catholics and accused them of libel and misrepresentation, the Sweeneys scurrilously denounced the clergy for trying to hush up the affair. They blamed the priests for all the misery of the church and slyly added that Martin Luther had once been an Augustinian. The priests then attacked the Sweeneys from the pulpit and an Augustinian in Andover called John Sweeney "a persecutor" who would "soon have rope enough to hang" himself. The *Journal* replied coldly that a priest who lost his temper was not competent to rule a parish. It added that the Augustinians in Lawrence were a "set of pious frauds" who would "hobnob with rumsellers to defraud the poor working people."

The unity of the Catholic church in Lawrence reached its nadir. When the fathers asked depositors to raise their hands in church to indicate that they would not sue, few would comply. In spite of personal visits from the priests, many Lawrence Catholics began to file suits, some for over a thousand dollars. Feeling was so high that many would not contribute when the parish began a drive for funds to settle the debt and on several other occasions parishioners refused requests of their priests. Politically the fight divided the Irish into two groups, one led by the Sweeneys and the other by John Breen, and this schism was to plague them for the next decade.[13]

As Breen's third term neared its end, the great boss moved from the local arena to the Democratic national convention of 1884. Though originally pledged to Ben Butler, he switched over to Grover Cleveland. John Sweeney, on the other hand, after dismissing the charge that the Republican candidate James G. Blaine was anti-Catholic and convincing himself that Blaine would do something to free Ireland, came out for him. Now Sweeney and his followers were against the church, against Breen, and against the

13. *Lawrence Journal*, April 6, 1878, Mar. 3, 17, 24, May 5, July 21, Oct. 4, 1883; *The Essex Eagle*, Feb. 7, 1874; *Lawrence American*, April 13, 1883.

Democratic party. The Irish split was complete. During the campaign the *Journal* attacked Cleveland for straddling the tariff issue, for being the "unrelenting foe of labor," and for keeping "Know-Nothing" advisers. It was rare irony that Blaine was himself associated with anti-Catholicism when Burchard made his famous "rum, Romanism, and rebellion" speech in New York just before the election. The *Journal*, already committed, ignored the blunder.

The Irish, who had suffered, fought, and matured during three years of Breenism, were not able to stand their three years of political prosperity; and the Sweeney-Breen rift led to the loss of the mayor's seat in four of the next seven elections down to 1890. The first disaster was the defeat of Breen's hand-picked successor, Alexander Bruce, in December of 1884. But though the *Journal* declared the "ring broken" and "Breenism repudiated," the machine held so many non-elective jobs that it survived the year out of office. When Bruce won the two following years, the *Journal* admitted that Breen was "still Boss." His influence was clearly waning, however, when he was unable to get either the Congressional nomination or the postmastership and even lost an election for sheriff. When a group of leading Democrats signed a protest against him in 1886, it further reduced his power and accentuated the party split.[14]

The Irish squabbles encouraged the natives to resume their attacks. In 1884 the School Committee rejected an Irish Catholic by the name of Owen H. Conlin as submaster in one of the schools, an action that several newspapers blamed on the "bigoted puritan families" who dominated the committee. The *American* then defended the committee on the grounds that all teachers should be capable of "instructing the scholars in the principles of American freedom," an impossible task apparently for Roman Catholics.

The native Republicans determined to gerrymander the city as they had done in 1875. Their victory in 1884 gave them the chance and they proposed a complete redistricting of the city with seven wards running east and west instead of the six that were perpendicular to the river. The additional ward would be the

14. *Lawrence Morning News*, May 23, 1884; *Lawrence Journal*, July 26, Sept. 27, Nov. 1, 15, Dec. 6, 1884, Dec. 12, 1885, Jan. 1, 1887; *Lawrence American*, Jan. 2, 1885.

solidly Irish Democratic district on the "plains" between Haverhill Street and the Spicket River, which the Republicans would concede to the opposition. They would also give the Democrats the two other central wards but expected to carry the four on the outskirts and win the important council. Since they were currently never sure of more than three of the six wards, the new plan was appealing.

So enraged were the Irish that even fourteen years later James O'Neill, President of the Hibernians, drew a pistol when enemies taunted him for voting for this plan to "corral all the Irish in one ward." At the hearings an Irishman named Hannegan said that Ward Four would be "Irishtown," while Councilman Murphy maintained that it would contain two-thirds of the Irish vote. Murphy shouted: "Was this bigotry, or accident?" The *Journal* then commented: "The real facts are that some Republicans are horror-stricken because a few gentlemen of foreign birth or parents have held offices; they insist that the atmosphere of city hall has been contaminated and must be purified." M. S. O'Sullivan then "showed the intrigue which had been resorted to in arranging the school districts, and claimed that the era of race prejudice was being revived." As invariably happened in Lawrence, national background determined the result. With just one exception the council vote was along ethnic lines: voting "yea" were Abbott, Somerville, O'Neill, Hinchcliffe, Haberle, Wheeler, Haseltine, Auty, Smith, Brackett, Abbott, Lyell; voting "nay" were O'Brien, Murphy, Cooney, O'Hearn, Sullivan, Hill. In the cases of Murphy and Cooney, Republicans, ethnic considerations outweighed party benefits. Since a twelve to six vote was not sufficient to carry the redistricting, the votes of the two Irish Republicans were decisive in defeating this Republican scheme.[15]

And so in spite of the Breen-Sweeney split the Irish stuck together sufficiently to thwart nativist efforts to curb their power. After 1885, nativism declined for a few years only to rise even more vigorously against the new immigrants after 1890. The gerrymander failure left the Irish in a strong political position.

15. *Sunday Despatch* (Lawrence), June 29, 1884; *Lawrence Morning News,* July 2, 1884; *The Evening Tribune,* Nov. 30, 1894, Mar. 7, 1898; *The ₌Sunday Register,* Mar. 19, 1899; *Lawrence Journal,* Oct. 24, 31, Nov. 7, 14, 1885, Jan. 23, 1886. See Map III, p. 50.

Intellectually also, the Irish had arrived. Already they were sending boys away to such colleges as Villanova and Ottawa. The Sweeney *Journal* reflected the views of at least part of the Irish population. The Catholic Friends Society had a lecture program to match the White Fund lectures. As the Irish became interested in their own tongue, the Irish Benevolent Society sponsored a lecture on Irish literature and language, which led to a talk in Gaelic on Saint Patrick's night in 1882. Fairly pretentious were John Sweeney's biographical sketches on Roger Taney. Katie O'Keefe, however, best represented the intellectual advances of the Irish. Whether composing a eulogy for Garfield, giving a talk on Motley or Tennyson, or reciting poetry at various meetings, this Irish-born school teacher and newspaper woman reflected the busy, but hardly profound, mind of her fellow Irish immigrants in the city.[16]

Evidence that the Irish had arrived socially was the abrupt decline in the number of newspaper articles accusing them of brawling and other crimes. Back in the 1850's the newspapers had been full of lurid stories of Irish misdeeds. Now the French Canadians were under the same kind of attack from the native press. A group of them, according to one article, maltreated a woman in a way that "would shame a community of savages"; French urchins stole apples; a young Canadian stoned a policeman; and a crowd of drunken Frenchmen drove down Essex Street insulting pedestrians. The climax came in 1890 when within a single month the *Tribune* blamed the "fighting Français" for a Lawrence-Haverhill brawl, referred to a "cantankerous Frenchman on a rampage," and reported another for indecent exposure. Many of the Canadian fights were with aggressive Irishmen who tormented them, but the newspapers stressed the Canadian participation. But while the Canadians got the blame, the record of arrests between 1874 and 1881 showed that a very small percentage of them were being arrested. Actually the Irish were still the ones getting arrested. The percentages read as follows:

16. *Lawrence Journal,* Feb. 2, Dec. 14, 1878, Jan. 18, Sept. 20, 1879, Sept. 4, 1880, July 9, 1881; *The Lawrence Sentinel,* Dec. 26, 1868, Jan. 24, 31, Feb. 7, 14, 21, 1874; *The Evening Tribune,* Feb. 16, 1895, Oct. 14, 1897; *The Evening Tribune,* Centennial Edition, 1953, Women's Section.

Nativity of Father	Percentage of arrests	Percentage of population 1880
Irish	72	42
British	6	17
Canadian	3	10
German	1	5
All foreign-born except Irish	10	32
Total foreign-born	82	74
Native-born	18	26

The newspapers, however, ignored the Irish record because the Irish were socially more acceptable than in the 1850's.[17] The Irish were also better able to weather the reputation of drunkenness and here the record showed them no worse than several other groups. The two Irish wards in 1871 voted to restrict the sale of liquor to those with licenses; while the German and British wards wanted no restrictions at all. Possibly the strongest organization against drinking was Father O'Reilly's Temperance Society. The only immigrant group supporting the open sale of all beverages was the German Personal Liberty League. In 1887, however, when the city decided to eliminate the sale of liquor entirely, it was too much for the Irish, and their precincts along with those of the Germans and Canadians voted against the proposal.[18]

17. *The Lawrence Sentinel,* Aug. 31, 1872; *The Essex Eagle,* Aug. 15, 1874; *Lawrence Journal,* June 11, 18, 1881; *The Evening Tribune,* June 16, July 17, 21, 1890; Bureau of Statistics of Labor, "Fall River, Lowell, and Lawrence," p. 258; *Census of Mass., 1880,* p. 50. See Table VIII.

18. The total vote in 1871 was 978 for restriction and 871 against. Wards Three, Four, and Six, all with heavy Irish population were for; Wards One and Two (German) and Five (English) were against. In 1887 the vote was 2,688 against the sale of liquor completely and 2,460 for the sale with licenses. *Lawrence Journal,* Dec. 10, 1887.

The Vote on The Restriction of The Sale of Liquor 1871

	For Restriction	Against Any Restriction
Ward One (German)	152	179
Ward Two (German)	195	202
Ward Three (Irish)	222	132
Ward Four (Irish)	236	150
Ward Five (English)	92	151
Ward Six	81	57
Total	978	871

The Lawrence Sentinel, May 6, 1871. See also Cole, "Lawrence," pp. 112-13

While the Irish were making steady progress, the city's leaders were trying desperately to make Lawrence the model city it had started to be. Recognizing that the city had not fulfilled the promise of 1845, they took steps to develop its intellectual side. The White Fund continued to bring speakers such as Wendell Phillips, Phillips Brooks, and Henry George to elevate the city, but unfortunately few workers attended the talks. Even though the trustees gave free tickets to the mills, the workers did not get them because the overseers gave them to their friends.[19]

The School Committee kept up with new developments by giving up slates and experimenting with a kindergarten. It took the side of the pupils by ordering less memory work and reducing the numbers in each class. When one teacher put mustard in the mouth of a whispering student, the committee dismissed her. It added a course in American history. But when the committee became too modern and suggested free textbooks, the *Essex Eagle* sarcastically asked whether it was planning a "noontime collation" in the near future.[20]

The establishment of a public library in 1875 was another brave effort by the city to elevate its workers. The total number of books read in its first year was so high that only New York, Boston, Cincinnati, and Philadelphia outranked Lawrence. From 1873 to 1878 the annual circulation averaged over four books per person registered and it remained over three through 1888. Among the favorites were James Fenimore Cooper, Sir Walter Scott, Oliver Optic, and Horatio Alger. Rags to riches and romance were as popular in Lawrence as elsewhere in the United States.[21]

As a result of these efforts the city enjoyed a mild intellectual revival shortly after the Civil War. The Riverside Literary Society vied with the Unitarian Shakespeare Club in the field of belles-

19. Edward Everett, Richard Henry Dana, Frederick Douglass, Henry Ward Beecher, Horace Greeley, Lucy Stone, Julia Ward Howe, and John Fiske also spoke in Lawrence. *Sunday Sun,* Sept. 30, 1906, Jan. 6, 1907.

20. School Committee of . . . Lawrence, *Annual Report,* XXIV (1870), 20; LI (1897), 20-21; LXV (1911), 26, 30; *The Essex Eagle,* Feb. 21, 1874; *Lawrence Journal,* Jan. 13, 1883; *The Evening Tribune,* July 1, 1892, Dec. 29, 1893, Nov. 23, 1894.

21. *The Essex Eagle,* Dec. 27, 1873; Librarian of the Free Public Library of the City of Lawrence, *Report, 1873* (Lawrence, 1874), pp. 11, 16; Librarian, *Report,* III-V (1874-76); VII (1878); IX (1880); XII-XXI (1882-92).

lettres, while the Natural History Society and the Young Men's Catholic Lyceum set the tone in other areas. In 1875 there was a series of spelling matches. The Lawrence Mozart Association and the Choral Union were native efforts in a field dominated by the Germans. By 1890 at least eleven inventions were patented in Lawrence. But Lawrence was not destined to become the Athens of America. In 1877, for example, the *Journal* complained that the patrons of the theater had little taste because they flocked to see Kit the Arkansas Traveller but ignored the performance of Madame Janauschek.[22]

Meanwhile better houses were going up around the city. The Germans with their garden cottages in Hallsville and the British with their frame houses along Broadway lived as well as the natives. The shacks above the dam vanished and even the "plains" boasted superior homes. More than one "spacious mansion" adorned Prospect Hill and one priest lived in a handsome building that cost $8,500.[23]

The city government did its part to improve the appearance of Lawrence. Essex Street, the shopping center, was macadamized in 1861 and paved with stone blocks a decade later. By 1890 almost all of the streets were paved, but they were still muddy when it rained because most had only a gravel covering. Street lighting and sprinkling made travel about the city safer and more pleasant. The city also turned its attention to sewage. Waste, which drained into the Merrimack or Spicket, left the river banks a redolent breeding place for flies. When the Spicket was high, the sewers backed up into cellars; when it was low, a disgusting array of slime and carcasses was revealed. The newspaper outcry was such that the city undertook to clean up this menace in 1883. And three years earlier it had begun to cart away the noisome garbage that filled every alley.[24]

22. *The Essex Eagle,* May 23, 1874, Aug. 12, 1876; L. Frederick Rice, *Report on General System of Sewerage for the City of Lawrence* (Lawrence, 1876); *Lawrence Journal,* Aug. 10, 1878, Sept. 11, 1880, Jan. 1, 1881, Nov. 3, 1883; *Anzeiger und Post,* Aug. 5, 1905; *Sunday Sun,* June 27, 1909; Robert E. Todd, *The Report of the Lawrence Survey* (Lawrence, 1912), pp. 225-36.

23. *The Lawrence Sentinel,* May 8, 1869; *Lawrence American,* Dec. 10, 1864; *Lawrence Journal,* Jan. 27, 1883.

24. *The Lawrence Sentinel,* Sept. 14, 1861; *The Essex Eagle,* Sept. 17, Oct. 15, 1870; United States Census Office, *Eleventh Census of the United States: 1890, Report on the Social Statistics of Cities* . . . (Washington, 1895), pp. 60,

These efforts to trim up Lawrence made the city a healthier place, but the problem of pure drinking water still remained. The completion of a large pumping plant in 1876 provided the residents with a steady supply of water from the Merrimack. No one was much concerned that ten miles above the city the mills and tenements of Lowell dropped vast quantities of chemicals and sewage into the river because studies had erroneously shown the water to be pure by the time it reached Lawrence. The state even made the river a free receptacle for waste and the city government decided to filter the water only when it had too much silt. From then on immigrant and native alike drank diluted sewage in Lawrence.[25]

By 1886 the high disease rate prompted the state to establish an experiment station in Lawrence to explore the related problems of sewage and drinking water. When an unusually severe typhoid fever epidemic came in 1891, Hiram Mills, who was in charge of the station, soon diagnosed the source of the infection. He was amazed at first that Lawrence did not have its fever peak in the early fall with the rest of the state, but suffered most heavily in mid-winter, when its deaths often equalled those in Boston. After carefully plotting the fever deaths in the various Merrimack Valley cities, he was able to prove that the disease came down the river from Manchester and Nashua to Lowell and then moved on to Lawrence. His report was for years the most widely known work on water purification in the world because it proved that streams could not purify themselves within short distances and that typhoid fever was easily carried in sewage-polluted rivers. He urged the immediate construction of a plant that could filter all the water used in the city.

When the new filter was put to work in 1893, the results proved

65; Bureau of Census, *Special Reports, Statistics of Cities . . . 1907* (Washington, 1910), pp. 477, 481, 486.

25. Joint Standing Committee on Water Works, *Report on . . . the Reports and Estimates of the Water Commissioners* (Lawrence, 1875); Water Commissioners, *Final Report* (Lawrence, 1876), pp. 4-14, 23-24; Morris Knowles and Charles Hyde, *The Lawrence, Mass., City Filter . . . .* , reprinted from *Transactions of the American Society of Civil Engineers*, XLVI (1901), 258-66. The state Board of Health in 1887 maintained that "the Merrimack is a good instance of the ability of a large river to receive . . . polluting material . . . without becoming seriously polluted." Massachusetts Board of Health, *Annual Report*, XIX (1887), Mass. Pub. Doc. 34, pp. 36-37.

all of Mills's contentions. The typhoid fever averages dropped from forty-three cases and twelve deaths a year before the filter to fifteen cases and fewer than three deaths after. And the general death rate dropped correspondingly. Three-quarters of the typhoid fever cases after 1893 came from unfiltered water, particularly the canal water that mill workers insisted on drinking.[26]

State help also brought Lawrence closer to ending the smallpox menace, which in 1866 attacked between two hundred and three hundred persons. For years a debate raged between those who favored compulsory inoculation and the others, mostly Germans, who felt it was an invasion of privacy and a scheme to make doctors and druggists rich. When the School Committee finally required inoculations in 1893 and the city doctors agreed to do the work free of charge, within a year all but five hundred of the three thousand school children were protected. Emil Stiegler defeated efforts by the city's Board of Health to pass a general order, but a mandatory state law eliminated all loopholes. The Canadians as well as the Germans were unpopular in this issue because the public believed that the epidemics had originated in Canada. Although the water filter and the compulsory vaccination did not come until three years after the end of the 1865-90 period, the progress taken in those directions before 1890 helps explain why these decades were decades of hope.[27]

Even those who contracted serious diseases had more of a chance because of the Lawrence General Hospital, which the Ladies Union Charitable Society opened in 1882. The immigrants

26. The typhoid fever cases and deaths were for 1887-92 and 1894-99. The typhoid fever annual death rate was three times that of the state before the filter and the same as the state's after it was built. The general death rate went from twenty-four per thousand to twenty. Lawrence Experiment Station, *Proud Heritage, 1886-1953* (Lawrence, 1953), pp. 6-12; H. W. Clark and Stephen Gage, *A Review of . . . Purification of Sewage at the Lawrence Experiment Station* (Boston, 1909), p. 3 (reprinted from Massachusetts Board of Health, *Report*, XL (1908); Hiram F. Mills, "The Filter of the Water Supply of the City of Lawrence and its Results," Massachusetts Board of Health, *Report*, XXV (1893), 545-46, 560; Knowles and Hyde, *Filter*, pp. 268-69, 307-17; M. F. Collins, "The Lawrence Filter," *New England Water Works Association*, XVII (1903), 295; Lawrence Board of Health, "Report, 1906," p. 12, *Lawrence City Documents 1906-1907.*

27. *The Evening Tribune*, May 26, Dec. 13, 23, 1893, Jan. 26, 1894; *Anzeiger und Post*, Dec, 28, 1901, Jan. 28, Mar. 15, Sept. 13, 1902, Feb. 25, 1905.

used the hospital more than the natives. Between 1886 and 1888, for example, even though the immigrants made up less than half of the city, they contributed 62 per cent of the patients. But the more recent immigrant groups did not use it as much as the earlier ones. The Irish, for example, provided more cases than the Canadians.[28]

As a result of these efforts Lawrence made great progress between the 1850's and the 1880's. The death rate dropped from twenty-nine per thousand to twenty-three, while the average age at death rose from fifteen to twenty-five. Parents had less cause to worry as the percentage dying before the age of two fell from 44 per cent of all deaths to 35 per cent. With fewer babies dying this period ended on an optimistic note. It was a better city in which to live than it had been in 1865.[29]

It was also a better place in which to enjoy life partly because

28. Ladies Union Charitable Society, *Report . . . of the Lawrence General Hospital . . .*, XI-XVI (1886-91).

PERCENTAGE OF TOTAL NUMBER OF PATIENTS
AT THE LAWRENCE GENERAL HOSPITAL

Nativity	1886–1888	1889–1891	1894–1896	1899–1901	1904–1906	1910–1911
American	38(56)*	47(54)	36(53)	39(54)	52(54)	54(52)
Irish	33(20)	22	21	15	8	6(7)
English	14(10)	14	14	11	6	8(7)
Canadian	7(6)	8	7	9	9	9(11)
Scotch	3	3	3	4	2	
French			4	3		
German	3	1	6	4	5	2
Italian		1	1	3	6	7(8)
Russian			1	2	2	5(5)
Armenian			3	2		
Polish					3	
Syrian			1	4	4	4(2)
Total Foreign	62(44)	53(46)	64(47)	61(46)	48(46)	46(48)

* In parentheses are the proportions of each ethnic group in the total population of the city.

29. The death rate averaged exactly 22.5 for the five census years 1870-90. It was 29.4 for the census years 1855-65. *Report . . . relating to the Registry and Return of Births, Marriages, and Deaths . . .*, XLIX (1890), Mass. Pub. Doc. 1, p. 373. The average age at death was twenty-five for the census years 1880-90. *Ibid.*, XXIX (1880), vii; XLIV (1885), vii; XLIX (1890), 7. In the period 1867-69, 44 per cent died before the age of two. It was 41 per cent 1877-79, and 35 per cent 1887-89. *Ibid.*, XXVI (1867), xliv-xlv; XXVII (1868), xliv-xlv; XXVIII (1869), xliv-xlv; XXXVI (1877), xliv-xlv; XXXVII (1878), xliv-xlv; XXXVIII (1879), xliv-xlv; XLVI (1887), 52-53; XLVII (1888), 58-59; XLVIII (1889), 58-59.

it was close to the countryside. The half-rural Lawrence of the 1850's remained in the 1880's. A brisk walk out Jackson or Prospect or almost any street brought the immigrant, generally from a rural background, into an environment he could understand. The smell of hay, the sight of apple blossoms, the taste of grapes from the vines were there for all to experience. For some a simple walk across fields was enough, others took picnics up the river, and the more adventurous explored the beaches or mountains. In bad times berry picking and fishing offered food and therapy, in good times there were hills and valleys where a man with savings could build a home. Neither metropolitan nor agrarian, Lawrence offered the immigrants a chance to escape.

Within the city there were opportunities for relaxation. The city streets offered the excitement of a Saint Patrick's Day parade or simply a place for children to frolic and parents to gossip. Sports and games of every sort existed. The walking craze hit the city in 1879, roller polo in 1883, canoe racing in 1884, and horse racing in 1885; boxing, wrestling, dog fighting, and football were more enduring. Enthusiasm for the old swimming holes never waned. The first and second "sandys" in Stevens Pond near the Arlington Mill were exciting because swimmers could dive from the big mill wheel, but the more intrepid frequented the deep, icy-cold, first and second "stumps" in the Merrimack barely above the dam. By the end of these decades of promise cricket and baseball, symbolizing the old world and the new, had become the most popular sports in the city.[30]

Sports heroes and contests brought much color and excitement to the drab existence of the immigrant. Near the close of the Civil War, Frank McAleer of Lawrence fought Professor Levett of Boston to a draw in a prize fight, and the first baseball game took place two years after the Civil War, with the Lawrence team victorious over Lowell forty to thirty-six. One winter seventy-five sleighs met on Canal Street for a race. When the weather became

30. Alice W. O'Connor, "A Study of the Immigration Problem in Lawrence, Massachusetts" (unpublished social worker's thesis, Lawrence, Mass., 1914), pp. 35-39; *Lawrence American,* May 14, 1864; *Lawrence Journal,* Oct. 13, 1877, April 13, Nov. 23, 1878, Aug. 16, 1879, Sept. 4, 1880, April 2, June 25, 1881, Oct. 27, Nov. 3, Dec. 15, 1883, July 11, 18, 1885; *The Essex Eagle,* Dec. 13, 1873, Aug. 4, 1883; *Lawrence Morning News,* June 19, 1884; *The Evening Tribune,* 1890-93, *passim.*

warmer, a "select crowd" gathered to watch two big dogs, "Turk" and "Joe," fight each other for two bloody hours. Occasionally the city had record breakers: men such as J. S. Taylor, who was one of the best walkers in the country, and Barney Weefers, who led all the dash men. Not every one enjoyed the fun. The police made many efforts to suppress games on Sunday and *The Evening Tribune* condemned bicycle speeders who were "scorching" the highways at ten miles an hour.[31]

But while these were years of promise, Lawrence had not reached the millenium by 1890. All over the United States cities were making improvements, often more than in Lawrence. People were still getting sick and dying—thousands of them too early in life—in the immigrant city. The scarlet fever epidemic of 1876 was an unforgettable tragedy. In each major disease Lawrence had a higher death rate than the state as a whole between 1870 and 1890, and its general death rate was fifth in Massachusetts.[32] The disappearance of the shanties only ushered in the tenements. In one a mother and child suffocated while sleeping in a tiny room with two other children. Open staircases inviting a thirty foot plunge to certain death were common. The "stench and pollution of the average tenement traps" drove people out into the streets, where crime flourished. "Starvation alley" off Common Street was crowded with "hovels where sin and crime . . . [were] bred with equal facility." And contributing to all the evils was un-employment, for conditions were unsteady after the Panic of 1873.

Nonetheless, Lawrence had made great progress. The descriptions of the tenements were at least partly exaggerated. Most people did not fall down stairways and most did not catch scarlet fever. If one could only reach the age of two he was likely to live a long while in Lawrence. By 1890 almost a third of those surviving the first two years lived past fifty-five.[33] And the im-

31. The baseball game was held on the Common. *Lawrence American,* May 14, 1864; *The Essex Eagle,* July 27, May 21, 1870, Dec. 13, 1873, Feb. 14, 1874, Feb. 13, 1875, May 13, 1876; *The Evening Tribune,* Sept. 3, 1897, July 18, 1899.

32. Massachusetts Board of Health, *Report,* XXIII (1891), xx, lxxxiii, 785-91, 868-71; *Report of Births, Marriages, and Deaths,* XLIX (1890), 215, 373, 375. The death rate from measles in Lawrence was 74 per cent above the state's; typhoid fever, 70 per cent; diphtheria and croup, 68 per cent.

33. *Lawrence American,* April 16, Aug. 27, 1864; *The Essex Eagle,* Feb. 7, 1874; Wadlin, *Census of . . . Massachusetts: 1895,* I (Boston, 1896), 662-64;

migrants were sure that conditions would soon improve in the mills and then there would be jobs for all. As the decades of promise drew to a close, the city's future seemed bright.

Between 1865 and 1890 Lawrence changed from a city of native Americans and immigrant Irish, where the natives were in complete command, to a cosmopolitan city in which the Irish and the natives ruled the French Canadians and to a lesser extent the British and the Germans. Only the French Canadians among the newer immigrants actually suffered much abuse. The Germans and British, more skilled in the mills and wealthier, were never as unpopular as the French Canadians. The key to the promise shown by the decades between 1865 and 1890 lay in the operation of the immigrant cycle. Even the lowliest Canadian operative recognized the progress made by the Irish during those years and could hope to do the same in the years to come. The city's leaders were able to review the years following the Civil War with pride. The dismal Lawrence of the Know-Nothing riots, the Pemberton disaster, and the shanties was no more. Conscientious efforts had elevated the city's inhabitants and had improved the environment. People lived longer, had more pleasures, and read more. While clashes between ethnic groups occurred, the bitter hatred and ugly violence of the Know-Nothing period did not reappear in the two decades after the Civil War. Had the I.W.W. strike occurred in 1890, the writers would not have been able to paint such a dismal picture as in 1912. The invasion of the post-1890 immigrants was to change Lawrence again.

Lawrence Morning News, April 14, 1884; *The Evening Tribune,* Aug. 15, 1890, Jan. 11, 16, 1891, Feb. 10, 1897; *Lawrence Journal,* Dec. 29, 1877.

CHAPTER V

Decades of Despair, 1890-1912

In January of 1890 the Massachusetts Board of Health made a special report on "the conditions which attended an unusually high rate of mortality" in Lawrence; on Memorial Day the G.A.R. refused to take part in a flag raising ceremony at Saint Mary's parochial school; in June a state meeting of the Hibernians in Lawrence denounced the British; in late July a terrifying cyclone ripped its way through South Lawrence; and that fall the "Micks" opposed the "anti-Micks" in the city election. Thus the decades of promise faded quickly into those of despair. While the transformation was not complete—smallpox inoculations and the filter were still to come—a change began in 1890. Between that date and 1912 massive invasions of new immigrants doubled the city's population and posed problems that the city could not immediately solve. During the first five years about a thousand refugees from the Russian, Austrian, Italian, and Turkish empires arrived in the city, and the total rose to 2,500 in 1900 and 15,000 in 1910. Just before the 1912 strike southeastern Europeans made up one-third of the immigrant population.[1]

1. Massachusetts Board of Health, "Lawrence: An Inquiry Relative to the Conditions Which Attended an Unusually High Rate of Mortality in Lawrence in 1889, with Special Reference to Diphtheria," *Annual Report,* XXI (1889), Mass. Pub. Doc. 34, pp. 397, 399-412; *The Evening Tribune,* May 4, 10, 27, June 12, July 28-31, Aug. 5, 1890; Cyclone Relief Committee . . . Lawrence, Mass., . . . , *Report, April, 1891* (Lawrence, 1891); *British-American Citizen,* Dec. 7, 1889, Aug. 2, 1890, cited in R. T. Berthoff, *British Immigrants in Industrial America, 1790-1950* (Cambridge, Mass., 1953), p. 200; United States Census Office, *Eleventh Census of the United States: 1890,* I (Washington, 1895), 670; Horace G. Wadlin, *Census of . . . Massachusetts: 1895,* II (Boston, 1897), 607; United States Census Office, *Twelfth Census of the United States . . . 1900,* II (Washington, 1902), 796-97; United States Census Bureau, *Thirteenth Census*

The first Italians came in 1891, when the owners of the street railway imported forty-two to break a strike.   The immigrants spent the night on straw beds at the condemned "Bullfrog Tavern," where hundreds of curiosity seekers visited them the next morning. Not satisfied with watching their toilet, the crowds pressed so close as the work began that the Italians finally panicked and ran out of town.   A dynamite explosion injured another gang of Italian workers in 1902 as they were building the electric railway in North Andover.   Others from Boston dug a sewer in North Andover until the pay ran out.   In these years Lawrence was a substation in the *padrone* system originating in Boston.   The Italians who came to stay moved into the former Irish districts of lower Common Street and the "plains," where they had a Christopher Columbus Society in 1899 and other clubs by 1909.   Around Columbus Day lower Common Street was particularly alive as the Italians enjoyed a weekend of band music and dancing under colored lanterns.   The organizers of the celebrations were usually Jeremiah Campopiano, president of the Columbus Society, and Fabrizio Pitocchelli, treasurer of the 1901 festival, both bankers, as well as Father Milanese, the priest at Saint Laurence's.[2]

Several nationalities fled to Lawrence from Russia.   The Lithuanians dedicated a church in 1903 and six years later commemorated the fortieth anniversary of the arrival of the first Lithuanian in America.   Their principal spokesman was John Alosky, president of their Citizens' Club and organizer of the 1909 celebration.   The Poles, who inhabited the "Italian and Polack district" of Garden and Union Streets, built a church in 1905 and had a young men's club a year later.   A majority of them actually came from outside the Russian Empire, two-thirds from Galicia. The Jews were about evenly divided between those from Russian Poland and Lithuania and those from the other Baltic provinces and the shores of the Black Sea.[3]

---

of the United States . . . 1910: Abstract of the Census . . . with Supplement for Massachusetts . . . (Washington, 1913), p. 609.   There were 6,700 Italians and 4,400 Russians in 1910.

2. *The Evening Tribune,* June 13, 1891, Aug. 3, 1900, Feb. 14, 1902; *Sunday Sun,* July 18, 1909, Aug. 28, 1910.

3. W. J. Lauck, "The Significance of the Situation at Lawrence: The Condition of the New England Woolen Mill Operative," *The Survey,* XXVII (1911-12), 1773; *Sunday Sun,* Feb. 5, 1905, Nov. 25, 1906; *The Strike at Lawrence, Mass.*

From the Turkish Empire came the Syrians. These immigrants, who settled on the "plains," were from around Mount Lebanon, particularly the cities of Damascus and Beirut. The Chicago World's Fair of 1893 aroused their interest in America and the Presbyterian minister W. E. Wolcott, who was the son of a Beirut missionary, attracted them to Lawrence. There they made rapid progress, within a few years establishing a newspaper, a school, and several churches, while producing leaders such as Joseph Saliba, principal of their school, Joseph M. Khoury, editor of *Al-Wafa,* and Gabriel Bistany, priest at the Syrian Catholic Church.[4]

The influx of the southeastern Europeans forced the construction of more and more tenements that climbed higher and clustered closer together. At first they were only two stories high, but by 1895, 957 of the tenements were three stories or more, the great majority in the central wards where the immigrants lived. By 1910 even the four-story building was common with 268 in the center of Lawrence, a far greater number than in any other city of Massachusetts. In 1901 the *Tribune* observed: "Lawrence is growing steadily, but not so rapidly as the towering mushroom buildings grow on the back alleys." In an effort to end such construction, Councilman Kennedy deplored the "large number of great eight-tenement and sixteen-tenement blocks that had crowded into the little yards in the rear of the other buildings." Adjoining dwellings were even closer on the side than on the back. Some were so close that a woman in one would hang kitchen utensils on the outside wall of the next, so close that there was not even room enough for a garbage pail between houses, so close that agents

---

Hearings before the Committee on Rules of the House of Representatives . . . 1912, 62 Congress, 2 Session, House Doc. 671 (Washington, 1912), p. 291; *The Evening Tribune,* Mar. 14, 1904.

4. Chief of the Bureau of Statistics of Labor, *Census of . . . Massachusetts 1905,* I (Boston, 1909), 109; Nagib Abdou, *Dr. Abdou's Travels in America* (Washington, 1907), pp. 68, 80; *The Evening Tribune,* Aug. 3, 1900, Nov. 7, 1901; Lauck, "Significance," p. 1773; Board of Trade of London, *Cost of Living in American Towns,* 62 Congress, 1 Session, Senate Doc. 22 (Washington, 1911), p. 209; *Boston Evening Transcript,* Feb. 1, 1912; *Al-Wafa,* April 30, 1907; *The Lawrence Sun,* April 9, 1906; *Sunday Sun,* May 31, 1908, May 14, 1911. For Armenian statistics see *The Evening Tribune,* July 30, 1894, Oct. 27, 1900.

collected rents on the upper floors of two blocks at the same time by reaching across from one apartment to the one next door.[5]

Inside, the tenements were dreary and dark. The 1911 survey commented: "In the apartments of the front house, one or two rooms are well lighted from the street; the kitchen receives but little light; and the two rooms in the rear are almost as poorly lighted. . . . The front rooms [and] . . . the kitchens in the rear houses are almost entirely inadequately lighted." Many rooms had no outside light at all. In one of them, a bedroom used by five people, the survey discovered that an eight-month-old child had died of tuberculosis, a price that Lawrence paid for over-crowding its buildings.[6]

Another price was fire, which constantly threatened the lives of all, but particularly the two thousand who lived on the fourth floors of wooden buildings. Jammed close together with no fire escape and but one exit, the four-deckers trapped men like animals. In 1895 all but 453 of the city's 6,855 buildings were wooden, and fires once started raced rapidly through the most heavily populated areas. The habits of the dwellers also contributed to the danger. A child with an oil lamp in a dark cellar could easily set fire to the piles of rubbish that were always there; and school children at home alone who attempted to light stoves with matches and kerosene were also a menace. A tenement building with six apartments had six coal stoves, any one of which could destroy the structure.[7]

Men as well as buildings were packed closer and closer as Lawrence neared the strike of 1912. While the density of population rose only from seven to ten per acre between 1870 and 1890, it jumped all the way to twenty by 1910. The worst crowding was in the center of Lawrence, where one-third of the city's people lived on only one-thirteenth of the area or about 119 to the acre.

5. Wadlin, *Census of . . . Massachusetts: 1895*, I (Boston, 1896), 662-64; Robert E. Todd and Frank B. Sanborn, *The Report of the Lawrence Survey* (Lawrence, 1912), pp. 37-38, 59-60, 87-89, 96, 105; *Lawrence City Documents, 1897-1898*, p. 19; *The Evening Tribune*, Feb. 5, June 20, 1901; Charles P. Neill, *Report on Strike of Textile Workers in Lawrence, Mass. in 1912*, 62 Congress, 2 Session, Senate Doc. 870 (Washington, 1912), pp. 147-51. Lawrence had many of the dumbbell-shaped dwellings that made Boston notorious.

6. Todd and Sanborn, *Survey*, p. 61.

7. *Ibid.*, pp. 44, 105; *Census of Mass., 1895*, I, 662.

The land on which they huddled was a central district running from Essex Street north almost to the Spicket River and from Union Street west to the railroad tracks near Broadway.[8] Into this "conflagration center" the immigrant moved when he first arrived: the Irishman and later the southeastern European to lower Common Street, the Irishman and then the Syrian to Oak Street on the "plains," and the French Canadian to Valley Street. These three streets quickly became the most densely populated and poorest in the entire city. The 1911 survey studied five half blocks on these streets and found that each held from three hundred to six hundred people per acre. There were few blocks in the country more heavily populated. Even the thirty crowded blocks in Harlem in New York, visible from the train between 125th Street Station and the 110th Street tunnel, included only three with more than six hundred per acre. Almost all of the lots on the Lawrence blocks had more than 70 per cent of the land covered by buildings, leaving little for anything else. The two on lower Common Street, the heart of the Italian quarter in 1911, were the most congested three acres in the state except for a small part of Boston. And in Boston there was much less danger of fire because the houses were nearly all of brick.[9]

All reports and studies of Lawrence underscored the threat of overpopulation. Health inspectors reported six Syrians sleeping in their clothes on two beds in a tiny room eight feet by ten on Oak Street and nineteen more in four rooms on Valley Street. The Sanitary Inspector in 1912 found only four rooms without a bed in 214 tenements.[10] The Labor Commissioner's report on the

8. United States Census Office, *Eleventh Census of the United States: 1890. Report on the Social Statistics of Cities* . . . (Washington, 1895), pp. 53-57; United States Census Office, *Ninth Census of the United States* . . . *1870,* I (Washington, 1872), 380; *Thirteenth Census* . . . *Supplement for Mass.,* p. 596; Todd and Sanborn, *Survey,* pp. 54, 87; *The Evening Tribune,* Feb. 5, 1901; *Sunday Sun,* June 24, 1906. See map, p. 25.

9. Todd and Sanborn, *Survey,* pp. 54-60. These half blocks were on one side of the street only and included all the land back to the alley. They averaged an acre and a half in size. Actual density of each half block per acre in 1911: Common Street south side east from Newbury, 603; Common Street south side west from Newbury, 462; Valley Street south side east from Franklin, 348; Valley Street south side west from Franklin, 342; Oak Street north side west from White, 303.

10. *The Evening Tribune,* Mar. 30, Aug. 10, 1900, July 9, 1903; *Sunday Sun,* Aug. 11, 1912.

Lawrence strike of 1912 showed that most of the immigrant workers' households occupied four or five rooms with an average of 1.5 persons per room. In his study only three of the households with ten or more members had more than five rooms. No wonder Lawrence was near the top in number of persons per room and in every other category that related to overpopulation.[11]

Filth already present during the decades of promise became worse during the decades of despair. Swill and ashes were often in the halls in open buckets or on closet floors. Rats were all too common. When the Stanley Brewery burned, thousands overran the streets of western Lawrence and according to one poor fellow "attacked his house by dozens, came up through the cellar into the sink room, where they carried off everything edible—raw potatoes by the peck, apples, eggs, pies, bread. . . ." While almost every apartment in 1911 had a sink with running water and a water closet, only one out of twenty in the poorer areas had a bathtub and half of the water closets were dark, dirty, and wet. Landlords were responsible when paint, plaster, and whitewash were missing, when cellars were wet, when roofs leaked, and when water closets overflowed. But the landlords complained that dirty tenants destroyed plumbing and wasted water. Immigrants from rural parts of Europe were no less clean than others, but they needed time to learn how to care for a city tenement. The peasant method of throwing water on the floor and swabbing it with a broom was disastrous to the ceiling of the apartment below, and it was no longer possible to bury garbage or feed it to farm animals. References to "vermin," "filthy alleys," "voracious rats," and "evil smells" were common.[12]

11. Lawrence was in the top 10 per cent among American cities in persons per house in 1910. She ranked between fourth and sixth in the state in families per house in 1910, size of family in 1905, and persons per room in 1895. In 1910 there were 8.2 persons per house, 1.6 families per house; 5.0 persons per family in 1905. *Thirteenth Census . . . Supplement for Mass.*, p. 262; *Census of Mass., 1905*, I, lx. In 1895 there were 0.8 persons per room and 5.8 rooms per family. *Census of Mass., 1895*, I, 761, 784. Neill, *Report*, pp. 156-60.

12. Mary Heaton Vorse, "The Trouble in Lawrence," *Harper's Weekly*, LVI (1912), 10; Alice W. O'Connor, "A Study of the Immigration Problem in Lawrence, Massachusetts," (unpublished social worker's thesis, Lawrence, Mass., 1914), p. 26; *The Evening Tribune*, Feb. 14, 1895, Mar. 30, Aug. 10, 1900, July 9, 1903; Todd and Sanborn, *The Survey*, pp. 65-67; *Lawrence Journal*, July 12, 1879; *Le Progres*, Aug. 26, 1904, May 10, 1906; Lawrence Board of Health, "Report, 1885," p. 7, *Lawrence City Documents 1885-1886;* Massachusetts Board of Health, *Report*, XXXIX (1907), 471; *Sunday Sun*, April 8, 1906.

The trend toward better housing that had started after the Civil War had ended by 1890. But this was not the only way in which life in Lawrence became bleaker at the close of the century. Many immigrants had enjoyed hearty meals in Lawrence during the period of French-Canadian immigration—some in their own homes, others in the boarding houses. As the southeastern Europeans moved in, almost all found their way to the tenements and the boarding house became less typical. Within their dismal tenements the immigrants no longer ate the hearty food that some had enjoyed in the past. At the government strike hearings in 1912 the city missionary said that his office had to feed the children bread and karo corn syrup in school because many arrived without breakfast. The pride with which he depicted the meal of hard bread and karo led Congressman Foster to comment acidly: "As I understand the testimony here, there are two very desirable luxuries in the city of Lawrence, Mass., among the mill operatives, that is, molasses on their bread, and water." A Polish mender said the people lived on bread, syrup, molasses, and beans, and rarely had meat. A weaver testified that when he was earning only $3.00 a week, he lived on bread and water, and even at best never had meat more than two or three times a week. The workers were also, he said, "trying to fool . . . [their] stomachs" with a "kind of molasses" in place of butter.

Food was so expensive in 1912 that the city set up a store to provide it more cheaply for the poor. Though the Syrians liked lamb and mutton and the Poles sausage and smoked shoulder, they and the other immigrants ate little meat. As a substitute the Italians consumed macaroni, vegetables dressed in oil, and rye bread; the Poles had tinned fruits, bakery products, and rye bread; and the Syrians filled up on rice, vegetables, and fruit. Greens and berries, readily available in the countryside, supplemented the workers' diet. Milk was so expensive that the immigrants replaced it with tea, coffee, or, in the case of the Italians, wine.[13]

13. *Strike at Lawrence*, pp. 32, 154-55, 244, 380-86. Another striker said he had meat once a week and otherwise nothing but black bread, coffee, and molasses at each meal. Once he was reduced to bread and water. *Sunday Sun*, Feb. 4, 1912; *Lawrence City Documents 1911-1912*, p. 651; Board of Trade of London, *Cost of Living*, pp. xxv, 217-18. Meat was so expensive it was not sold by the joint. Neill, *Report*, pp. 26, 165-78; O'Connor, "Study," pp. 30-32.

And so in the decades before the strike the immigrants found themselves crowded into dirty tenements where the hazard of fire put their lives in jeopardy. Poorly-fed and ill-clad they left their homes daily to work in the mills. Here they found an existence even worse than their home lives because the mills maimed and killed them in many ways. The case of one Polish girl with beautiful long hair was not unusual and received only cursory attention. Carelessly chatting with her fellow workers she allowed her flowing hair to get caught in her machine and seconds later lay writhing on the floor with part of her scalp torn off. After placing her scalp carefully in a paper bag, her friends carried her to a doctor, and happily or unhappily she survived. Other machines sucked in arms and legs; some even whole bodies. The Pacific Mill had 1,000 accidents in less than five years and even though most were considered slight, the steady succession of injuries was depressing to the immigrants, who suffered 788 of them. With an average of forty-three persons working above the ground floor for every stairway or fire escape, the Lawrence mills were next to the worst in the state in 1877. Four of the large plants employing workers above the second floor had only a single exit and that inside. By 1912 conditions were even worse. The sight of terrified operatives nerving themselves for the breath-taking plunge to a net or the street below was not uncommon.[14]

The very nature of the textile industry caused less spectacular deaths. In the ring spinning and carding rooms, for example, dust, dried sputum, heat, moisture, poor air and light, and carbon monoxide produced unhealthful conditions. The humid, confined air of the weaving rooms was filled with fine particles of fiber that cut years from the weavers' lives. Elizabeth Shapleigh, who studied the city's vital records for the socialist *New York Call* in 1912, found that a third of the spinners died before they had worked

---

Oxtails, pig's plucks, and lamb's plucks were eaten. Butterine, leaf lard, and suet replaced butter. Condensed milk replaced fresh milk.

14. *Strike at Lawrence,* p. 170; *The Evening Tribune,* Sept. 23, 1897, Mar. 25, 1899; Charles Harrington, "Report on Sanitary Conditions of Factories, Workshops, and Other Establishments," Massachusetts Board of Health, *Report,* XXXVIII (1906), 477-79; Bureau of Statistics of Labor, *Eighth Annual Report . . . 1877,* Mass. Pub. Doc. 31, pp. 239, 282. Actually Lawrence was the worst city in regard to number of fire escapes; the only city that had fewer was a small city employing only 769 workers. In Lawrence 8,421 worked above the ground floor and had only 195 exits.

ten years and half of them before they were twenty-five years old. Pneumonia, tuberculosis, and other respiratory infections carried off large proportions of the weavers, dyers, and combers, as well as the spinners. While these diseases killed almost 70 per cent of the textile operatives, they killed only 4 per cent of farmers, who consequently lived to be sixty while the textile workers could not reach forty. The Massachusetts Board of Health found that the death rate from tuberculosis and pneumonia in Lawrence from 1886 to 1910 was higher than in almost all of the non-textile cities.[15]

The same board made a special report on Lawrence in 1890 because an epidemic of typhoid fever, diarrheal diseases, and diphtheria, as well as the mill diseases, were making the city a death hole. The death rate, dropping steadily in the 1870's and 1880's, shot back up to 27 per thousand in 1890, placing Lawrence first in Massachusetts and sixth in the nation. The board found that most of those who succumbed to diphtheria and croup lived in immigrant areas, the dense Irish and French-Canadian district between Essex and Lowell Streets being the worst. Here, where ill-fed, poorly-clad families huddled in three rooms in six-family tenements, half of those who contracted diphtheria died. Additional plagues struck the city in 1891 and 1892, and a concentrated attack of diarrheal diseases in 1900 led to another study of the beleaguered city. This time the board found that only in deaths from consumption, heart disease, and cancer did the immigrants suffer noticeably more than the natives.

Disease hit the new babies so hard that the percentage dying in the first two years, which had dropped between 1870 and 1890, went up again to 44 per cent of all deaths after 1900. And with it the mean age at death dropped back down from twenty to fifteen. The decades of promise had indeed given way to those of despair.[16]

15. Harrington, "Report," p. 472; Elizabeth Shapleigh, "Occupational Disease in the Textile Industry," *The New York Call*, Dec. 29, 1912, p. 13; H. W. Clark and Stephen Gage, "A Study of the Hygienic Condition of the Air in Textile Mills with Reference to the Influence of Artificial Humidification," Massachusetts Board of Health, *Report*, XLIV (1912), 659-92. The record of the other textile cities was similar.

16. For death statistics see *Report . . . relating to the Registry and Return of Births, Marriages, and Deaths . . .* , XLIX (1890), Mass. Pub. Doc. 1, p. 373. See also Table VI. For the five census years 1870-90 Lawrence had the fifth lowest excess of birth rate over death rate in the state. *Ibid.,* XLIX (1890),

While the homes and the mills were full of dangers, so were the streets, where crime continued to prevail. But now the newspapers were blaming most outrages on the newcomers. While up to 1890 they had been filled with accounts of the Canadians' crimes, they now were concentrating on the misdeeds of the southeastern Europeans. One Italian was called a beggar, the two who followed were counterfeiters, and the *Tribune* connected another with an illegal liquor business. Police arrested an "Israelite" and a Syrian for peddling without licenses; Russian Poles "overindulged"; and a Syrian boy made the headlines by stealing $2.07. When seven Italians slashed an Irishman in 1894, the stories of fights and killings began. One Italian ran "amuck" in "Little Italy," while another threatened to stab a pretty girl whom he could not seduce. One Chinese chased two taunting boys with a long knife and a second routed four assailants with a brick. The press also twisted isolated events into mass movements such as a "Polander" riot and a Syrian-Portuguese "race war."[17]

215, 373, 375; *Eleventh Census . . . 1890, Social Statistics of Cities*, p. 55; United States Census Office, *Eleventh Census of the United States . . . 1890*, XVII, Part I (Washington, 1896), 554. The federal census called the 1890 death rate 29·1. Massachusetts Board of Health, "Lawrence," pp. 397, 399-412, tables 415f; *The Evening Tribune*, Mar. 15, 25, 31, June 11, 1892, May 4, 1893, Mar. 26, 1897; *Lawrence American*, Dec. 13, 1889; *Anzeiger und Post*, April 8, 1899. The statistics for the 1900 deaths are as follows:

DISEASES THAT KILLED PROPORTIONATELY MORE
FOREIGN-BORN THAN NATIVE-BORN IN LAWRENCE 1900*

	Native-Born	Foreign-Born
Consumption	55	69
Heart Disease	36	60
Urinary Diseases	26	27
Old Age	12	21
Cancer	10	24

* Foreign-born percentage of population was 46 per cent. United States Census Office, *Twelfth Census of the United States . . . 1900*, III (Washington, 1902), 365. The statistics for babies' deaths came from *Report of Births, Marriages, and Deaths*, XXVI-XXVIII (1867-69); XXXVI-XXXVIII (1877-79); XLVI-XLVIII (1887-89); LVIII-LX (1899-1901); LXVI-LXVIII (1907-9). The percentage was 44 per cent before 1870; 35 per cent 1870-90; 44 per cent again 1907-9.

17. *Lawrence Journal*, June 28, 1879, Feb. 12, 1887; *The Lawrence Sentinel*, Mar. 13, 1875; *The Evening Tribune*, June 16, 1890, Sept. 1, 10, 1894, July 18, Aug. 16, 1896, June 3, 1899, Feb. 25, 1901, July 6, Sept. 17, 1903; *Sunday Sun*, Aug. 19, 1906. According to *The Evening Tribune* there was trouble in the "Hebrew Quarter," the Syrians "shed blood," and there was a "hot Syrian row." *The Evening Tribune*, June 26, 1901, Aug. 18, 1902.

The crimes of the post-1890 immigrants were actually quite similar to those of the Irish, French Canadians, and others before them. National animosity led to the more serious brawls. The Irish-French fights of the early period blended later into clashes involving Italians, Syrians, and other southeastern Europeans. As before, the newly-arrived immigrants tended to resist police authority. Examples were the early French and Irish attacks on policemen and the later attempt of two hundred Poles and Lithuanians to tear a prisoner away from the police. Most of the immigrants, particularly the Italians, Irish, French Canadians, Poles, Lithuanians, Syrians, and Armenians had come over hating the government back home and were in the habit of resisting its wishes. It is remarkable that they obeyed an alien law force as well as they did. Tragically ironic was the number of deadly riots that accompanied weddings. At Lithuanian "drunken orgies" the members of the wedding parties used bottles, black jacks, stove covers, and stones on each other. There were also Irish, French, Polish, and Syrian wedding brawls. The major change came in weapons. With the Irish, conflict was a matter of fists or blunt objects, but the later immigrants turned to knives, guns, and even razors. When Patrick Mulvaney exchanged taunts with some Italians who were walking with a girl, a crowd gathered and shouted, "Here's yer dagoes, Kid, go get them," and with that one Italian slashed Mulvaney with a razor.[18]

Although the amount of crime did not actually increase, it remained fantastically high. Six per cent of the population was arrested in 1880 and 1890, and it was still 5 per cent in 1910. It is hard to imagine six persons out of one hundred with a police record in one year. Between 1889 and 1891, 56 per cent of the arrested were immigrants and even though the proportion of immigrants in the population grew during the next two decades, their percentage of arrests was identical for the years 1909 to 1912. Once again the newspapers were unfairly stressing the misbehavior of the more recent arrivals.[19]

18. *Sunday Sun*, July 30, 1905. Concerning the Irish see *The Lawrence Courier*, April 24, 1855; French, *Lawrence Journal*, June 18, 1881; Syrian, *The Evening Tribune*, Aug. 26, 1903; Polish, *Sunday Sun*, Feb. 4, 1906. The razor quotation is in *ibid.*, July 5, 1908.

19. Bureau of Statistics of Labor, "Fall River, Lowell, and Lawrence," *Thirteenth Annual Report . . . 1882*, Mass. Pub. Doc. 31, pp. 193-415; *Lawrence*

The intellectual climate of the city was much less favorable in 1912 than it had been in the 1880's. Once again the hopes of the founders of the model town and the promise of the 1870's and 1880's had been in vain. The workers were still not attending the lectures set up for them by the early builders. Nor was the great library interest maintained. While mill workers made up 37 per cent of those holding library cards in 1873, an encouraging figure, the percentage for the 1890's was 30 per cent and for 1900-10 only 22 per cent. At the same time the proportion of non-fiction and non-juvenile literature read dropped from 29 per cent in 1875-84 to 19 per cent in 1912. Conditions were little better in the school system where Lawrence spent in 1891-92 less per child than any city in the state but one. Truancy, a nightmare for the principals, averaged 8,500 cases a year. And those students who did come to class were frequently older than the generally accepted age levels. The median Italian and Syrian student had not advanced beyond the first grade in 1896.[20]

Illiteracy and inability to speak English, which were both related to the decline in intellectual standards, were sharply on the rise after 1900. While less than 1 per cent of the native population was illiterate in both 1890 and 1910, foreign-born illiterates numbered 15 per cent in 1890 and 22 per cent in 1910. And this was an increase over the 14 per cent of the foreign-born who were illiterate in 1865. As a consequence one-eighth of the city could not read or write any language just before the strike. Among the natives those with foreign parents had three times as many il-

City Documents 1889-1890, p. 305; 1890-91, pp. 280-81; 1891-92, pp. 253-54; 1899-1900, p. 183; 1900-1, pp. 151-52; 1901-2, p. 235; 1909-10, p. 6; 1910-11, p. 4; 1911-12, p. 72; *Eleventh Census . . . 1890*, I, cxxvii; United States Census Office, *Twelfth Census . . . 1900*, II, 621; *Thirteenth Census . . . Supplement for Mass.*, p. 609.

20. *The Essex Eagle*, Jan. 3, 1874; *Catalogue of the Free Public Library of . . . Lawrence* (Lawrence, 1873), p. 332; Librarian of the Free Public Library of the City of Lawrence, *Report*, 1873 (Lawrence, 1874), p. 9; Librarian, *Report*, IV-V (1875-76); XIV-XV (1885-86); XIX (1890); XXI (1892); XXV (1896); XXIX (1900); XXXI (1902); XXXIII (1904); XXXVII (1908); XXXIX (1910); XLI (1912); School Committee of . . . Lawrence, *Annual Report*, XLVI (1892), 91; XLVIII (1894), 19-20; L (1896), 9-11, 46-47; LVI (1902), 9-11; LXV (1911), 26, 30, 71. One-fifth of the pupils in the first eight grades were above the normal age. *Ninth Census . . . 1870*, p. 446; *Eleventh Census . . . 1890*, I, 172-80. Immigrants made up 18 per cent of the public school students in 1870; 16 per cent in 1896. The median student in Lawrence was in the fourth grade in 1896.

literates as those with native parents. The figures for the factory workers studied by the Immigration Commission in 1909 were about the same. The immigrant who could not read or write his own language often had the added difficulty of not being able to speak English. It was bad enough in 1890 when about 10 per cent of them could not speak English, but in 1909 almost 40 per cent of the woolen and worsted workers had that added handicap.[21]

The immigrant city sought to remedy the situation through its schools. In the regular day-classes natives mixed freely with foreigners. Not one of the city's schools in 1896 had a dominant number born in any one country and most had students from five to seven ethnic groups. Only the Syrians were confined to one school. Segregation was the rule of course in the Free Evening School, which taught English to immigrants, where only two classes out of sixteen were mixed. There were two separate German classes, seven French, and one each of Italians, Syrians, and Armenians. A school of six hundred in 1870, it doubled its size by 1912. The city also set up an industrial school in 1909 to teach the immigrant a trade. Situated within the city, it was a great improvement over the previous arrangement whereby tired workers left the mills at 6:30 P.M., went nine miles to the textile school in Lowell, returning to a midnight supper. But in spite of all efforts Lawrence was a city of poorly educated and frequently illiterate immigrants in 1912.[22]

21. "Illiterate" means "cannot read or write" or "cannot write" any language. Oliver Warner, *Abstract of the Census of Massachusetts,—1865* . . . (Boston, 1867), p. 94; *Ninth Census* . . . *1870*, I, 446; Carroll D. Wright, *Census of Massachusetts: 1880* . . . (Boston, 1883), p. 470; United States Census Office, *Eleventh Census of the United States: 1890*, II (Washington, 1897), cxix-xccii; *Thirteenth Census* . . . *Supplement for Mass.*, p. 597. Exact native illiteracy was 0.7 per cent 1890 and 1910. Exact total of illiteracy 1910 was 13.2 per cent. Immigration Commission, "Woolen and Worsted Goods in Representative Community A," *Immigrants in Industries, Part 4: Woolen and Worsted Goods Manufacturing*, II, Immigration Commission, *Reports*, X, 61 Congress, 2 Session, Doc. 633 (Washington, 1911), pp. 775, 789; *Eleventh Census* . . . *1890*, II, lxv, 270. Factory worker illiteracy 1909: native-born, native parents, 0.2 per cent; native-born, foreign parents, 0.5 per cent; foreign-born, 21.9 per cent. See Table IX.

22. School Committee, *Report*, L (1896), 46; LXVI (1912), 89; *The Evening Tribune*, Mar. 1, 1894; *The Essex Eagle*, Nov. 12, 1870; William Dooley, "Practical Education for Industrial Workers," *Educational Review*, XXXVIII (1909), 261-72. Those enrolled in evening School were: 600 in 1870; 900 in 1894; 1300 in 1912.

As the gap between immigrant and native grew, nativism, dormant for a few years after the gerrymander failure of 1885, arose again. The ugly prejudice displayed in the Saint Mary's flag raising episode in 1890 only foreshadowed worse ethnic clashes to come, for after several decades of relative peace, the city returned to the fierce passions of the 1850's. The Saint Mary's affair began when members of the G.A.R. would not take part in a Decoration Day ceremony at Saint Mary's school and were called "bigots" by the Irish. Patrick Sweeney, donor of the flag that was to be raised, then offered the city $1,000 for prizes at Saint Mary's school. Since many thought he only wanted to influence the schools, they felt the city should not accept his offer. The positive stands of the G.A.R. and Sweeney focused attention on the flag raising ceremony in which only Catholic societies participated. Father O'Reilly, the prominent priest at Saint Mary's, probed the religious issue with these words:

We find here and there, the smoldering embers of intolerance and bigotry, fanned into a flame of religious hatred.
No sect or creed, no native nor foreign-born class can claim upon this soil to be the loyal men or women of America.
. . . We are not ashamed to assert it, God first, country second. And he who serves God well, the better serves his country.
[But why have we parochial schools?]
We believe that a religious education should go hand in hand with a knowledge of the sciences of the material and physical world. This is no new doctrine of America. The Puritan founders of Massachusetts insisted in having their parish schools alongside their parish church.

The idea that what was good for the church was good for America and the parallel drawn with New England Puritanism did little to ease tension. Nor was the situation relieved a few days later when the Hibernians attacked the British Americans, whom they believed had kept the G.A.R. away from the flag raising. A British American extended the controversy by replying, "We are sorry for our neighbors . . . that they cannot adapt themselves to the institutions as they find them. . . . They are ruled by scheming and tricky politicians and demagogues. . . ."[23]

The Saint Mary's affair touched off five years in which the nativist issue dominated politics, a period comparable to the six

23. *The Evening Tribune*, May 5, 10, 27, 31, June 14, 1890.

years between 1854 and 1860. Party labels became "Mick" and
"anti-Mick" or "A.P.A. and "anti-A.P.A." The Democratic *Evening Tribune* felt that the only way the Democrats could win in
1891 was to nominate a native for mayor because even the second-
generation Irish wanted one. Its poem accentuating this point was
one of the high spots of the campaign:

The Boston democrats	Go to the polls
Elected an	Today from
American democrat	Four to 9 o'clock
For mayor.	And vote to restore
The example is	Democratic harmony,
Worthy of emulation	Democratic unity
By the democrats	And win a
Of Lawrence.	Democratic victory.

The Republicans at the same time considered the Germans, the
so-called "Bremen Line," an equal handicap. The campaign song
used to get the German Gesing off the Republican ticket was as
well known as the *Tribune's* ditty:

> Arra, Gesing, dear, and do you hear the cry that's going
> round:
> "Get off the ticket, laddy buck, or you surely will be
> drowned.
> There's a German weight at one end that makes a round
> shouldered stoop;
> Get off! Get off! Get off! or the ticket's in the soup."

Prejudice reached its high point on the day of the election
when twenty-eight women in Ward Six united to vote against the
Irish Democratic candidates for the School Committee and succeeded in defeating a Catholic named Kennedy by the scant margin
of eleven votes. The Democrats, who followed the *Tribune's* cue
by nominating the native-born Lewis P. Collins for mayor, carried
the city, but controversy continued over appointments to office.
"Nominate a Mc or an O, Mr. Mayor," said the *American*; "the
fellows [the Democratic Aldermen, mostly Irish Catholics] will
recognize him at once." The Irish Democrats then combined

with the Republicans on the board to defeat any of the mayor's Democratic nominees who were not Irish.[24]

Later that year prejudice arose in a different area when a few native members of the swank Canoe Club voted not to admit a half dozen Irish because they imagined a "studied attempt" to make it an Irish club. The Irish members had been in Lawrence too long for such treatment, however, and succeeded in passing the following resolution: "Whereas it is apparent that at a recent meeting of this club certain members thereof voted to reject applicants for membership solely through race prejudice: Be it resolved, That we distinctly repudiate the spirit of bigotry thus manifested . . . as hostile to the best interests of the club and that we denounce their action as narrow, illiberal, and un-American. . . ."[25]

But the next year a different slur against the Irish was not officially rebuked. Former Senator Patterson addressed a Lawrence meeting of the Essex County Teachers' Association and made remarks that the Catholic teachers of the city held to be "offensive." He attacked the sale of indulgences and not only ridiculed the "superstitious . . . reverence of Catholics for sacred relics" but also said he had seen enough of them on his travels "to build a house." The School Committee's discussion of the teachers' resolution against him revealed intense religious feeling. While a Protestant member named Brewster suggested tabling the resolution, Catholics McCarthy and Breen wanted to endorse it. Brewster saw no reason for Catholic irritation and pointed out that he had done nothing when people accused his Puritan ancestors of whipping naked women through the streets. Breen, however, thought this irrelevant, saying that Brewster's ancestors had actually whipped women, while Patterson's remarks were false. After additional acrimony, the committee voted along strictly religious lines not to condemn the Senator's references. When Brewster in his campaign for mayor later said it was necessary to protect the schools against Catholic foreigners, Breen and McCarthy used his statement to defeat him.[26]

24. *British-American Citizen,* Dec. 7, 1889, Aug. 2, 1890, cited in Berthoff, *British Immigrants,* p. 200; *The Evening Tribune,* Nov. 11, 14, 27-28, Dec. 3, 9, 17, 1891, Jan. 14, 30, 1892, Nov. 23, 1894.

25. *Ibid.,* June 9, 21, 1892.   26. *Ibid.,* April 28, Nov. 28, Dec. 9, 1893.

After the controversy over the role of the Catholic church in education and politics, Lawrence became the scene of a series of American Protective Association lectures in the fall of 1893 and throughout 1894. This organization, the Know-Nothing movement reborn a half century later, was organized in 1887 in the Mississippi Valley and spread to the northeast on the heels of the depression of 1893. A harbinger of the A.P.A. lectures was a meeting back in 1886 when Patrick Welch spoke in City Hall on "Why I left the Roman Catholic Church and Became a Protestant," amid hisses, stamping of feet, and calls of "How about that, Paddy Welch?" But there was nothing more until 1893.

The A.P.A. in Lawrence was more concerned about Catholicism than immigration. Out of ninety-five references in the lectures, fifty-two were about the menace of the Catholic church to America, while only fourteen took up the dangers of uncontrolled immigration. While the lecturers, most of whom were Protestant ministers, feared the power of the church over education and other American institutions, they were particularly worried about its political influence. To the rhetorical question: "What power is it that has corrupted our municipalities?" the Reverend Wheeler replied: "It is that very power that has its grip on Mexico, and has demoralized Italy, Canada East and the South American republics." One A.P.A. lecturer so feared the divided loyalty of a Catholic, split between Papal dogma and the Constitution, that he asked: "What constitutes a loyal citizen of the United States?" When he added, "Can one who owes allegiance to the pope . . . be one?" he felt obliged to answer, "No! No man can serve two masters." To guard against the threat the speakers urged their listeners to demand an educational qualification for all voters and to elect only those whose primary allegiance was to the United States.

Although the A.P.A. denied any objection to parochial schools, it did not want public money supporting them. If the Catholic church "chooses to have such a school," said Reverend Bates, "she must not come like a pauper and ask state aid." Nor did the A.P.A. want Roman Catholics on public school boards. To defeat the Catholic threat the A.P.A. called for frequent inspections of all public schools.

Closely related to the menace of Catholicism was the danger from unrestricted immigration. According to Reverend Nathan Bailey there were "two dangers—the first . . . Romanism and the second . . . immigration. The first is dependent upon the second. If another immigrant did not come in it wouldn't take Romanism long to die out from natural causes." The A.P.A. believed that the new immigration was swamping New England upsetting its basic American institutions. The United States could never teach such immigrants to understand America, it said, because "what can you do with people who have a vague idea that our liberty is license?" The A.P.A. opposed Catholicism and immigration because they menaced its particular interpretation of the American way of life.

In order to define this way of life the typical A.P.A. speaker would open his talk with a rhetorical question such as: "Why is it that . . . these meetings are being held. . . ?" To this he would respond: "It is because they feel that there is danger somewhere, and we have come together . . . ready to make any sacrifices that our institutions may be preserved and perpetuated." For the A.P.A. these institutions included individual liberty, the public school, the separation of church and state, the Constitution, and the Supreme Court. They were opposed to anarchism and other radical movements. They continually called upon the immigrant to be an American. When the Reverend Blackburn introduced the theme, "Who shall carry the flag?" he said they had gathered "not as Protestants or as Catholics, but simply as Americans." When he asked "What sort of people are to carry the flag?" a voice answered, "American."

The Lawrence A.P.A. speeches usually closed with a tolerant gesture. The movement was not, said the speakers, an attack on the Catholic church but only on its evil influence for they "would not destroy the Roman Catholic church" if they could. When speakers referred to the loyal service of the Irish in the Civil War, they were simply repeating the tolerance that Lawrence had shown during the war. But the generosity was frequently patronizing. "When I walk through the streets and see the character of the people pouring in upon us," said one speaker, "I am convinced that that church is needed to touch them—that the whip of her priesthood is necessary to keep these people within the bounds of moral decency."

Immigrant Lawrence, led by the Catholic *Sunday Register* and its editor, Katie O'Keefe, responded to the A.P.A. attacks. Miss O'Keefe was silent at the May 14 meeting, but members of the Young Men's Catholic Association carried her burden by passing out pamphlets. When Miss O'Keefe sat in the front row, notebook in hand, at the next lecture, she so irritated the speaker that he ended one of his more extreme sentences with "Take that down, sister." When he quoted a statement from the *Catholic World,* Katie in vain demanded the number of the issue. After a brief exchange, hisses rose from the audience, and the speaker challenged his tormentors to come down front. There were no takers, but hissing continued at the next lecture. In another, Reverend Scott Hersey sharply criticized Roman Catholic canon law and when the *Register* contradicted his statements, he defended his position by quoting from a book on ecclesiastical law. The nonsectarian *Tribune,* which often sympathized with the immigrants, called the A.P.A. views "narrow" and "un-American."

Not all Lawrence opposed the movement, for many attended the meetings and vigorously applauded references to Americanism and attacks on Catholics in education. An Englishman wrote in to the *Tribune* urging the abandonment of parochial schools. But while some who filled the lecture hall were supporters of the A.P.A., most were either curiosity seekers or active opponents. The A.P.A. found little religious favor in Lawrence.[27]

For a while, however, the movement had great political importance. The *Tribune* referred darkly to its effect on the city election of 1893, but not until the fall of 1894 did its significance become evident. During the next twelve months over forty articles appeared in the *Tribune* concerning the political role of the A.P.A., generally connecting it with the Republicans. Jeremiah T. Sullivan and Charles A. DeCourcey, both Irish Democrats, denounced the movement, and DeCourcey even suggested that it might be a group of Tories returned from Canada. Although they could not carry Lawrence in November, 1894, the Democrats did manage to

27. *Lawrence American,* Nov. 21, 1886; *Lawrence Journal,* Nov. 13, 1886; for lectures see *Tribune,* Nov. 27, 1893, May 14, 21, 28, June 4, 11, 18, Sept. 6, 19, Oct. 4, 18, Nov. 1, 1894. For analysis of lectures see Table X.

defeat the one Republican candidate who was openly for the A.P.A. The Democratic candidate who was suspected of A.P.A. leanings also lost.

In spite of its November rebuff, the A.P.A. exerted great influence on the city election the following month. The Democrats, already suffering from the religious split between Breen and Sweeney, tried to prove that the Republicans were the intolerant ones. John Breen compared the A.P.A. with the Know-Nothing party; a Lowell Democrat tied it to the Orangemen; and others connected it with the British-American club. All agreed that the A.P.A. was in control of the Republican party and planned to gerrymander the city and register women to vote against Catholics on the School Committee. The result: an important Democratic victory.

After this election the Republicans abandoned the A.P.A. and wisely put two Irish Catholics on their ticket the next year to combat the balanced Democratic slate. Their smashing victory meant the end of the A.P.A. in Lawrence. While the Democrats lost this particular election and a few that followed, they were not to lose many more. Shortly afterward they healed their own religious schism and were able to nominate and elect Irish Catholic mayors.

And so one year after the final A.P.A. lecture the movement came to the end of its political importance. Even though school children still called each other "A.P.A.'s" or "anti-A.P.A.'s" and in spite of continuing bitterness in the mills, the organization had lost its vigor. When the Lawrence School Committee replaced two Protestant principals with Roman Catholics, it was the Boston A.P.A., not the Lawrence group, that accused the committee of planning to "Romanize" the schools. By 1898 Katie O'Keefe was able to ask sarcastically where the A.P.A. people had gone now that there was a war. The strength of the immigrant society in Lawrence had killed the A.P.A. several years before it died in other New England cities.[28]

The A.P.A. was one in a series of movements against the immigrant, and like the others its principal concern was religion.

28. *The Evening Tribune*, Sept., 1894-Dec., 1895, particularly Oct. 6, 23, 31, Nov. 3, 7, 20, 28, Dec. 5, 1894, Nov. 26-27, Dec. 4, 1895. For the decline of the A.P.A. see *ibid.*, Nov. 23, 1894, Jan. 22, July 2, 3, 1895.

While the Know-Nothing riot and the Breen election posed the problem of the Irish Catholic in politics and the Saint Mary's affair focused attention on sectarian education, the A.P.A. lectures covered the entire relationship of immigration and Catholicism. In retrospect, it is remarkable that so little violence arose from these and other incidents. Possibly the steady intolerance of the city had dulled the immigrant's sensibilities. When the Irish themselves in 1912 began to echo the A.P.A. attacks on anarchy and the A.P.A. adulation of the flag, the persecuted had become the attacker and the immigrant cycle had been completed in Lawrence.

As trouble between the natives and Irish waned, more vicious battles among different immigrant groups arose. While these conflicts were not completely new, they came to a head after 1890. The Irish-British antagonism grew in the decades after the Civil War until finally in 1888 the Lawrence British-Americans asked the Irish-Americans to stop supporting the rebels in Ireland. "A great nation . . . on whose dominions the sun never sets," they said, "is not going to yield to a few agitators." The *Journal* then snapped back that the only purpose of the British-American societies was to persecute the Irish. Two years later in 1890 a state meeting of the Hibernians vigorously denounced the British. The main battle, however, awaited the Boer War.

The officers of the Irish legal societies in a secret meeting at Christmastime in 1899 decided to help the Boers in their revolt against the British. When they sponsored a mass meeting, Germans and other immigrants joined them in condemning the British. John Breen began with a broad attack on the British Empire, comparing the situation in South Africa with that in India and Ireland. At the same time he praised Secretary of State Olney's courage in denouncing Britain in the Venezuela boundary dispute. When Reverend Francis Page said that the Boers were more anti-Catholic than anti-British, he stung Father Fleming into a hot denial. The *Tribune* kept the agitation alive by calling attention to the large number of Scots at a British celebration and commenting: "This is peculiarly a British practice. In South Africa the Irish and Scotch brigades lead the van." But the furor subsided even more suddenly than in the A.P.A. movement.[29]

29. *Lawrence Journal*, Feb. 25, June 23, 1888; *The Evening Tribune*, June 12,

The Irish continued to plague the French Canadians, with whom they had had so many fights in the 1880's. Life for the immigrant *habitants* in Lawrence was particularly difficult. People called them dirty and germ-laden; they did not have the same chance as the Germans or Irish to get city jobs; the newspapers scorned and ridiculed them. Between 1899 and 1906 the French newspaper *Le Progrès* carried at least thirty articles complaining about the Irish, a third of which were based on religious antagonism and another third on political friction. The basis for the religious conflict was the issue of whether bishops in predominantly Canadian districts should be Canadian or Irish. *Le Progrès* protested for example, that while the Canadians comprised two-thirds of the diocese of Portland and three-fifths of Manchester, New Hampshire, they had no high church officials in those cities except a great vicar who was part Irish at that. It warned that the clergy was driving Canadians to apostasy by tyrannically suppressing the French language. In politics it accused the "democrats irlandais" of bribing Canadian leaders in order to get Canadian votes. To solve this problem *Le Progrès* urged its readers to get naturalized and join the Republican party in a bloc.

Le Progrès was sensitive about slights and insults, real and imaginary. When the Board of Health put Doctor Magee instead of Doctor Beauchamp in charge of all smallpox patients, the newspaper accused the two Irishmen on the board of not being able to see "further than their prejudice permitted them." *Le Progrès* assumed that errors made by Irish city officials in French names were intentional. It was also unhappy about Irish domination of Catholic societies, particularly the Catholic Foresters. On one occasion, however, *Le Progrès* gave this grudging tribute to its enemy: "What an admirable race are these Irish! What fire! What assurance! What confidence! . . . they doubt nothing, and no one doubts them."[30]

1890, Dec. 23, 30, 1899, Jan. 12, Mar. 12, 1900; *Anzeiger und Post,* Jan. 13, 1900.

30. See reference to *Le Progrès* in Donald B. Cole, "Lawrence, Massachusetts: Immigrant City, 1845-1912" (Doctoral dissertation, Harvard University, 1956), pp. 173-75. More important references are *Le Progrès,* May 12, June 9, 1899, Jan. 25, 1901, June 3, 1902, Mar. 30, 1905; *The Evening Tribune,* June 16, July 21, 1890.

The trouble between the Jews and the French was economic. *Le Progrès* attacked the Jewish peddlers for capturing the confidence of the naïve Canadians and pictured them swarming into Essex, Common, Broadway, and Hampshire Streets and threatening the French sections. The French, whom others had attacked for bearing germs, now insisted that the dirty Jewish junk shops were the sources of "spotted fever."[31]

When *Le Progrès* praised the "heroic battle for liberty" of the Boers and attacked Rhodes scholarships, the French Canadians were in the strange position of supporting the Irish against the British. Their feeling, however, was entirely anti-British and not pro-Irish. Almost pathetically *Le Progrès* told its readers that they need not fear comparison with the British and pointed out the glories of the age of Louis XIV and the contributions of the French to American history. While admiring British perseverance, it condemned British materialism.[32]

Although the earlier immigrants and natives fought each other, they joined together against the new arrivals. "When intoxicated," said the *Tribune*, "these people go along the streets insulting and abusive to law-abiding citizens." Whether they were "cheap foreigners" stealing vegetables on their way to the Glen Forest Park on the river or "drink-frenzied foreigners" accosting women, the natives and the earlier immigrants did not like them. The *Telegram*, always anti-immigrant, said: "These Italians should be taught a severe lesson. Our gates have been thrown open to them, but they should not be allowed to perpetrate the old country habits which have made their fair land the bloodiest in Europe."

Much of the opposition was simply prejudice against a strange people. While the *Tribune* did not find it "entirely pleasant to contemplate the change that is going on in the character of the immigration," *Le Progrès* more bluntly stated that "these immigrants . . . belong to a less desirable class." The *Anzeiger und Post* feared that the new immigrant would become a public ward. When a Chinese tried to violate the immigration act, the headline read, "Sly Chinaman caught," and when a Chinese-native marriage failed, the *Tribune* commented on "the failure of mixing races."

31. *Le Progrès*, Feb. 7, 1902, May 14, 1903, April 5, 1906.
32. *Ibid.*, April 12, 1901, April 8, 1902.

The Lawrence press frequently repeated the traditional stories about the Chinese: they did not bathe; they killed two hundred children a year from special towers; they were superstitious about cockroaches; they loved watermelon; they gambled; and they smoked opium. To the Lawrence newspapers they were "Celestials," "Chinks," or "Pigtail Laundrymen." The French Canadians called the Jews "sheenies" and the Catholic Literary Society held up Shylock as the typical Jew. "Shakespeare's indomitable pen," said one member, "has painted . . . [Shylock] in all the loathing of his basest nature . . . ," and others commented on the Jew's "low cunning," his "base individuality," and his "hard, icy intellectuality." The Irish hated all other immigrants, particularly the Italians. Typical was Davy Roach, who "had a well known aversion" to "Dagoes," "Celestials," and Armenians.[33]

Because of its native-immigrant friction Lawrence had long opposed immigration, but the feeling did not become vocal until the decades of despair after 1890. The arguments then foreshadowed those used by restrictionists in 1912. The *Tribune,* unhappy about the "forty-two Dagos" who came to Lawrence as strike breakers in 1891, proclaimed three years later that "the protection which mill workers in Lawrence need is protection from foreigners who thus pauperize labor." Although the Lawrence Central Labor Union voted in 1902 only to keep paupers and criminals out and to punish violators of the contract labor law, nine of its member unions wanted much stronger restriction. *Le Progrès* and the *Anzeiger und Post* feared the increased use of child labor as well as violations of the contract labor law. Both the *Journal* and the *Tribune* pointed out the inconsistency of free trade in labor and protection for goods. The "protectionist manufacturer," according to the *Journal,* demanded the right "to import from the markets of the world the cheapest labor that can be got, while for the products of the factory he claim[ed] the most rigid protection." Harbingers of 1912![34]

33. *The Evening Tribune,* April 14, May 2, 8, 1890, Jan. 20, Feb. 7, April 18, June 12, Sept. 9, 1891, Aug. 4, 1893, Jan. 2, 1894, Jan. 16, 1895, June 27, 1896, Nov. 15, 1897, June 8, 1899, July 17, 1900, Sept. 2, 1902; *Sunday Sun,* July 30, 1905, Mar. 4, July 29, 1905, Aug. 4, 1907; *Le Progrès,* June 14, 1904, *Anzeiger und Post,* Dec. 31, 1910.

34. *The Evening Tribune,* June 13, 1891, May 29, 1894; Committee on Immigration, United States Senate, *Report on the Bill (H.R. 12199) to Regulate*

An unforeseen result of the antipathy toward the southeastern Europeans was the way in which it helped the immigrants who had arrived between 1870 and 1890. Just as the French-Canadian arrival strengthened the position of the Irish, so now the southeastern Europeans increased the Canadians' security. The immigrant cycle was operating and they were no longer at the bottom. The publication of *Le Progrès* in 1890 symbolized their new strength. "Le petit Jimmy" Cloutier was now prominent in politics and every one knew about the French Cooperative, the Lafayette Court of Foresters, and the Congrégation Des Dames of Saint Anne's.

Amidst the flood of anti-immigrant feeling, a strong undercurrent of good sense and tolerance held firm. The *Tribune* condemned those who would restrict immigration, "many of whom would not be here if the doctrine they now preach had been practiced half a century ago." When the *Tribune* showed that the "same treatment now accorded Russian Jews and the later classes of immigrants" was once the "portion of the Irish [and] . . . Germans," they were underscoring the cyclical nature of prejudice in Lawrence. A member of the Central Labor Union said that constant immigration meant new ideas for the country and recalled that many remarkable men had once been immigrant criminals. And the *Anzeiger und Post* denounced the "Jingoes and Nativists" who wanted to "surround our land with a Chinese wall and let no one else in." Occasional references to "intelligent" Swedes, "progressive" Lithuanians, "fine-looking Italian maidens," "intelligent-looking" Italian boys, and the "great Hebrew race" helped prevent more serious explosions.[35]

The economic side of ethnic friction in Lawrence hinged on the alleged violation of the 1885 law forbidding the importation of contract labor. During a federal investigation two Lawrence workers testified that they had been part of English groups to which

---

the *Immigration of Aliens into the United States* . . . , 57 Congress, 2 Session, Doc. 62 (Washington, 1902), p. 347; *Le Progrès,* May 31, 1904, Mar. 29, 1906; *Anzeiger und Post,* Dec. 16, 1905, May 12, 1906; *Lawrence Journal,* April 12, 1882.

35. *The Evening Tribune,* July 28, 1892, Aug. 23, 1901, Oct. 5, 1903; *Lawrence Journal,* Feb. 24, 1883; *Anzeiger und Post,* June 2, Dec. 8, 1906; *Sunday Sun,* Nov. 21, 1909.

agents had promised jobs in America. James Denby said that the following advertisement back in Yorkshire had attracted him: "Wanted for America—five hands for drawing, six spinning. . . . Families preferred having four or more girls. Wages from three shillings two pence. . . ." Though the agent promised to pay for the passage of the whole family, Denby later denied that the law had been violated, rationalizing that none of the transactions had been person to person. The pattern of advertisement, inducement, and group passage, was repeated in the case of George Foster. Although Andover mills, not Lawrence, were the guilty parties in each instance, Denby and Foster did later move to Lawrence.

But there were frequently direct references to Lawrence. The *Tribune* spoke of "inducements held out to" workers and of the "almost forgotten alien contract labor law. . . ." *Le Progrès* said flatly that the Arlington and Wood companies had "taken a contract with Europe to rid her of her worker surplus" and the *Anzeiger* called the contract law a "farce." The Immigration Commission heard testimony from two union officials, two clergymen, and one mill officer that a Lawrence company had advertised in Europe for worsted workers, but found the evidence to be second hand. One informant, for example, had a cousin in Glasgow who had seen pictures of the mills, and an Italian clergyman "understood" that promises of ten-dollar wages had appeared in English and Italian newspapers. All agreed that the corporations had agents in Boston to corral labor from the ships.

The workers particularly feared the use of imported labor against them in strikes. When the Arlington woolsorters struck in 1891, they cabled Bradford, England, urging sorters not to come. Striking Pacific engravers actually sent a representative to Bradford to forestall the coming of other strike breakers. The owners succeeded, however, in importing scab labor in 1902 to break up a spinners and doffers strike and also sent a group from Lawrence to end a strike in Camden, Maine. It is obvious why immigrants feared immigration and the corporations' use of it.[36]

36. *Lawrence Journal*, Aug. 25, 1888; *Testimony Taken by the Select Committee of the House of Representatives to Inquire into the Alleged Violation of the Laws Prohibiting the Importation of Contract Laborers. . .* , 50 Congress, 1 Session, House Doc. 572 (Washington, 1888), pp. 578-91; *The Evening Tribune*, Feb. 9, 1894, Nov. 24, 1897; *Le Progrès*, Mar. 29, 1906; *Anzeiger und Post*,

But in spite of their fears the immigrants had turned against the corporations in a major way only once during the half century before 1890; that was in the Pacific strike of 1882. When they rose in mass protest twice within eight short years (1894-1902), it showed how desperate they had become. The Washington Mills strike, which began in February, 1894, originated in a wage reduction. As in 1882, the strikers raised relief money, but this time it was insufficient and they had to return to work in May. Even more than in 1882 the immigrant played a leading role, with the part of the Armenians and Italians particularly decisive. "Our Armenian friends," as the strikers called them, voted to stay out six months if necessary, joined the Textile Workers Union, and paraded. In a like manner the Italians, most of whom spoke no English, went on strike and joined in parades. Because of their loyalty, the Armenians and Italians, once "distrusted as 'cheap foreign laborers,'" became the "heroes" of the fight, and during the parade of February 17 "the most flattering reception was reserved" for them. But among them there were fights between strikers and scabs. The Germans were still important, and when their weavers voted to return to work, the strike ended. As in 1882 the Canadians stayed out of the struggle, many of them returning to Canada.[37]

In the Washington strike of 1902 the Germans held the undisputed lead, particularly at the start when they demanded a 20 per cent raise and the abolition of the premium system. The newly arrived Franco-Belgians, who later helped to organize the strike of 1912, were among the first to go out. To appeal to them and others, labor agitators made speeches in German, French, and Polish. But all immigrants did not support the strike. The *Anzeiger und Post,* in urging the Germans to return to their jobs, argued that they lacked funds and that Asian scabs might replace them. Furthermore, it begged the German workers not to be responsible for the suffering of thousands in an economic disaster. And the parish calendar at Saint Mary's presented the Irish view

May 12, 1906, July 6, 1907; Immigration Commission, "Community A," pp. 770-73; *Strike at Lawrence,* pp. 81-82, 257, 396. For strike breakers see *The Evening Tribune,* May 29, 1891, April 12, 15, May 4, 1892, Jan. 16, 1902; *Anzeiger und Post,* Feb. 23, 1901; *Sunday Sun,* Mar. 20, 1910.

37. *The Evening Tribune,* Feb. 10, 12, 13, 15-17, 23, Mar. 14, April 17, 25, May 5, 1894; *The Lawrence Sentinel,* Mar. 30, 1894.

that in the end only the workers would suffer. As a result of the immigrant split the strike ended with only a slight concession in the premium system in May of the same year. Unlike the two earlier strikes this one was generally unpopular. The newspapers called some of the strike leaders "extremists" and others "red button Socialists." The earlier immigrants, particularly the Irish, were now so well established that they were beginning to oppose strikes. Another harbinger of 1912![38]

By 1912, then, the formation of the immigrant city was complete. Of the 86,000 inhabitants in 1910, 74,000 were either born abroad or had foreign-born parents. Since 1905 Lawrence had had the highest proportion of immigrants in its population of any city in the state. The immigrant cycle had made a complete revolution as the Irish, once the despised shanty dwellers of 1850, were now in complete control of the city's politics and were in many ways indistinguishable from the natives. Less prominent but well established were the British and German immigrants already four decades in the city. And while the French Canadians were still insecure, they now had immigrants below them on both the social and economic scales. Since 1890 the southeastern Europeans had doubled the city's population, thereby creating the much-deplored slums and drastically lowering the intellectual standards of the city. Anti-Irish-Catholic nativism had its last great splurge in the A.P.A. lectures of 1894 and was then submerged by the attacks against the newcomers. During the decades after the Civil War, Lawrence made great progress as the Irish rose to power and the city's leaders tried in every way to make it the model city that the founders had intended. Even nativism was less brutal than in the 1850's. The problems of Lawrence after 1890 were too much for its leaders, and the city entered the black decades in which poverty and anti-immigrant feeling were more severe than in the 1870's and 1880's. As wages dropped and men lost their jobs, the misery led to the strikes of 1894 and 1902. A decade later it would bring about the strike of 1912.

But terms "decades of promise" and "decades of despair" are not absolute because they depend wholly upon the immigrant's

38. Both *The Evening Tribune* and the *Anzeiger und Post* felt the Germans were the key to the strike. *The Evening Tribune,* April 18, 26, May 1, 6, 7, 9, 1902; *Anzeiger und Post,* April 19, 26, May 3, 1902.

search for security. While the trembling jobless *habitant* of the 1880's did not see the hope of those years, his wage-earning son may not have felt the despondency of 1910. When the immigrant felt secure, he believed in the promise of the city, when insecure, there was only black despair. Before going on to the strike of 1912 we must determine just how successful the immigrant felt he had been in finding security in Lawrence. By studying the city's history we have placed the strike of 1912 in its historical perspective, but we still have not looked at the immigrant's life from his own point of view.

The strike observers who painted such a doleful picture of notorious Lawrence in 1912 would probably look at the city differently after reading its pre-strike history, but they would not necessarily change their minds. While they would be surprised by the model town of 1850 and the decades of promise after the Civil War, they would insist that the decades of despair confirmed their views. The immigrant cycle, they would say, might have given hope and a better life to some after 1865, but it also meant misery for the thousands of immigrants who doubled the city's population after 1890. And furthermore, they would point out, the cycle brought with it recurring episodes of the most savage intolerance. But the narrative of the years down to the strike does not tell the whole or even the most important story. While hinting at the immigrants' efforts to find security, the narrative fails to determine whether he believed he had found it. Even the most miserable shanty Irishman or Neapolitan Italian may have found his own forms of security in Lawrence, and if so, the 1912 strike observers' concept of the city was completely false. During the seven long decades from the building of the dam to the strike the immigrant sought security in many places. To these places—the home, the mill, and the club—we must go. And before we are through we must also determine whether the immigrant found the deepest form of security that his new country offered—the sense of belonging, of being an American.

Part Two

The Search for Security, 1845-1912

CHAPTER VI

Security in the Family

No immigrant could succeed alone in Lawrence. While some may have talked of individualism, they all needed and sought for help. For most immigrants—conditioned by the peasant traditions of Europe and Canada—it was natural to look first to the family. Since many came to Lawrence alone, they tried desperately to maintain ties with their families back home. Duncan Wood, the Lawrence travel agent, appealed to them with this notice:

A Word in Season
Remember
The Promise
You Made to
Father or Mother
When Leaving
The Old Country
And Receiving
Their Blessing:
"God bless you! I
will never *for-*
get You."
You can Now
Redeem That Promise
By
Sending
Some Article as
a
Xmas [sic] Present
I am Now Prepared

To
Forward
Small Parcels
From Lawrence to
Your Home
at
Very Low Rates
. . .
Make the Hearts
of the
Old Folks at Home
Rejoice
Picture Your
Good Old Mother or Father
opening a
Parcel from You
in this Country, and
exclaiming
With Tears of Joy
in their eyes

"God Bless Them. I knew   of
they would not forget me."   Foreign Parcels
Duncan Wood   499
Forwarder   Essex Street., Lawrence.

For those with wives and children across the sea the desire to keep
the ties unbroken was even greater. Just before the strike about
one married immigrant mill worker in eight had a wife in the old
country. The earlier arrivals—the Irish, English, Germans, and
Canadians—almost invariably had their wives with them, but over
a quarter of the most recent immigrants had their wives back home.
No matter what nationality, the longer an immigrant had been here
the less likely he was to have his wife abroad. Less than 5 per cent
of those here ten years were without their wives.[1]

The immigrant responded faithfully to his obligations by
making visits home. J. T. Murphy, a travel agent, advertised in
1861:

Old Black Star Line—Liverpool to Lawrence
Adults $19, Children under 12 $14, Infants under 1 $3
New York and Liverpool Steamship 3rd Class $30 Cabin $75
Bills of Exchange in any amount payable in England, Scotland,
    Ireland, Wales.

In 1884 the Cunard Line charged only $15 for steerage passage
to Ireland from Boston. The Irish, not content with individual trips,
formed an excursion club to raise money for a group voyage. Italians often went home for the winter to participate in festivals and
to avoid the cold as well as to see their families. And Canadians,
not facing the dangers of an ocean voyage, were frequent visitors.
One-sixth of all immigrant workers in Lawrence had made at least
one trip home by 1912, and about one-third of those who had been
here over ten years had made such a trip home. Half of the French
Canadians, a quarter of the English, and a sixth of the Germans and
Irish had visited their old homes. Even a few of the southeastern

1. *Lawrence Journal*, Jan. 13, 1883; Immigration Commission, "Woolen and
Worsted Goods in Representative Community A," *Immigrants in Industry, Part
4: Woolen and Worsted Goods Manufacturing*, II, Immigration Commission,
Reports, X, 61 Congress, 2 Session, Doc. 633 (Washington, 1911), pp. 781-82.
For more details see Donald B. Cole, "Lawrence, Massachusetts: Immigrant City,
1845-1912" (Doctoral dissertation, Harvard University, 1956), Table VII, p. 391.

Europeans had already made a trip back. Since these statistics refer only to visits and not to permanent returns, they show how tenaciously the immigrant held on to his family abroad.[2]

The great majority of immigrants faced the equally difficult task of holding their families together in the new and forbidding world. Family spirit did not develop easily when a dozen other households within earshot destroyed privacy. It was maintained with difficulty when boarders and roomers shared the table and the bed. A mother could hardly bring up her children properly when all had to work in the mills, and young people could not be kept at home. When the son found a job while his father was unemployed, it was disastrous to old-world discipline. For the daughter the utter lack of privacy was demoralizing. Bathing in the sink, living in a home where every room was a bedroom, sharing sleeping quarters with male roomers, knowing that every word she uttered was public, all combined to dull the feeling of family unity.

The French Canadians in particular found life difficult for their families. *Le Progrès* complained that fathers neglected their children while they gambled, drank, and sought "long hours of sleep, and short hours of work." Children, accustomed to the pure country air and the simple joys of rural life, became ill in the infectious atmosphere about the machines or joined gangs of "toughs" who roamed the streets. They no longer respected parental authority and after they married they forgot their vows. But even so, the French newspapers stated that the only way to save their traditions was to start with the family in which the parents could read the old stories around the fire. The Canadians, indeed all immigrants, knew how hard it was to hold a family together, but they also realized how essential it was for their security. The

2. *The Lawrence Sentinel*, April 6, 1861; *Lawrence Morning News*, June 11, 1884; *The Evening Tribune*, May 1, 1897; Amy A. Bernady, "The Aliens Rush Home," Immigration Restriction League, Scrapbook of Clippings, 1907, Widener Library, Harvard; *The Strike at Lawrence, Mass. Hearings before the Committee on Rules of the House of Representatives . . . 1912*, 62 Congress, 2 Session, House Doc. 671 (Washington, 1912), p. 367; Immigration Commission, "Community A," p. 783. Percentage having visited home: 17.2 per cent of all immigrant workers; 6.1 per cent of those here under five years; 19.1 per cent of those here five to ten years; 31.6 per cent of those here over ten years; 27 per cent of the English; 16 per cent of the Irish and Germans. See Cole, "Lawrence," Table VIII, p. 392.

immigrant community challenged the integrity, in fact the very existence, of the family, but at the same time made it a necessity.[3]

The marriage rate in Lawrence was always high, particularly during the more difficult years before the Civil War and after 1890. While there were about thirteen marriages each year per thousand population between 1856 and 1865, the average dropped to eleven during the next twenty-five years, only to climb again to twelve between 1890 and 1910. A higher proportion of immigrants than natives were marrying, thus providing the impetus for the high marriage rate of the city. The percentage of immigrants in the total who married started high at 56 per cent in 1855-65, dropped to 53 per cent in 1875-85, and rose again to 62 per cent after 1890. Thus during the years of the shanty Irish and the decades of despair, the immigrants sought security in marriage more frequently than during the decades of promise. And at any given time in the history of the city about 60 per cent of the marriageable immigrants were married and only about 40 per cent of the natives. In 1909 the French Canadians and the English led the others with two-thirds married.[4] In an unfriendly city the immigrant did not dare remain single.

3. *Le Progrès,* April 6, 1900, Feb. 8, 22, Mar. 1, 1901, Aug. 15, 1902, Oct. 16, 1903, May 4, Sept. 14, 21, 1905, April 25, 1907; *Le Courrier de Lawrence,* Dec. 14, 1911, Jan. 11, 1912.

4. *Report . . . relating to the Registry and Return of Births, Marriages, and Deaths . . . ,* XIV (1855), Mass. Pub. Doc. 1; XIX (1860); XXIV (1865); XXXIV (1875); XXXIX (1880); XLIV (1885); XLIX (1890); LIV (1895); LIX (1900); LXIV (1905); LXIX (1910). See Tables XI and XII. Carroll D. Wright, *The Census of Massachusetts: 1885,* I, Part 1 (Boston, 1887), 224-25; United States Census Bureau, *Thirteenth Census of the United States . . . 1910. Abstract of the Census . . . with Supplement for Massachusetts . . .* (Washington, 1913), p. 588. Immigration Commission, "Community A," pp. 778-79.

MARRIAGE STATISTICS FOR WORKERS*

	14 and over 1885	20 and over 1909	15 and over 1910
Native-born of foreign-born father	—	34.3 per cent married	—
Native-born of native-born father	—	44.1	—
Total native-born	41	37.0	42
Foreign-born	55	55.7	61
Men	—	62	—
Women	—	45	—

* More details in Cole, "Lawrence," Table XXV, p. 411.

It followed that immigrants married earlier than natives. Irish brides and grooms were about three years younger than their native counterparts before 1850. In 1885 over 2 per cent of the foreign-born under twenty were married but less than 1 per cent of the natives. Among mill operatives in 1909 over a third of the immigrants in their twenties were married and only a fifth of the natives.[5]

In selecting his mate the immigrant could theoretically marry either within or without his own particular group, but he rarely considered the choice. Endogamy prevailed. Immigrant married immigrant and native married native because there was greater security that way. When there was a little less need for security during the last years of the decades of promise, endogamy went down with the marriage rate, but both rose again during the decades of despair. The percentage of endogamy was as follows:

Husband	*Wife in Same Category*		
	1860 & 1865	*1885 & 1890*	*1910*
Native-born	91%	69%	77%
Foreign-born	91%	84%	89%

Even within narrower ethnic groups intramarriage was the rule. The city marriage records for ten scattered years between 1847 and 1912 reported about 4,500 marriages from which the following chart was derived:

PERCENTAGE OF MARRIAGE WITHIN OWN GENERAL
ETHNIC GROUP

Birthplace of Husband	Wife Born in Same Area							
	1847-49	1854	1865	1875	1882	1894	1902	1912
United States		92	90	85	75	71	63	73
Northwestern Europe	74	67	72	54	76	70	51	64
Ireland	96	98	88	74	70	60	74	65
Canada				59	71	70	67	48
Southeastern Europe							95	96

5. The Essex Institute, *Vital Records of Lawrence, Massachusetts, to the End of the Year 1849* (Salem, Mass., 1926); *Census of Mass., 1885*, I, Part 1, 224; Immigration Commission, "Community A," p. 779. In 1909 actually 36 per cent of the foreign-born and 22 per cent of the natives in their twenties were married.

For those born in northwestern Europe, mostly in Britain and Germany, the percentage of endogamy fluctuated about the 70 per cent mark (except for 1875) until it dropped off in 1902 only to climb again in 1912. The Irish showed a steady decline down to a low point in 1894 and then went up again in the twentieth century. The Canadian figures were inconclusive until 1882, but from then they fell steadily until 1912. Those from southeastern Europe married almost exclusively within their own group.

When immigrants first came to America, they married their own kind. And when their religious or physical characteristics were most different from those in America, as in the case of the Irish and the southeastern Europeans, the amount of exogamy was at first negligible. Intramarriage declined as time passed, but then it increased again as the nationality became established. Those who had been here the longest or the shortest period of time married endogamously most frequently. In 1912, for example, both the native Americans and the southeastern Europeans were more exclusive than the nineteenth-century immigrants. A reason for the increase in native endogamy in 1912, however, was that by then the term "American" included many second- and third-generation Americans who preferred to marry each other rather than natives of longer standing or the more recent immigrants.

There were certain definite marriage habits. Natives took wives from Canada or northwestern Europe if they could not find American girls, while northwestern Europeans favored Americans after members of their own group, as did the Irish and the Canadians. It meant that an immigrant preferred to marry another from the same general area but failing that would wed a second-generation American whose parents were from his group. Marriages in Lawrence were divided into three broad classifications: first, those between persons within the same group (77 per cent); second, those involving immigrants and Americans (19 per cent); and third, those between foreigners from different areas (4 per cent). An immigrant would either come to America with his wife or, if he married in Lawrence, would select a mate from his own group or from the ranks of the native-born. Rarely did he marry an immigrant from another country. There was certainly no melting pot in Lawrence.[6]

Immigrant marriages meant frequent childbirth. Families had to have two or three members working to survive and children could often get jobs in the mills when their parents could not. Immigrant families, therefore, tended to be large, particularly before the Civil War and after 1890. In 1856 the parents in 70 per cent of the births were foreign-born, mostly Irish, and in 1865, 78 per cent. No wonder the *American* contended that the native stock had exhausted itself. The proportion of immigrant parents dropped during the decades of promise—65 per cent in 1885—but

6. *Report of Births, Marriages, and Deaths*, XIV (1855); XIX (1860); XXIV (1865); XXXIV (1875); XXXIX (1880); XLIV (1885); LIV (1895); LIX (1900); LXIV (1905); LXIX (1910); Record of Marriages City of Lawrence, MSS, City Clerk's Office, Lawrence, Mass., I (1850-59); II (1860-66); IV (1872-77); V (1878-82); VI (1882-86); VIII (1891-95); XI (1902); XVI (1912-13); Essex Institute, *Vital Records*. See Tables XIII, XIV, XV.

The most frequent marriages were as follows:

1. American husband and American wife	1300
2. Irish husband and Irish wife	682
3. Southeastern European husband and southeastern European wife	593
4. Northwestern European husband and northwestern European wife	495
5. Canadian husband and Canadian wife	276

These 5 plus number 12 totaled 3418 endogamous marriages or 77% of the total

6. Northwestern European husband and American wife	186
7. American husband and Canadian wife	168
8. Canadian husband and American wife	136
9. American husband and northwestern European wife	135
10. American husband and Canadian wife	118
11. Irish husband and American wife	86

These 6 plus number 16 and a few scattered marriages involving Americans totaled 861 marriages between native-born and foreign-born or 19%

12. Asian husband and Asian wife	72
13. Irish wife and northwestern European husband	56
14. Northwestern European wife and Irish husband	42
15. Northwestern European husband and Canadian wife	28
16. Southeastern European husband and American wife	23
17. Canadian husband and Irish wife	20
18. Canadian husband and northwestern European wife	19
19. Irish husband and Canadian wife	9

These marriages (13, 14, 15, 17, 18, 19) plus a few scattered totaled 187 or 4%

The censuses of 1880 and 1895 showed that in 90 per cent of the cases a person's father and mother were from the same nationality. Again no melting pot. Carroll D. Wright, *The Census of Massachusetts: 1880* . . . (Boston, 1883), p. 126; Horace G. Wadlin, *Census of . . . Massachusetts: 1895*, II (Boston, 1897), 95.

went up again to 70 per cent in 1910. Consequently the city's birth rate dropped from about thirty-three per thousand population before the Civil War to twenty-seven in the 1870's and 1880's and climbed back to thirty-one in the period 1890-1910.[7] The immigrant seemed to need the security of a big family more during the periods of Irish and Italian predominance than during the era of the French Canadians. But even during the decades of promise immigrant families were larger than those of the natives. In 1875 nearly as many mothers with one child were natives as immigrants, but as the number of children grew larger, foreign-born mothers were more and more in the majority. Among those with four children, for example, there were 211 native mothers and 499 foreign, while in families with more than six it was 163 to 1,139.[8]

So many of the newborn, particularly those with immigrant parents, failed to survive birth or early childhood that 40 to 45 per cent of the deaths in Lawrence were children under three.[9] The year 1878 was unusually bad as measles, whooping cough, diptheria, and typhoid fever took a heavy toll. The last week of July, during which thirty-one children died, was the most horrible of all. Few cities had a record as bad as Lawrence where up to two hundred of a thousand newborn babies died each year. The

7. [Lemuel Shattuck], *Sanitary Survey of the Town of Lawrence* (Boston, 1850), p. 20. In 1864, 650 of the parents of newborn babies were Irish, 240 were from other foreign countries, and only 268 were natives. *Lawrence American*, Mar. 22, 1862, Jan. 28, 1865; *Municipal Records and Memoranda 1856-1859*, II; *The Essex Eagle*, Jan. 8, 1876.

	Percentage of Population That Was Immigrant	Percentage of Births in Which Both Parents Were Foreign-Born	Percentage of Births in Which One Parent Was Foreign-Born
1865	42.5	78.3	5.3
1875	44.5	68.0	9.8
1885	44.0	64.5	12.6
1895	46.6	71.2	14.4
1905	46.1	64.9	19.1
1910	48.1	70.8	14.1

Report of Births, Marriages, and Deaths, XXIV (1865); XXVIII (1869); XXXIV (1875); XLIV (1885); XLIX (1890); LIV (1895); LIX (1900); LXIV (1905); LXIX (1910). See Table XVI.

8. Carroll D. Wright, *Census of Massachusetts: 1875*, I (Boston, 1876), 392-93.

9. Essex Institute, *Vital Records; Report of Births, Marriages, and Deaths*, 1857-59; 1867-69; 1877-79; 1887-89; 1899-1901; 1907-9. See Tables VII, XVI.

carnage continued into the next century when Lawrence ranked seventh in the state in the infant death rate.[10] Even if the child survived his first two years, those which followed were made hazardous by the filthy environment. A sensational infant starvation case in 1866 revealed conditions that were not unusual. In an alley between Essex and Common Streets a woman lived who took in babies, some of them illegitimate, for pay. The discovery of the dead, maggot-covered body of one of her infants in the alley led to a series of indignant articles, but the city missionary maintained that her home was no worse than a hundred tenements in the city. There were frequent stories of abandoned babies thrown into the canal or the Spicket, stories of infanticide and abortion. One young country girl murdered her illegitimate child in a boarding-house room; another threw hers into the vault of an outhouse.[11] Even the wanted babies suffered, for soon after childbirth their mothers returned to the mills leaving them alone in damp cellars and later loose in the streets. In a society where children were numerous and mothers had to work to support them, neglect was the natural result. It was ironic that the immigrant's search for security in a family led also to acute suffering.

But once marriage and childbirth had formed the family, the parents struggled to protect and strengthen it. Needing a place where all could gather to perform the simple rituals, they turned to the kitchen. Since it was the only heated room, it was ordinarily in the middle of the tenement with two rooms in front and two in back. Here, instead of the peasant hearth, was the stove that warmed the cold, fed the hungry, and cheered the unhappy. And here, too, were beds because the room was warm, the household large,

10. Massachusetts Board of Health, *Annual Report,* IX (1877), Mass. Pub. Doc. 34, p. 417; United States Census Office, *Tenth Census of the United States (1880)*, XII, Part II (Washington, 1886), 180-83; United States Census Office, *Eleventh Census of the United States . . . 1890,* XVII, Part I (Washington, 1896), 554. Massachusetts Board of Health, *Report,* XXVIII (1896), 753; Statistics Department, City of Boston, *Monthly Bulletin,* II, Nos. 1-3 (Mar., 1900), p. 32; *Sunday Sun,* July 10, 1910; Charles P. Neill, *Report on Strike of Textile Workers in Lawrence, Mass. in 1912,* 62 Congress, 2 Session, Senate Doc. 870 (Washington, 1912), p. 27.

11. These stories were as disgusting as they were commonplace. A two-weeks old child was abandoned by her mother. A male infant was found buried on the south bank of the Merrimack. *The Lawrence Sentinel,* July 4, 1868; *The Essex Eagle,* May 21, Nov. 12, 1870, Nov. 29, 1873, May 30, 1874; *Lawrence Journal,* May 22, Mar. 31, 1883.

and the apartment small. The scene of all domesticity and the place for recreation, the kitchen more than any other spot provided security for the frightened and lonely immigrant.

The essentials for this room and the others in the home were a stove, table, chairs, and beds, costing initially up to $45.00. Beds were normally of iron, but the Italians and Syrians preferred brass. The interior of an Italian home in 1912 showed "pleasing vistas of spotless beds piled high in the old world fashion, the frames . . . surmounted with feather beds rising high to enormous heights and crowned with crochet-edged pillows." This family was obviously more prosperous than most and others like them often had curtains, lamps, rocking chairs, rugs, bureaus, and even gramophones. The dangerous stoves burned wood, but coal gradually came into use, and kerosene was the lamp fuel.[12]

Into such an apartment in 1912 Polish families packed an average of nine persons, Lithuanians eight, and Italians seven. Privacy, difficult to attain within the family, became an impossibility when roomers also crowded in.[13] Most often the boarders bought their own food and sometimes even prepared it themselves. The city missionary painted vividly the picture of the boarder system: ". . . there will be what is called a central family; that is, lodgers occupy rooms in the house for so much a week, and each individual has his own loaf of bread and makes his mark on it, and lays it on the table, and it is his bread until it is eaten; he may have some cucumbers with it in the summer or may have some cheese with it, or he may join in purchasing some meat and make a stew; but he eats his own bread, and he does not butter it. . . ." They paid $2.00 or $3.00 a month for their rooms. While the system strained the family ties as much as having the mother work, it was such an economic necessity that about half of the worker households in 1912 had boarders and roomers.[14] Since they were usually of

12. Only four of eighty immigrant apartments studied in 1912 had heat other than from the kitchen stove. Neill, *Report*, p. 152   The furniture would include two beds, two mattresses and springs, a stove, four chairs, four yards of oilcloth, and a table. If new, the cost might reach $45.00. *Ibid.*, pp. 180-82. Alice W. O'Connor, "A Study of the Immigration Problem in Lawrence, Massachusetts" (unpublished social worker's thesis, Lawrence, 1914), p. 28.
13. Neill, *Report*, pp. 156-60. See Table XVII.
14. O'Connor, "Study," p. 49; *Strike at Lawrence*, p. 381; Neill, *Report*, p. 155.

the same nationality, ethnic unity was maintained even if the family integrity was threatened.

Since the family depended so completely upon the home, it was encouraging to immigrants to know that their homes were likely to get better. Sometimes it took several generations, but the Irish did not remain in their shanties forever and the Germans and English soon had attractive homes. The immigrant cycle brought newcomers into the undesirable dwellings in the heart of Lawrence and enabled the earlier immigrants to move to better sections closer to the outskirts of the city. Geographically Lawrence was like a bowl. The low land between the Merrimack and the Spicket (Wards Two, Three, and Four) was the bottom and Prospect Hill (Ward One), Tower Hill (Ward Five), South Lawrence (Ward Six), and the surrounding towns the sides. (See map, page 110.) The characteristic immigrant movement between 1845 and 1912 was up from the bottom of the bowl.

In 1855 the Irish were strongest in Wards Two and Three, where the boarding houses and the "plains" were situated. While these wards did not add much foreign-born population in the next decade, Wards One, Four, and Five grew rapidly as the Irish moved into them. The influx of French Canadians following the Civil War began in Ward Three, but by 1875 many of them had also shifted into Ward Four. During the same period the English had pushed west from the central wards to Ward Five and the Germans east into Ward One.

A comparison of the 1880 and 1910 figures demonstrated the up and out phenomenon more clearly. While the percentage of immigrants in the wards at the bottom of the bowl increased tremendously, that in the outside wards either remained constant or dropped, showing that the new immigrants were entering the center of Lawrence, while the second-generation Americans were moving to the outside. Many Irish-Americans moved across the Merrimack into Ward Six; the French-Canadians who had moved out into Ward Four continued on to the slopes of Tower Hill in Ward Five. While one-quarter of the members of a French-Canadian women's club lived in Ward Four between Common and Bradford Streets in 1908, a larger group occupied an area in Ward Five across the railroad tracks and up Tower Hill. The Italians,

Map IV
ETHNIC SHIFTS IN LAWRENCE AND WARD BOUNDARIES

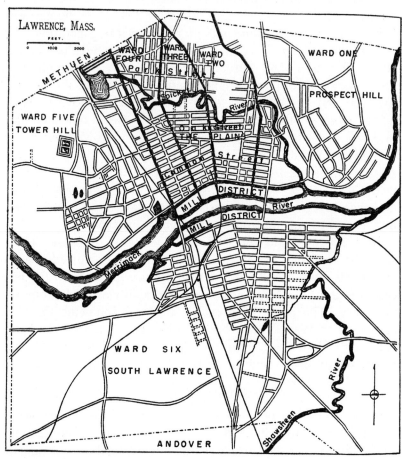

Park St. Polls	1884	1912
British or American	58	60
Irish	48	150
Post-1890 Immigrants	0	23

Oak St. Polls	1884	1912
British or American	43	30
Irish	357	127
Post-1890 Immigrants	0	358

Common St. Polls	1884	1912
British or American	198	79
Irish	257	35
Post-1890 Immigrants	4	655

meanwhile, had pushed the Irish out of the lower end of Common Street and the Syrians had ousted the Irish from Oak Street on the "plains." And before 1910 one street had even shifted from an Italian quarter to a mingled Jewish, French, and Portuguese colony.

A study of three well separated and parallel streets cutting across the three interior wards showed the same movement up from the Merrimack to the edges of the city. These were Common Street just one block above the shopping center of the city, Oak Street on the "plains" north of the Common, and finally Park Street on higher ground close to the Methuen line. A comparison of the names on the street lists for various years between 1884 and 1912 showed population shifts.

There were 257 persons with Irish names on Common Street in 1884, but only 35 in 1912. On Oak Street the number dropped less drastically, from 357 to 127. The Irish names on Park Street, meanwhile, climbed from 48 in 1884 to 150 in 1912. The British and native Americans, whose names were indistinguishable, also deserted Common Street for the hills but had not moved to Park Street. While 198 of them inhabited Common Street in 1884, only 79 were left in 1912. On both Oak and Park Streets their totals remained constant. The post-1890 immigrants adhered to the pattern by moving into the lowest street, Common Street, in the greatest numbers. Only a few of them lived on Oak Street in 1912 and hardly any had penetrated Park Street.

The shifts within parts of Common Street were also revealing. Two-thirds of lower Common Street in Ward One was made up of Irish names in 1884, but a decade later the invasion of Italians, Poles, and Armenians had cut the Irish proportion in half. In 1902 almost none of the names were Irish, while one-tenth were Polish, and half Italian. The dominance of the Italians was complete by 1912 when they comprised four-fifths of the names. Ward Three Common Street started in 1884 as a section of Irish, French Canadians, British, and Americans, but by 1902 the French Canadians dominated it with over half of the names. Ten years later the southeastern Europeans had driven almost everyone out.[15]

15. The shifts in ward population were derived from Oliver Warner, *Abstract of the Census of Massachusetts,—1865* . . . (Boston, 1867), pp. 62-63; *Census of Mass., 1875*, I, 288-311; *Census of Mass., 1880*, p. 50; *Thirteenth Census* . . . *Supplement for Mass.*, p. 609. See Table V. Paroisse Sainte-Anne, Lawrence,

Moving to a better section was just one of the ways in which the immigrant strengthened his family in Lawrence. Visits home, early marriage, endogamous marriage, and frequent procreation also helped him protect his family from the unfriendly city. Family life in Lawrence conformed to the pattern established by the immigrant cycle between 1845 and 1912. The rate of marriage, the degree of endogamy, and the birth rate tended to be high during the difficult years of the shanty Irish and the southeastern Europeans and lower during the years between. When security was most difficult to attain, the miserable immigrant found it in his family.

Mass., *Congrégation des Dames de Ste. Anne* (Salem, Mass., 1908) gives French addresses. O'Connor, "Study," pp. 19, 36-37, 40-41, 44. Since five of the six wards were parallel to one another running north and south above the Merrimack River, it was impossible to determine the northward migration up from the river merely by examining ward figures. While such ward statistics demonstrated the shifts out to Ward Six and up to Wards One and Five, they did not indicate the great movement of immigrants from the low areas of Wards Two, Three, and Four to the hilly outskirts of the same wards. The source of all information regarding Common, Oak, and Park Streets was the Lawrence Assessors' Street Lists of Polls, which listed all adult males liable for poll taxes. *Assessors' Street List of Polls . . . 1884 . . .* (Lawrence, 1884); *Assessors' Street List of Polls . . . 1894 . . .* (Lawrence, 1894); *Assessors' Street List of Polls . . . 1902 . . .* (Lawrence, 1902); *Assessors' Street List of Polls . . . 1912 . . .* (Lawrence, 1912). See adjoining map. See also Cole, "Lawrence," Table VI, pp. 387-90, for statistics.

CHAPTER VII

Security in the Mills

When the mill whistles blew before six o'clock in the morning, the Lawrence immigrant got out of bed; when they blew again, he marched into the factory; a final blast sent him home at night. He had little choice but to obey the whistles because in Lawrence almost every one had to work in the textile mills. In 1860 the woolen and cotton factories employed one-third of the 18,000 inhabitants. At the beginning of the 1912 strike half of the population fourteen years of age and over worked in the factories, and three-quarters of the city depended on them for their livelihood. The Immigration Commission studied Lawrence because it was the leading worsted center in America and because the textile industry dominated the city.[1] The mills at the same time depended heavily on the immigrants for their working force. In 1872, 3,800 of 4,700 employees at the Pacific Mill and at the Atlantic Mill were foreign born. Six years later all the Lawrence factories employed only 3,000 natives out of 9,000 workers. Of the remainder, 2,800 were born in Ireland, 1,400 in England, 700 in Canada, and 400 each in Germany and Scotland.[2] In his search for security the immigrant had to look

1. A. W. Doe, *Statistics of Lawrence (Mass.) Manufactures, January . . . 1861* (Manchester, N.H., 1861); Oliver Warner, *Abstract of the Census of Massachusetts,—1865 . . .* (Boston, 1867), p. 65. Charles P. Neill, *Report on Strike of Textile Workers in Lawrence, Mass. in 1912,* 62 Congress, 2 Session, Senate Doc. 870 (Washington, 1912), p. 9; Immigration Commission, "Woolen and Worsted Goods in Representative Community A," *Immigrants in Industries, Part 4: Woolen and Worsted Goods Manufacturing,* II, Immigration Commission, *Reports,* X, 61 Congress, 2 Session, Doc. 633 (Washington, 1911), p. 741.

2. Bureau of Statistics of Labor, *Third Annual Report . . . 1872,* Senate Doc. 180, p. 164; Bureau of Statistics of Labor, "Fall River, Lowell, and Lawrence," *Thirteenth Annual Report . . . 1882,* Mass. Pub. Doc. 15, p. 205.

to the mills, and in their search for manpower the mills had to look to the immigrants. Thus were their fates combined.

Since most of the immigrants had not previously worked in mills, the adjustment was difficult. The Immigration Commission report showed that only the English, German, and Scotch males had much previous experience.

NATIVE-LAND OCCUPATIONS BY PERCENTAGE

Males	Textile Manufacturing	Other Manufacturing	Farming	General Labor	Hand Trades, Trade, Other
Total	26	5	35	5	29
Canadian, French	9	4	53	9	25
English	55	9	2	8	25
German	72	5	4	2	17
Irish	16	5	48	10	21
Italian	2	3	45	5	45
Polish	8	3	74	3	12
Russian	11	1	65	9	14
Scotch	43	18	6	6	27

The one-third who had formerly been farmers found work in the mills particularly unpleasant. This dislocation in part accounted for the chronic dissatisfaction expressed by the French Canadian in *Le Progrès,* for the difficulties of the Irish, and for the abuse showered on the later immigrants. Those who had the least trouble in Lawrence were the ones whose past experience had included mill work, notably the Germans and English. And the fact that the Germans and English were predominantly Protestant and generally spoke English made their acceptance of, and by, America all the easier. The former farmers on the other hand were most often Catholic and frequently could not speak English. Since half of the female operatives had previous experience in the mills, their adjustment must have been simpler.[3]

3.
NATIVE-LAND OCCUPATIONS OF FEMALES BY PERCENTAGE*

	Textile Manufacturing	Other Manufacturing	Farming	Domestic Service	Other
Total	50	1	27	5	17
Canadian, French	33	4	35	6	12
English	91	2	—	3	4
Irish	49	4	12	24	11
Italian	14	1	19	6	60
Polish	7	3	71	11	14

* Immigration Commission, "Community A," pp. 755-56.

Peasants who had once depended upon their landlords now relied completely on the mill owners. The line between success and failure was a thin one, and a manufacturer's whim could determine the future of hundreds of immigrant families. His influence reached far beyond America because many nations had a stake in Lawrence prosperity. So many came to Lawrence from Bradford, England, that it was called the "Bradford of America." The *Bradford Observer* quoted from the Lawrence newspapers and carefully followed the career of Joseph Walworth, a Pacific Mill wool buyer who was born in Bradford. When two Montreal cotton mills shut down in 1883, the *Lawrence Journal* announced that 1,500 would be seeking jobs in Lawrence and Lowell. The Canadian *Soleil* spoke sadly of the closing of the Pemberton Mill. An attempt by outsiders to buy a cotton mill in Lawrence, where Russian Jews could work unmolested, reflected the hope that the immigrant city held out to the world.[4]

The mill owners continued the policy of the model town by exercising strict control over their workers. Often it was to the employees' advantage. The Pacific Mill made so many contributions to the "material, intellectual, and moral welfare" of its workers that it won a prize at the Paris Exposition of 1867. For many years the Washington Mill gave each operative a turkey or a skirt for Christmas. William Wood was merely following an old tradition when he built his model Wood Mill in 1905 and put in many conveniences for the workers.

The influence of the owners on elections was less admirable. In 1870 the *Sentinel* accused the paper manufacturers of sitting at the voting table to intimidate their employees. It was natural that the mill owners should oppose the secret ballot. When Mark Hanna ordered all McKinley supporters to fly an American flag before the election of 1896, the Washington owners forced their workers to contribute five cents each and Thomas Dolan and John McKenna, who refused, were discharged. The *Tribune* maintained that other mills let men go for not joining McKinley gold clubs and that the Boston and Maine railroad got rid of one for giving to a

4. *Ibid.,* pp. 745-46; *The Evening Tribune,* Feb. 23, 1892, Feb. 9, 1894, Feb. 21, 1895; *Lawrence Journal,* Nov. 3, 1883; *Le Progrès,* June 28, 1904.

Bryan flag fund. The members of the B & M Gold Club paraded to jeers of "That's right, boys! Hold on to your jobs!"[5]

To restrain possible labor agitation the corporations used private detectives and often pitted one immigrant group against another. William Forbes discharged some of his plumbers when they joined a union. To guard against such tactics the Knights of Labor told its members to remain unknown and to "refrain from any . . . petty strikes." Owners occasionally evicted strikers from their boarding houses and often would not rehire strike leaders. The employment of children also served to control adult labor.

Inside the mill the foreman's word was law. Since he was generally American, British, or Irish, he was not sympathetic with the more recent arrivals. Recognizing the antagonism between the older and newer employees, he believed that if he started to hire southeastern Europeans for one department, he would find no one else who would work there. One worker reflected the feeling of many when he stated: "The little jests that break the monotony of millwork are impossible when a 'dago' is working next to you; if you joke him, he will stick a knife into you." As a result, the foremen usually put the "impulsive, industrious, erratic" Italians by themselves in the spinning room. There were frequent complaints against domineering foremen, particularly concerning the way they counted up the amount woven or spun. One foreman at the Washington threatened to discharge workers who protested his reckoning of the cuts. Operatives in all the mills complained about the excessive number of machines they had to run. No immigrant in the Lawrence factories believed himself to be a free man.[6]

5. Pacific Mills, *Statement Presented to the Special Jury of the Paris Exposition of 1867* (Lawrence, 1868), pp. 12-13 and notes. For material on mill welfare see *The Lawrence Sentinel*, Dec. 27, 1862; *Journal*, May 2, 1885, May 21, 1887; Lawrence City Mission, *Annual Report*, XXVI (1883), 42; *The Lawrence Sun*, Dec. 3, 1909. For influence of corporations on politics see *The Lawrence Courier*, Dec. 7, 1857; *The Lawrence Sentinel*, Nov. 11, 1865, Dec. 10, 1870; *Lawrence Journal*, Feb. 3, 1883. The corporation said the two men were discharged for laziness. *The Evening Tribune*, Oct. 16, 24, 26, Nov. 2, 1896.

6. The use of scab labor to break up strikes in Lawrence was not uncommon. When the Arlington wool sorters struck in 1891, they were so afraid of strikebreakers from England that they cabled Bradford, England, urging sorters there not to come to Lawrence. Strikebreakers were imported in 1902 to end a spinners and doffers strike. *The Evening Tribune*, May 29, 1891, Jan. 16, 1902. The Knights of Labor quotation is in the *Lawrence Journal*, Mar. 10, 1888.

But since they were poor the immigrants had to accept the mills and their officials. Thousands arrived as paupers. Deep in the winter of 1877, with the temperature below zero, the city missionary found one of these families in a filthy shack. Four of the children were covered by a single shawl in one bed and in another the father and mother tried to keep the baby warm with a quilt. "Cold, hunger, nakedness, with no work, no credit in a land of strangers, made that home one of the most desolate of places." And there were many others equally naked and fully as hungry. While the foreign-born population was less than half of the whole, it contributed about two-thirds of the mission cases. At the start of the Civil War the Irish and the English, with only a third of the population, had two-thirds of the cases. Four decades later native Americans made up only 30 per cent of the new cases reported by the Overseers of the Poor.[7] One Common Street pawnbroker started with only ten dollars, another came without even a proper pair of pants, and forty Rumanian Jews arrived without any money at all. *Le Progrès* complained that even though the French Canadians entered the city poor, the church bled them of whatever they had. The Boston authorities found that only twenty-five of seventy Genoese who had come to Boston destined for Lawrence during the 1912 strike had bank accounts. These were immigrants seeking security in Lawrence.

For treatment of workers inside the mills see Immigration Commission, "Community A," pp. 770-72.
   7.
THE PERCENTAGE OF THE TOTAL RELIEVED BY CITY MISSION
BORN IN CERTAIN COUNTRIES*

	1861	1890	1900	1910
United States	30	38	36	42
Ireland	43	28	20	14
England	21	22	16	9
Scotland	4	5	8	3
Canada	2	5	11	14
Germany	1	1	1	1
Poland or Russia			2	6
Italy				4
Foreign-born	70	62	64	58

* The 1861 figures are for families relieved; those for 1890 and after for new cases. For additional details, dissertation copy, Table XL. City Mission, *Report*, III (1861), 5; XIX (1877), 11; XXI (1879), 5; XXXI (1890), 24; XLI (1900), 13-14, 22-23; XLII (1901), 14-15; LI (1910), 20-21. Overseer

On his arrival in Lawrence the poverty-stricken immigrant found that wages were not as high as he had expected. Nor were they steady because with the long layoffs he could never count on more than forty weeks of work a year. Wages went up from the start of the Civil War until about 1875, when the panic of 1873 began to drive them down. Even at this peak the average Lawrence wage of about $400 a year was far below the state average of $476. Men of course did better than women and children and could count on about $500 a year, compared to about $250 for women and $150 for children. Ten years later the average in Lawrence had fallen to $325 a year, lower than all except eight other cities in Massachusetts. The bottom was reached in 1893 when pay in Lawrence was below $300 a year and was one-quarter less than in Fall River and Lowell.[8]

In terms of individual jobs the decline after 1875 was even more startling. The Pacific was paying dressers only $10.00 a week in 1896 compared to $17.00 previously. The aristocratic loom fixers and wool sorters in another mill went from $13.00 and $11.00 a week in 1889 to $12.00 and $10.00 in 1894. Arlington weavers, who received $10.00 a week for two looms in 1875, got only $7.00 in 1896 for five. And the lowly doffers were down to a bare $3.60 a week in 1894. In one mill the average pay for all jobs was only $7.00 a week.[9]

At best the pay was inadequate. Even during the Civil War an operative earning $11.00 a week said he could not save. A group of poor Lawrence families in 1869 had an average of $20.00 more in expenses than in income. At the high point in 1875 the average male in Lawrence earned $500 a year for 250 days of work. Since his total expenses were over $600, he could not survive unless his

of Poor figures from *ibid.*, XLI (1900), 24; *Municipal Records and Memoranda 1856-1859*, IV.

8. The Lawrence average wage in 1875 was actually $392. Constance Green, *Holyoke, Massachusetts* (New Haven, Connecticut, 1929), p. 56; *Lawrence Journal*, June 21, 1879; Bureau of Statistics of Labor, *Fourteenth Annual Report . . . 1883*, Mass. Pub. Doc. 15, pp. 346-47, 365, 372-73; Carroll D. Wright, *Census of Massachusetts: 1875*, II (Boston, 1877), 354, 436, 444, 447, 577, 583; *Tribune*, Oct. 14, 1893.

9. Bureau of Statistics of Labor, *Report . . . 1870*, Senate Doc. 120, pp. 117, 380-86; *Census of Mass., 1875*, II, 436, 444, 449, 577, 583; *The Essex Eagle*, June 17, 1876; *The Evening Tribune*, Oct. 29, 1892, Aug. 18, Oct. 1, 1896; Immigration Commission, "Community A," pp. 757-60, 773.

wife worked.[10]   And prices fell much more slowly than wages after 1876. Tenement rents in 1893, when wages dipped below the $300 mark, were often $200 a year. By this time a man had difficulty surviving unless his children as well as his wife worked.[11]

As wages hit their low point in 1895 the immigrant, who sought security in the mills, had apparently failed. Trapped at a job for which he was not trained, accepted only reluctantly by his foreman, ruthlessly controlled both inside and outside the mill, caught between dropping wages and more stationary prices, he faced a desperate situation. Here early in the decades of despair the immigrant seemed to have no chance for economic security.

Fortunately the mills recovered from their economic nadir and wages began to rise again after 1896. Wages had always fluctuated with the business cycle. After an initial boom connected with the building of the city, Lawrence suffered her first major depression after the panic of 1857. Hard times were the rule until the Civil War, when a boom began which lasted until the panic of 1873. Difficult conditions prevailed down to 1885, when mild prosperity took over until 1893. On the morning of April 12, 1893, 15,000 workers were out of jobs and for the first time in the memory of most citizens every mill was closed. Though unemployment never exceeded this figure, Lawrence wallowed in the depression until 1896, when it began to climb toward the great

10. A survey of over 1,000 Lawrence workers in 1876 showed how narrow the margin was between earnings and expenses. The figures for males and females were as follows:

	Male	Female
Average number dependent on each worker	2.84	1.74
Days employed per year	252.83	239.19
Daily wages	$ 1.93	$ 1.01
Yearly earnings	$504.84	$238.57
Rent paid	$130.85	$ 78.82
Remaining cost of living	$481.17	$197.30
Total expenses	$612.02	$276.12

Bureau of Statistics of Labor, *Report . . . 1870*, pp. 116-18, 407; Bureau of Statistics of Labor, *Sixth Annual Report . . . 1875*, Mass. Pub. Doc. 31, pp. 376, 381; Bureau of Statistics of Labor, *Seventh Annual Report . . . 1876*, Mass. Pub. Doc. 31, p. 102; *Lawrence City Documents 1906-1907*, p. 8.

11. Bureau of Statistics of Labor, *Tenth Annual Report . . . 1879*, Mass. Pub. Doc. 31, p. 83; Board of Trade of London, *Cost of Living in American Towns*, 62 Congress, 1 Session, Senate Doc. 22 (Washington, 1911), lxxviii; *Anzeiger und Post*, Sept. 25, 1909; *Sunday Sun*, Sept. 8, 1907; *The Evening Tribune*, Jan. 27, June 5, 1893, Aug. 7, 1902; *The Sunday Register*, Feb. 26, 1899; Neill, *Report*, pp. 158-60. See Table XVIII.

peak year of 1909. Thanks in part to the construction of the giant Wood Mill in 1905, the population increased so dramatically that the press called it the biggest boom in Massachusetts and asserted that within two years Lawrence would be the first industrial city in the state. In sum, prosperity was dominant in the period 1845-73, depression in 1873-96, and prosperity again in 1896-1912. Population increases went hand in hand with the periods of prosperity.[12]

Wages followed the business cycle until by 1909 the city was about level with the 1875 peak average of $400 a year. Loom fixers and wool sorters at $15.00 a week were higher than ever before. Even the doffers were making $5.50. The average weekly wage throughout the city was between $8.50 and $9.00, with men at $9.50, women at $8.00 and children averaging $6.00.[13]

There was hope as soon as wages began to go up. The strike observers believed that the workers' pay was intolerably low in 1912 and it was; but from the immigrant's point of view, wages were much higher than in 1894. With the hope of even more increases after the strike and with evidence of a business boom all about, the immigrant was finding more security in the mills than anyone might have guessed.

He derived some consolation also from a steady reduction in hours. As early as 1847 the Labor Reform organization met to demand a ten-hour day, but the real drive came between 1865 and 1870, when the Short Time movement and the Ten-Hour Clubs flourished. Partly because of this pressure and in part owing to the depression, hours dropped in 1873 from 64 a week to 62.5, and a year later they were down to 60. Here they re-

12. For complete documentation see Donald B. Cole, "Lawrence, Massachusetts: Immigrant City, 1845-1912" (Doctoral dissertation, Harvard University, 1956), pp. 279-81. Population 1850-75: up 306 per cent; 1875-95: up 49 per cent; 1895-1910: up 65 per cent. See Table II.

13. Immigration Commission, "Community A," pp. 757-60, 773. The median figures for all jobs studied at one mill were: 1889—$6.45; 1894—$5.85; 1909—$8.10. The average was: 1899—$7.50; 1894—$7.00; 1909—$9.50. For 1909, therefore, there were three figures given for mill wages in Lawrence: $9.50 (the average of the specific jobs studied in one mill); $8.10 (the median of the specific jobs); and $8.75 (the average of all mill wages in the city). Since $8.75 is between $9.50 and $8.10, it is probably the best figure. The average person in the Lawrence textile mills was earning $8.75 a week in 1909, the high point since 1875. Bureau of Statistics of Labor, *Fourteenth Annual Report . . . 1883*, pp. 372-73. *Anzeiger und Post,* Mar. 9, 1907.

mained until about 1890, when Massachusetts began to lower the maximum number of hours women and children could work. During the next two decades the hours went from sixty to fifty-eight, to fifty-six, and finally in 1911 to fifty-four. Since about half of the operatives were women and children, the mills found it convenient to set the hours for all employees at the same limits. The way the corporations handled the reduction to fifty-four hours incited the strikers in 1912.[14]

In addition to the business cycle and the steady reduction in hours the immigrant cycle made the immigrant feel that his search for security in the mills would not be in vain. He knew that the arrival of new immigrants improved the position of the older ones. His own pay might not be much, but he had reason to believe that his son would do better. The figures of the Immigration Commission in 1909 bore out his faith. While native male workers with native fathers averaged a little over $11.00 a week, those with foreign fathers received something less than $11.00 and the foreign-born got only about $9.25. Though an Irish immigrant was making only $10.21, his son was up to $10.54, and the Germans showed the same improvement over a generation. The earlier immigrants, notably the English and the Germans, were earning the most and the later ones, such as the Italians and the Poles, were getting the least. The longer a person had been in the United States, the higher his earnings. Among men who had been here over ten years only the Syrians had a median wage of less than $7.50, while for those here less than five years four of the southeastern European nationalities were below the $7.50 level. The immigrant cycle brought hope to those who were suffering in Lawrence.[15]

The immigrant father hoped more than anything else that his son would abandon the mills and turn to the crafts, because skilled artisans in Lawrence often earned two to three times as much as

14. *Lawrence Journal*, Feb. 22, 1879; *The Lawrence Courier*, July 24, 1847, Feb. 7, 1852; *The Lawrence Sentinel*, Sept. 2, 1856, April 13, 1867, Aug. 7, 1869, April 16, 1870; Bureau of Statistics of Labor, *Report . . . 1870*, pp. 390-91; Bureau of Statistics of Labor, *Fourth Annual Report . . . 1873*, House Doc. 173, p. 315; *The Essex Eagle*, April 13, 1867, Sept. 26, Oct. 3, 1874; *The Evening Tribune*, April 21, 1891, Oct. 22, 1892, Dec. 15, 1896, April 22, 1899; *Sunday Sun*, Jan. 7, 1912.

15. Immigration Commission, "Community A," pp. 757-65. See Table XVIII.

the ordinary mill workers. About 1900 horseshoers and painters had a minimum weekly rate of $15.00. Newspaper workers and paperhangers got $12.00 to $18.00 a week. When the carpenters and plumbers began to demand $2.00 to $3.00 a day, *Le Progrès* complained that it was too much and that soon they would be asking $5.00 a day. From skilled brewmasters at $23.00 a week down, the craftsmen were in a favored position.[16]

Not all the immigrants could become craftsmen, but the federal census reports proved that they improved their jobs after several decades in the city. The following chart taken from the reports of 1880 and 1900 establishes definite trends in the occupations of different nationalities. It shows the percentage of the workers of each nationality in four job categories. The statistics for 1880 are according to the nativity of the worker, while those for 1900 show the nativity of the worker's parents. This variation is useful. Take the Irish, for example. The 1880 statistics cover the immigrants who came about the time of the Civil War, while those for 1900 include both them and their children as well as later Irish immigrants. This makes it possible to compare the occupations of the Irish-born in 1880 with both first- and second-generation Irish-Americans in 1900. The four job categories were not completely satisfactory because they lumped a wide variety of jobs under the same heading. "Manufacturing and mechanical pursuits" covered mill labor, skilled craftsmen, and mill owners; "trade and transportation" went from banker to street railway employee. But generally the best jobs were the "professional services"; second, "trade and transportation"; third, "manufacturing and mechanical pursuits"; and last, "personal service." Those employed in agriculture were never more than 1 per cent of any group and so were not listed in the following table.[17]

16. Bureau of Statistics of Labor, *Thirty-fourth Annual Report . . . 1904*, Mass. Pub. Doc. 15, p. 370; Bureau of Statistics of Labor, *Thirty-sixth Annual Report . . . 1906*, Mass. Pub. Doc. 15, p. 477; *Le Progrès*, April 26, 1906.

17. See Tables XIX and XX. These percentages and the material on occupations that follows were derived from United States Census Office, *Tenth Census of the United States . . . 1880*, I (Washington, 1883), 882; United States Census Bureau, *Twelfth Census of the United States, Special Reports, Occupations* (Washington, 1904), pp. 588-91. The total number gainfully employed in 1880 was 19,153; in 1900, 30,254. The native-born figures for 1900 were for whites only, and though the other figures included the other races, there were so few non-whites in Lawrence that the discrepancy is meaningless. The

PERCENTAGES OF EMPLOYED 1880, 1900

Occupation	Nativity						
1880	Total	United States	Ireland	Great Britain	Ger-many	Canada	Italy Poland Russia
Professional Services	2	4	1	1	1	1	—
Trade and Trans-portation	9	13	7	5	6	5	—
Manufacturing	78	75	72	90	90	80	—
Personal Service	11	8	20	4	3	13	—
1900	Parent Nativity						
Professional Services	3	8	3	2	2	1	0
Trade and Trans-portation	15	29	14	12	11	12	12
Manufacturing	70	48	66	78	80	74	77
Personal Service	12	14	16	8	6	12	10

The over-all figures reveal what immigration meant to a city such as Lawrence. Within twenty years the percentage in professional service went up 50 per cent and that in trade and transportation rose 67 per cent. For those who had been in the city in 1880 the change was even greater, the Irish, for example, tripling their percentage in the professions. Bearing the burdens relinquished by the early immigrants and natives were the southeastern

Canadian figures stood for British America in 1880, but Canada in 1900. Professional Services included clergymen, dentists, journalists, lawyers, musicians, physicians, surgeons, officials, and civil employees. Trade and transportation embraced clerks, salesmen, dealers, bankers, teamsters, street railway employees, grocers, and sailors. Manufacturing and mechanical pursuits included such artisans as blacksmiths, shoe makers, carpenters, engineers, machinists, masons, painters, plumbers, and printers, but also such persons as bakers and butchers, as well as the nebulous cotton, woolen, and worsted mill operatives. Personal services meant barbers, bartenders, hotel keepers, janitors, policemen, firemen, and ordinary laborers. Clearly the professional service people had the best jobs, and in general the personal service individuals were at the bottom of the economic ladder. The groups between were difficult to rank. The bankers, brokers, and highly skilled craftsmen in the mills received higher pay than the remainder of the trade, transportation, and manufacturing groups. For a more complete study of Lawrence occupations including material on 1847-49, 1870, and 1912 see Cole, "Lawrence," pp. 236-46 and Table XXXVIII, pp. 436-40. This work lists the first ten or twelve occupations of each nationality in both 1880 and 1900. It breaks the Canadians in 1900 into French Canadians and English Canadians; the southeastern Europeans into Italians, Poles, and Russians; and the native-born into native-born with native parents and native-born with foreign parents.

Europeans, who could boast of no one in professional service. As the immigrant cycle worked, the whole city raised its level of employment because of the efforts of the most recent arrivals.

Since at first the Irish were laborers and domestics, they outranked the other nationalities in personal service and were economically at the bottom of city employment. By 1880 they were working in the factories instead of building them. Twenty years later in 1900 they were much better off with one out of six employed professionally or in trade. While it required only two occupations to employ two-thirds of the Irish in 1880, showing how dependent they were upon menial labor, nine jobs were necessary to account for two-thirds of them in 1900. Though the total employed had doubled, the number of laborers and servants did not change. Many more had become salesmen, merchants, and clerks. The percentage of Irish workers in their leading occupations in both years are in the following chart. Only the occupations necessary to employ two-thirds are listed.

Irish

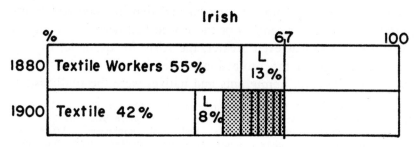

L -- Laborers

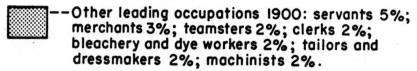
-- Other leading occupations 1900: servants 5%; merchants 3%; teamsters 2%; clerks 2%; bleachery and dye workers 2%; tailors and dressmakers 2%; machinists 2%.

The British meanwhile showed a much smaller percentage of laborers and servants and a much larger proportion in the mills. Between 1880 and 1900 the latter went down while that in trade and transportation rose. Like the Irish, the British spread out into a wider range of jobs and were placed more frequently in stores and other businesses. The British percentages:

British

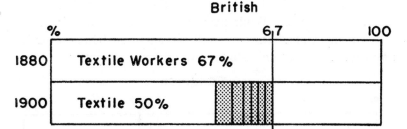

Other leading occupations 1900: machinists 5%;
clerks 3%; carpenters 3%; salesmen 2%; merchants 2%;
bleachery and dye workers 2%.

German occupations formed a pattern similar to those of the British: the percentage in trade and transportation, low at first, rose steadily; that in manufacturing, originally high, dropped; and the proportion in personal services was minimal. The Germans could not match the Irish in trade, but they were ahead of them in manufacturing because so many German wool weavers came to Lawrence. While the percentage of Germans in the textile mills dropped, the percentage in manufacturing remained relatively high because of an increase in German carpenters and machinists. As was the case with the Irish and the British, the variety of German occupations increased greatly between 1880 and 1900. The German statistics:

German

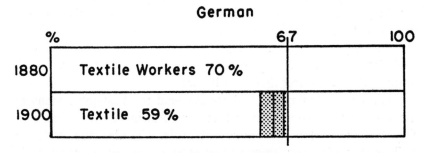

Other leading occupations 1900: carpenters 4%;
salesmen 3%; merchants 3%.

The Canadians had a high percentage in trade and transportation. Like the other early immigrants many were in the mills at first, but the proportion dropped by 1900. The large percentage doing personal service placed the Canadians down with the Irish on the economic scale. While their range of occupations increased by 1900, many Canadians were still servants and laborers, underscoring their low economic status. Canadian occupations:

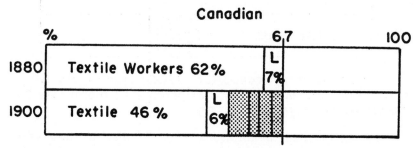

Canadian

Other leading occupations 1900: carpenters 6%; salesmen 3%; servants 3%; dressmakers 3%.

For the later immigrants there was a similar pattern. Like the early Irish they had almost none in the professions and few in trade and transportation; most of their workers were in the textile mills. Only the Russians, with their numerous junk dealers, could claim many merchants. The large number of southeastern Europeans in manufacturing indicated that they had replaced the older immigrants in the mills. The Italians, Poles, and Russians combined had 64 per cent of their workers in the textile mills in 1900 and 8 per cent doing day labor—two occupations accounting for 72 per cent of those employed. The majority of the Syrians, too, found work in the mills, but there were also many Syrian grocers and restaurant keepers. As the southeastern Europeans took the jobs once held by the shanty Irish, the effect of the immigrant cycle was clearer than ever before.

The native Americans had always held the best jobs, many of them in the professions and in trade and transportation. But even they benefited from the immigrant cycle. Trades and crafts as well as teaching were among their most numerous occupations in 1880, but these were joined by manufacturing and banking in 1900. As early as 1880 two-thirds of the native-born were spread among seven jobs. By 1900 the same proportion of natives with native parents needed sixteen types of work. The leading occupations were as follows:

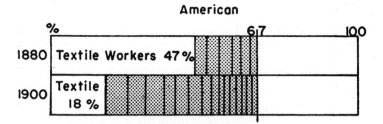

Other leading occupations 1880: tailors 4%; clerks 4%; traders 4%; machinists 3%; carpenters 3%; domestics 3%.

Other leading occupations 1900: bookkeepers 7%; salesmen 6%; carpenters 6%; merchants 4%; machinists 4%; steam railroad workers 4%; dressmakers 3%; servants 3%; teachers 2%; painters 2%; draymen 2%; laborers 2%; shoe workers 2%; manufacturing 2%; policemen and firemen 2%.

Not only did the native Americans with native parents have better jobs than the immigrants, but they also had better jobs than the native Americans with foreign-born parents. In this respect the census report of 1900 revealed the same order of economic success as the Immigration Commission figures on wages in the mills in 1909. Those with the best occupations were the native-born with native parents; next were the natives with foreign parents; last were the foreign-born. The following chart demonstrates the differences among the three groups:

Percentage of Each Group Engaged in Certain Pursuits, 1900

	Native-born with Native Parents	Native-born with Foreign Parents	Foreign-born
Professional Services	8	4	1
Trade and Transportation	29	17	10
Manufacturing and Mechanical Pursuits	48	71	74
Personal Service	14	8	14

The number of occupations necessary to employ two-thirds of each group also showed the same order. The more recent arrivals in America were confined to a small number of jobs, while the early immigrants had begun to spread out into many more occupations.

Number of Occupations	1880	1900
16-20		Native-born with Native Parents 16
11-15		
6-10	Native-born 7	→Native-born with Foreign Parents 8 Foreign-born (No. Eur. & Canada) 7
1- 5	Foreign-born 4 (No. Eur. & Can.)	Foreign-born (Southeastern Eur.) 2

The arrows demonstrate the progress made by each group in twenty years. As each group lived in America longer and longer its occupational range widened. It is likely that the later nationalities found jobs for two-thirds of their workers in six or eight occupations by 1929 and that those from Germany, Ireland, Great Britain, and Canada needed fifteen or more. The natives of long standing by that time had probably spread into at least twenty-five jobs for two-thirds of their workers.[18]

Still further evidence appeared in a 1935 history of Essex County, Massachusetts, which carried biographies of its prominent citizens. Only 14 of the 130 "successful" men connected with Lawrence were foreign-born, 67 were second-generation Americans, and 49 were native-born with native parents. Most of the 130 had been young men in Lawrence at the turn of the century. There were more natives with foreign parents than those with native parents because the former group was much larger in Lawrence. Proportionately the native-born with native parents were the most "successful." The longer one's family had been in America the more likely he was to get a good job.[19]

The earlier immigrants and natives dominated government

18. Cole, "Lawrence," pp. 237-38, 436-40, has material derived from a study of the death records of 1912, which gave the occupations of those who died and their parents. These figures provided the basis for comparing the occupations of first and second generation Americans with those of native-born Americans with native-born parents. They revealed the same pattern of economic success as that established by the 1900 figures. City of Lawrence, Deaths, XII (1911-13), 67-133.

19. Scott H. Paradise and Claude M. Fuess, The Story of Essex County (New York, 1935), III, IV, passim.

service and the professions, the best jobs the city offered. The politicians elected to office were almost invariably native-born citizens or Irish. In thirteen administrations selected out of the decades of promise, three-quarters of the officials were native citizens, over an eighth were Irish, and most of the rest English.[20] The same pattern appeared in the census reports of 1900, which showed the birthplace of the parents of the workers:

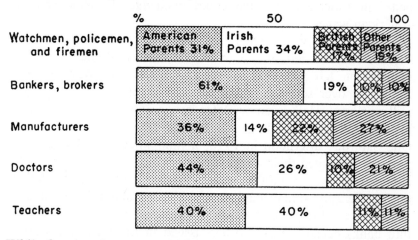

While few immigrants could hope to become bankers or doctors, the immigrant cycle made it possible for the next generation to do so. Even the poorest Italians or Poles were willing to exist in the slums of a city that brought immigrants from the bottom to the top within a few generations.[21]

And even if he and his sons never advanced beyond the mills, the immigrant liked to think that he was better off than he would

20. *Lawrence American,* Jan. 9, 1864, Jan. 7, 1865, Jan. 5, 1866, Jan. 11, 1884, supplement; *The Lawrence Sentinel,* Dec. 7, 1867, Jan. 7, 1871, Jan. 6, 1872, Jan. 3, 1874; *The Essex Eagle,* Jan. 10, 1874, Jan. 2, 1875; *Lawrence Journal,* Jan. 12, Dec. 7, 1878, Jan. 11, 1879, Dec. 31, 1881; Carroll D. Wright, *The Census of Massachusetts: 1885,* I, Part 2 (Boston, 1888), 124; City Marshal, "Report, 1903," pp. 13-22, *Lawrence City Documents 1903-1904,* showed 50 native policemen, 10 Irish, and 15 others.

21. The material for 1900 came from the same census reports cited in footnote 17. A Lawrence school manual lists the teachers for 1913 and the names show that the Irish were prominent in that profession. Of the 416 names 194 appeared to be Irish. In the high school all thirty-one teachers had Irish names. City of Lawrence, *Manual of the Public Schools* (Lawrence, 1913), pp. 26-41. Of the lawyers in 1912, 70 per cent American or British names, 18 per cent Irish. *Lawrence Directory, 1912* (Boston, 1912), pp. 800-1.

have been in the old country. The *Courier* cheered the early arrivals by stating that wages were 33 to 50 per cent lower in Manchester and Leeds, England, than in New England. Later the *American* carried lurid descriptions of the squalid conditions in the British factories. While some responded that hours in England were shorter and prices lower and others doubted that conditions could be anywhere worse than in the "dirty, dusty, miserable human pens" in Lawrence, no one could challenge the superiority of American wages.[22]

Since wages were higher, workers were better able to save. Patrick Murphy left an estate of $50,000; a French Canadian named Coté left $10,000. At the end of the Civil War the Essex Bank had over seven thousand deposits in one year, many from mill workers. Half a century later immigrants ranging from Irishmen to Italians held a large number of the accounts at the Essex. One Saturday afternoon in 1910, a time when mill workers customarily deposited their wages, the Essex had almost 400 deposits, aggregating over $10,000. Back in the 1880's the revelations during the Augustinian bank failure showed about seven hundred accounts, totalling over $400,000. But not all the money went into banks because money orders issued in Lawrence for sending money abroad amounted to $150,000 a year about 1910. And many newspaper articles spoke of immigrants who carried about large sums of money.[23]

The savings were soon invested in property. When the Essex Company offered land at auction before the Civil War, so many

22. *The Lawrence Courier*, Nov. 19, 1859, *Municipal Records,* VI; Bureau of Statistics of Labor, *Third Annual Report . . . 1872*, p. 399; *The Evening Tribune*, Oct. 14, 1893; *Lawrence American*, Aug. 31, Sept. 14, Oct. 12, 1888; Board of Trade of London, *Cost of Living*, p. lxi.

23. *Lawrence Journal*, Mar. 3, 17, Oct. 4, 1883; Essex County, Mass., Registry of Probate, Nos. 92541, 71887; *The Essex Eagle*, Oct. 12, 1867; Bureau of Statistics of Labor, *Fifth Annual Report . . . 1874*, Mass. Pub. Doc. 31, p. 167; *Le Progrès*, April 19, 1906; *The Strike at Lawrence, Mass. Hearings before the Committee on Rules of the House of Representatives . . . 1912*, 62 Congress, 2 Session, House Doc. 671 (Washington, 1912), p. 409; Neill, *Report*, p. 210; *The Evening Tribune*, Aug. 30, 1894. Newspaper articles depicted fairly affluent immigrants. A weaver was robbed of $69. An Italian foreman was found dead with $80 to $100 on him. Two Armenians had $800 and $600. Another Armenian had bankbooks with accounts totaling $500. *Lawrence Journal*, Aug. 27, 1881; *The Evening Tribune*, April 3, 1891, Feb. 21, 1894, Nov. 5, 1903. Ninety-two of the accounts at the Augustinian Bank were over $1,000.

immigrants bought land and built houses that Lawrence became known as the "city of homes." By 1882 Lawrence mill workers, mostly immigrants, owned as much property as those in Fall River and Lowell combined. Patrick Sweeney, owner of the *Journal*, bought large holdings and, when prices rose, made a great profit; his tax bill in 1884 was the highest of any resident. Joseph Saliba in 1900 was buying up all available real estate for the fast growing Syrian colony, and prosperous Italians invested heavily in Pleasant Valley. Other Syrians and Italians were assessed for over $400,000 in another area. The assessed valuation of real estate belonging to Armenians, Syrians, Poles, Lithuanians, and Italians was over a million dollars in 1912. French Canadians alone were assessed for another million.[24]

Immigrant churches and clubs were also prosperous. The Catholics collected about $3,000 on Easter in 1878 and the same at Christmas in 1880. As Father Devir left to visit Ireland, his parishioners gave him a purse of $1,000. When their convent became inadequate, 1,200 Catholics contributed an average of about $9.00 each to build a new one. The Germans easily raised $3,000 to alter Turn Hall and the French Canadians mustered $33,000 for the Saint Jean de Baptiste building in 1906. Even the Chinese laundrymen were able to gather a few dollars for a Fourth of July float. When immigrants contributed a large percentage of the $27,000 collected to aid the sufferers from the 1890 cyclone and a significant proportion of the San Francisco earthquake fund, it was only additional evidence of immigrant wealth.[25]

A few final examples indicate the manner in which some of the

24. *Sunday Sun*, June 2, 1907; Bureau of Statistics of Labor, "Fall River, Lowell, and Lawrence," pp. 296-97; United States Census Office, *Eleventh Census of the United States . . . 1890*, Bulletin 31 (Washington, 1893), p. 9; *Lawrence City Documents 1906-1907*, p. 8; *The Evening Tribune*, Aug. 10, 1900; *The Strike at Lawrence*, pp. 409-10. Citizens' Association, Lawrence, Mass., *Lawrence, Massachusetts: A Story of Protest, Patriotism, Thanksgiving, and Truth* (Lawrence, 1912), pp. 8-11. For further references to immigrant property see Cole, "Lawrence," pp. 59-60, 272.

25. *Lawrence Journal*, April 27, 1878, Jan. 3, 1880, April 9, 1881, Jan. 31, 1885; *The Evening Tribune*, Feb. 17, 1892, May 5, 1903; *The Essex Eagle*, June 18, 1874; *Le Progrès*, May 31, 1906; Cyclone Relief Committee . . . Lawrence, Mass. . . . , *Report April, 1891* (Lawrence, 1891); *List of Contributors to the Fund for the Sufferers from the Earthquake that Destroyed . . . San Francisco . . .* (Lawrence, 1906).

new Americans behaved. When Patrick McCarty got out of jail in 1873, he gave a reception for 200 people. The funeral of John Breen was the largest in the history of the city; and even the funeral procession for two little Syrian boys who drowned had thirty-two carriages. There were also happy occasions upon which the immigrants could display wealth: the gifts at Maurice Curran's marriage were particularly costly; Peter Holihan, the Breen sisters, and John Ford all built elegant homes; and many of the Irish went on expensive vacations in America and Europe. Wealth and an immigrant's station were not necessarily exclusive. While most were poor, there were sufficient examples of immigrant success to give the rest hope.

And most important, not all of the immigrants felt trapped. The half-rural setting of Lawrence, with open countryside but a mile or two in any direction, eliminated the closed-in feeling that frustrated European peasants in a metropolis such as Boston. Every miserable newcomer could escape for an afternoon to the wooded hills and fresh streams in the vicinity of Lawrence, and when a man was out of work the countryside offered a way of forgetting and occasionally a place to find food as well. The constant surge of new immigrants moved, as we have seen, the earlier immigrants up and out of the heart of the city. Some moved to Tower and Prospect Hills, others to South Lawrence, and the more fortunate to Pleasant Valley in Methuen and Shawsheen Village in Andover.

For those whose future seemed completely hopeless there was the possibility of moving west. Although this was a difficult process, Lawrence was never cut off from the frontier. Letters from the west and advertisements for tickets to California reflected a continuing interest. When Boston emigration agents inserted articles in the *Journal* about settlements in Kansas, Colorado, Nebraska, Minnesota, and the Dakotas, the editor urged his readers to go. The editor of another newspaper left in 1880 for Marshall, Minnesota, where he established a printing office. In 1890 the *Lowell News* said that after a Lawrence man made some money, he invested it in southern or western land speculation or went to a town in the middle west. When the San Francisco earthquake and fire took place, at least eleven residents of Lawrence had relatives in the stricken city.[26]

Instead of going west other immigrants simply packed up and went home when conditions were too bad in Lawrence, and this possibility made some immigrants feel less trapped. Unemployment in the 1850's sent Irishmen to the agents for tickets home. French-Canadian departures, common in the 1880's, became an exodus by 1893, when "hundreds" of railway tickets to Canada were sold. Many left for homesteads that the Canadian government offered in the west to attract the habitant back home from the United States. The Lawrence Congrégation des Dames listed forty-four former members living in Canada in 1912. But while many Canadians went home, the stereotype of the Canadian "birds of passage," who came to the United States only to raise a little money with no intention of staying, is not accurate. This impression dates back to the 1880's, when Carroll Wright of the Massachusetts Census Bureau dubbed them the "Chinese of the East." Actually the Canadians had no monopoly on permanent departures, and when they did go, it was because of unemployment in the textile mills. More than any other group the French Canadians were family conscious and they tried hard to make permanent homes for their families in Lawrence. When they took them back to Canada, it was generally a necessity. Italians more than Canadians were deserting Lawrence in 1907, 1908, and 1911, again because of mill difficulties. The chance of possibly going home made the city much more tolerable.[27]

But for the vast majority of immigrant workingmen, who were committed to Lawrence on a permanent basis, the only way to at-

26. *Lawrence American*, Aug. 2, 1862, Dec. 31, 1864, Feb. 11, 1865; *The Lawrence Sentinel*, July 17, 1869; *The Essex Eagle*, June 6, 1874; *Lawrence Journal*, April 5, 1879, Sept. 25, 1880, Aug. 18, 1883, Jan. 24, April 18, 1885, July 7, 1886. The announcements included references to Florida and Texas. *The Evening Tribune*, Oct. 23, 1890; *Sunday Sun*, April 22, 1906.

27. *Lawrence Journal*, Aug. 19, 1882; *Lawrence Morning News*, May 9, 1884; *Lawrence American*, Sept. 17, 1886; *The Evening Tribune*, Aug. 9, 1893; *Le Progrès*, Sept. 1, 1899, April 29, May 10, 1904, April 25, 1907; *The Lawrence Sun*, Feb. 6, 1912; Paroisse Sainte-Anne, *Congrégation des Dames de Ste. Anne*, 1912-13 (Salem, Mass., 1913); Amy A. Bernady, "The Aliens Rush Home," Immigration Restriction League, Scrapbook of Clippings, 1907, Widener Library, Harvard; Immigration Commission, "Community A," p. 652; *Strike at Lawrence*, p. 367; *Sunday Sun*, Oct. 22, 1911.

tain real security in the mills was to organize. For a long time, fear, ignorance, and inertia kept most of them out of the labor movement even though all of the national labor unions tried to organize the city. The Workingmen's party, which took part in the city elections of 1865-70, called for a ten-hour day and higher wages. In 1870, three thousand workers formed a branch of the National Labor Union in Lawrence and passed a resolution against coolie workers. The Knights of Saint Crispin met in 1869 and 1874. Formed shortly after the strike of 1882, the Knights of Labor grew slowly until 1886, when a district convention met in Lawrence. From then on its decline was as rapid in Lawrence as it was throughout the United States. The silversmiths combined against it, the corporations tore up its holiday petitions, and the police took its hall away, all by 1891. Its more radical demands, such as cooperatives, child labor restrictions, and an eight-hour day, were far too advanced for Lawrence. All it left behind was the Central Labor Union, a meeting place for most unions in the city.

Through the help of the C.L.U. the American Federation of Labor came to Lawrence about 1900, but it made little progress and few of its unions lasted any length of time. While there were references to almost 150 different unions in the city press and the Bureau of Statistics of Labor reports, only four were mentioned ten times or more and lasted more than twenty-five years: the Moulders, Mule Spinners, Loom Fixers, and Barbers.[28]

Even less successful were efforts to establish a union of all textile operatives. Early in the 1890's the National Union of Textile Workers set up a local, which in 1898 joined the A.F.L. Samuel Gompers, president of the A.F.L., and John Golden, head

28. *Lawrence American,* Mar. 11, Sept. 15, 1865, Feb. 23, 1866; *Lawrence Journal,* Nov. 17, 1877, Feb. 9, Nov. 30, 1878, Nov. 29, 1879; *The Lawrence Sentinel,* Sept. 10, 1870; *The Essex Eagle,* Feb. 27, 1869, Jan. 10, 1874. For Knights of Labor see the *Lawrence American,* Sept. 15, 1882; *Lawrence Journal,* Aug. 12, Sept. 23, 1882, July 26, 1884, Oct. 30, 1886, April 23, Oct. 29, Nov. 12, 1887, Jan. 28, June 9, 1888, Mar. 16, 1891. For C.L.U. and A.F.L. see *ibid.,* Nov. 12, 1887. The Central Labor Union was far more active before 1900 than after. *The Lawrence Sun,* Sept. 24, 1906; *Anzeiger und Post,* Oct. 13, 1906, Nov. 16, 1907. The statistics on labor unions were derived from Bureau of Statistics of Labor, *Annual Reports,* I-XLIV (1870-1913), *passim,* particularly the special sections entitled variously, "Hours," "Wages," "Labor Chronology," "Benefits," and "Working Rules and Agreements," which appeared 1893-1913, and from all the Lawrence newspapers.

of the Textile Workers, marched in parades and held conventions as they struggled to organize the city. Gompers tried to appeal to the innate conservatism of the workers by warning them against anarchism and socialism. Competing with the A.F.L. was the more radical National Industrial Union of Textile Workers of the Industrial Workers of the World, which set up a local in 1905 and five years later held a convention in Lawrence. The I.W.W. local disapproved of the wage system and was far to the left of the A.F.L. Although the I.W.W. boasted 1,000 members in Lawrence at the start of 1912, only 300 were paid up. The total membership of the various A.F.L. textile craft groups was about 2,500. Whether the A.F.L. or the I.W.W. would secure the loyalty of the remaining 30,000 textile operatives depended upon their ability to appeal to the immigrant worker. The Lawrence strike of 1912 held the answer.[29]

Within these labor unions the immigrant played only a modest role. The most important immigrant labor leader after the Civil War was Robert Bower, an Englishman, who fought for the ten-hour day through his Lawrence Amalgamated Short Time Committee. In 1869 the Labor Reform party nominated him for the House of Representatives and in 1870 he organized the National Labor Union in Lawrence. As the 1870's developed he became editor of a Lawrence labor weekly, worked at the Boston Customs House, and was president of the Massachusetts Ten-Hour Association. Associated with Bower were two other Englishmen, Richard Hinchcliffe, brother of an Illinois miners' leader and editor of Bower's newspaper, and Duncan Wood, the exporter. Still other English immigrants were active in the Weekly Payments movement and the Engravers and Printers Union. While the Irish had no outstanding labor leaders, they were strongly entrenched in the Workingmen's party, and John Breen came out vigorously for weekly wage payments. The Germans did their bit for the Workingmen's party by sponsoring an address by Dennis

29. Bureau of Statistics of Labor, *Twenty-fifth Annual Report . . . 1895,* Mass. Pub. Doc. 15, p. 314; Bureau of Statistics of Labor, *Twenty-sixth Annual Report . . . 1896,* Mass. Pub. Doc. 15, p. 731; *The Evening Tribune,* May 2, 6, 1896; *Anzeiger und Post,* April 22, 1905; *Sun,* Aug. 1, 1906; *Sunday Sun,* Oct. 24, 1909; *The Weekly People,* Dec. 16, 1905; *Solidarity,* Sept. 17, 1910, Feb. 4, 1911; Neill, *Report,* p. 11.

Kearney, the California labor agitator. With a cigar makers' group as well as brewery workers', bakers', and carpenters' unions, the Germans showed more interest in the labor movement than did any other nationality. There was also a French carpenters' union and the Italians had a coal handlers' organization as well as the Building, Laborers, Excavators, and Rockmen's Union.

But these groups did not represent the great mass of immigrants, who worked in the mills. The German Weavers did dominate the 1902 strike and there was a German branch of the A.F.L. textile union, but only the I.W.W. made a concerted effort to organize all the immigrant textile operatives. To court the apathetic Canadians the I.W.W. held a smoker in 1905 with speeches in French and a convention of all the French and Franco-Belgian branches of the I.W.W. in 1911. Simultaneously an Italian branch of Local 20 of the I.W.W. met and considered sending for Joseph Ettor, the Italian I.W.W. strike organizer. A year later Ettor came to Lawrence and took over the great textile strike.[30]

Stronger unions and a successful strike were needed before the Lawrence immigrant could find real security in the mills. Yet the immigrant could not quite understand the deep concern shown for him in 1912. Of course his life was grim and of course he desperately needed more money, but all was not despair. The business cycle and the immigrant cycle, which meant rising wages, better jobs, property ownership, and savings, combined to make his plight more tolerable. And even if everything failed, the

30. For the English see *Lawrence American,* Dec. 1, 15, 1865, Mar. 30, 1866; *The Lawrence Sentinel,* Oct. 23, 1869, Mar. 28, 1874; *Lawrence Journal,* Oct. 31, 1874, May 8, 1875, cited in R. T. Berthoff, *British Immigrants in Industrial America* (Cambridge, Mass., 1953), p. 243, n. 80; *The Lawrence Sentinel,* Mar. 11, Sept. 20, 1870, Nov. 11, 1871, Mar. 30, 1872, Feb. 20, 1875; *The Essex Eagle,* Oct. 1, 1870, Feb. 28, Mar. 28, June 25, 1874, May 15, 1875; *Lawrence Journal,* Sept. 2, 1882, Jan. 20, 1883. For the Irish see *ibid.,* Nov. 30, 1878, Nov. 29, 1879, Sept. 2, 1882. For Germans and others see *ibid.,* Aug. 10, 1878, April 10, 1880; Bureau of Statistics of Labor, *Twenty-fifth Annual Report . . . 1895,* pp. 314, 330; *The Evening Tribune,* Sept. 1, 1894, April 28, 1896, July 9, 1897, Mar. 17, Jan. 2, 1899, April 18, 1902; *Anzeiger und Post,* May 5, 1906. For mill workers see Bureau of Statistics of Labor, *Twenty-eighth Annual Report . . . 1898,* Mass. Pub. Doc. 15, p. 342; Bureau of Statistics of Labor, *Thirty-sixth Annual Report . . . 1906,* p. 527; *Sunday Sun,* Sept. 3, 10, 1905; *The Lawrence Sun,* Feb. 26, 1906; *The Weekly People,* Dec. 16, 1905; *Solidarity,* Mar. 18, July 1, 1911.

immigrant was buoyed by the knowledge that his children and grandchildren would be more prosperous than he. All about him examples of immigrant success gave him hope. His optimism, not understood by the native American strike observers of 1912, enabled him to find considerable security in the mills of the immigrant city.

CHAPTER VIII

Security in Groups

In 1890 Lawrence held a contest to determine the most popular club in the city. As the climax approached, some groups were adding two thousand votes a day while others were holding ballots back in order to surprise their opponents. Down to the final hour it looked as though the German Turners would win, but in the last minutes Father O'Reilly marched in with fifty thousand votes for the Saint Mary's Cadets, and Thomas Gilmanton followed with forty thousand for the Father Matthew Temperance Society. The result: both societies came in ahead of the Turners, over a quarter of a million votes were cast, and "good humor" prevailed.[1] The absorption of Lawrence in this contest and others like it reflected the importance of clubs to the immigrants of the city, particularly the new ones. When they first arrived, the scared, lonely Germans would join their fellow countrymen at the Turn Hall, where they were drinking beer and exercising. Irishmen after the long voyage from Dublin, Cork, or Liverpool found a haven at the Hibernians' clubhouse. All immigrants turned to organizations—large or small, formal or spontaneous, permanent or temporary—in their search for security. Whatever the form, the immigrant club was an indispensable part of immigrant life. They were established, not by chance, but according to a definite chronological order.

In determining this order the first year in which a nationality had a hundred immigrants in the city was considered the time of its "arrival" in Lawrence. The number of years from that date to

1. *The Evening Tribune,* Nov. 19, 1890-Jan. 10, 1891, *passim.* Contests to determine the most popular individuals resulted in Irish and English victories in 1893. *Ibid.,* Jan. 28-Aug. 19, 1893, *passim.*

the establishment of particular clubs was then tabulated and the pattern quickly emerged. Immigrants on first arriving in Lawrence were usually too weak and disorganized to accomplish much until the end of the first decade, when they managed to found a church. In the second decade a nationality established social clubs, protective societies, cooperative stores, and organizations that cemented ties with the homeland. The third decade produced intellectual achievements such as newspapers, debating circles, and political clubs; while in the fourth and fifth the immigrants began to unite with other societies throughout the state and form hyphenate clubs.[2]

Almost as soon as the Irish reached Lawrence, Catholic priests began to give services and within a few years a church was built. With its debating groups, temperance societies, cornet bands, and other affiliates, the Catholic church offered the Irish more than just religion. Not until 1869 or fourteen years after the first hundred had come to Lawrence were there enough French Canadians for separate worship and even then they met in the basement of the Irish Immaculate Conception Church. For the same reason the Germans were tardy in constructing their own church or even in holding separate services, but in 1872, seventeen years after their arrival, the Germans had a Presbyterian church.

The later immigrants worked more rapidly and with the help of the earlier Catholics produced nine new churches between 1900 and 1912. Many nationalities and dozens of Catholic organizations took part in the inauguration of the Polish and Portuguese churches. At the dedication of the Syrian Catholic Church, Father O'Reilly stressed the financial sacrifice necessary to build these

2. This paragraph and much of the first part of this chapter were derived from references to immigrant groups in the Lawrence newspapers. Twenty-six different types of immigrant organizations were decided upon, and the date of the first example of each for certain nationalities was determined. The number of years from the time the nationality first came to Lawrence to the time of the founding of its various organizations was ascertained. (The year that a nationality first came to Lawrence was the year in which it had 100 in the city.) The various lengths of time that elapsed before the formation of certain types of organizations were then averaged, and it was thus possible to determine in which decade a specific type of organization was most likely to arise. Newspaper references will follow each paragraph on the various types of associations. More details are to be found in Donald B. Cole, "Lawrence, Massachusetts: Immigrant City, 1845-1912" (Doctoral dissertation, Harvard University, 1956), Table XXXII, pp. 421-22.

churches and urged all to give part of their wages to lift the debt. In 1903 the *Tribune* mentioned Catholic services in eight different languages: English, French, Italian, German, Polish, Lithuanian, Syrian, and Portuguese.[3]

The older nationalities began social clubs in the second decade after their arrival in the city. The earliest for the Irish were the Ancient Order of Hibernians, established in 1863, and the Knights of Saint Patrick, formed about 1870. When each held a picnic in the summer of 1870, the Hibernians outdid the Knights by hiring Finn and Pfefferkorn's Full Quadrille Band. Even though the Irish were avid baseball players skillful enough to push natives off the Lawrence team, they failed to form their own athletic club until 1892, when they founded a branch of the Gaelic Athletic Association.[4]

The British, on the other hand, for many years had nothing but athletic societies. The Lawrence Cricket Club, founded by soldiers who played at Fort de Kalb, Virginia, was the first British organization in the city and the forerunner of other cricket clubs. And no Caledonian or Clan MacPherson picnic took place without running events and wrestling. At the 1878 Caledonian meet at Haggets Pond, Andover, the Lawrence club bested the Boston Caledonians in a tug of war and the burlier Scots competed in throwing the caber. Four years later 4,000 people, some from as far away as Canada and New York, saw Duncan Ross pin Donald Dennie twice out of three falls in the feature event of these games. The first English society not based on athletics was the Albion Club in 1886 and the English Social Club that followed. The many Ulster Irish, meanwhile, had formed the Orangemen group, which made itself so famous in the 1875 riot.[5]

3. Katherine O'Keefe, *A Sketch of Catholicity in Lawrence* (Lawrence, 1882), p. 61; *Lawrence American,* Jan. 12, June 29, 1866; *Lawrence Journal,* Nov. 10, 1877, Jan. 26, July 27, 1878; *The Essex Eagle,* Feb. 27, Oct. 9, 1875; *The Evening Tribune,* Feb. 4, Mar. 24, 1903. St. Anne's Church, the first French church, was not dedicated until 1884. *The Lawrence Sun,* April 9, July 2, 1906; *Anzeiger und Post,* Dec. 5, 1903. The Germans set up their own Catholic Church in 1887. *Lawrence Journal,* Oct. 15, 1887; *The Lawrence Directory 1912* (Boston, 1912), pp. 37-39; *Sunday Sun,* Feb. 5, 1905, Sept. 30, 1906.

4. *The Lawrence Sentinel,* Mar. 19, July 2, Aug. 13, 1870; *Lawrence Journal,* Aug. 11, 1883, April 16, 1887, Mar. 8, 1897; *The Evening Tribune,* Nov. 8, 1892, June 20, 1894, Jan. 18, 1896; *Sunday Sun,* May 28, 1905.

5. *Lawrence American,* May 30, 1863; *Lawrence Journal,* Sept. 7, 1878,

No one surpassed the German in his interest in sports. The Turner Society, started in the second decade of German migration to Lawrence, merely formalized German gymnastics which had been going on since 1853. By 1890 the Turners had one of the best gymnasiums in the state and their annual exhibition of tableaux, bar and ring calisthenics, work on the horses and parallel bars, and dumbbell drills was a high point of the Lawrence social season. But calisthenics was but one side of the Turners' activity. Socialism in Lawrence got its start at Turn Hall, where members of the German Socialist Labor party flew red and black flags to show sympathy for the anarchists arrested in the Haymarket Riot of 1886. There was also a Turner Choral Society. The Germans operated altogether eight musical clubs of which the Lyra, formed in 1871, was the oldest. With his game and song the German loved his drink. When the Lyra Society dedicated a new clubhouse in 1899, the president explained that the Germans were "different from other settlers in America in regard to social life" and that they did not "come together to have a good time by eating ice cream and drinking soda." He added that Germans found it hard to "have a social time without lager beer." Beer mug in hand, the new arrival lost his loneliness discussing socialism at Turn Hall.[6]

Like the earlier immigrants the French Canadians also had a band, marched in parades, went picnicking, and played games, particularly whist, during their second decade in Lawrence. The chief French group was the Saint Jean de Baptiste Society, founded in 1870, fifteen years after the first Canadian arrivals. Connected with their church were other social clubs such as the Congrégation des Dames and the Cercle Paroissial of Saint Anne's. Gathered safely around the whist table, the French Canadians found pleasure in an alien city.[7]

Sept. 9, 1882, Mar. 6, 1880; *The Essex Eagle,* Mar. 20, 1875; *The Evening Tribune,* Sept. 28, 1892; *Sunday Sun,* Nov. 19, 1905, Oct. 18, 1908; *The Essex Eagle,* Oct. 9, 1875. There was also a British Merrimack Social and Improvement Club and a Devonian Society.

6. The Turners started in 1866. *The Evening Tribune,* May 27, 1890, Nov. 23, 1894, April 23, 1900, Jan. 8, 1896, July 29, 1899; *The Essex Eagle,* June 8, 1867. Also the Arion, Mozart, Vorwarts, Glocke, Turner, and Liederkranz Singing Societies.

7. *Lawrence Journal,* May 7, 1881, Aug. 26, 1882; *The Evening Tribune,* April 3, 1891, Aug. 19, 1898, May 16, 1901, May 14, Nov. 27, 1893; Joseph-Edouard Fecteau, *Monographie du Cercle Paroissial Sainte Anne* (Quebec,

Church groups predominated also among the post-1890 immigrants. When the Italians paraded in 1910 in honor of Columbus Day, five of their eight societies were religious. The largest was the Christopher Columbus Society, started in 1899 a scant four years after the first Italians had come to Lawrence and a year before they had a church. The Lithuanians had at least five clubs participating in their 1909 celebration. For the Jews there was the Sons of Israel and later the Young Men's Hebrew Association.[8]

All the immigrant social groups, whatever their origin, had the same goal: uniting a nationality and somehow expressing its feeling of group consciousness. Immigrants in Lawrence did not want to be alone and did not wish to mix with those from other countries. Through religion and recreation they found security among their own people.

And since the immigrants looked also for economic safety among their fellow-countrymen, their clubs provided benefits more substantial than picnics and lager beer. In a society that talked of rugged individualism but wanted social security, the immigrant organizations offered life insurance, funeral benefits, and aid while out of work. The earlier benefit associations usually arose a few years after the social clubs, but the later immigrants set them up at about the same time. The Irish Benevolent Society with its motto, "We visit our sick, and bury our dead," was typical of the others. In return for an initiation fee of $1.00 and monthly dues of $0.25, members were certain of $4.50 a week when sick and $25.00 for burial.

The immigrant cooperative store was another means of finding security. English immigrants established the Arlington Association, a Rochdale cooperative, in 1866. Since it had open membership, a limit to the number of shares per person, and one vote per member, it was more democratic than most other cooperatives. It was also more practical because it sold goods at market prices and thereby avoided merchant hostility. With its 3,440 members

1925), p. 41; Paroisse Sainte-Anne, Lawrence, Mass., *Congrégation des Dames de Sainte Anne* (Salem, Mass., 1908).

8. For Italian societies see: *Sunday Sun,* Aug. 28, Oct. 9, 1910; Lithuanian, *Sunday Sun,* May 23, 1909; Jewish, *The Evening Tribune,* Oct. 25, 1897, Mar. 5, 1911; other, *The Lawrence Directory 1912,* pp. 37, 39, 40, 46, 48, 67, 68. There were also Syrian, Armenian, Polish, Portuguese, and Franco-Belgian societies.

and three stores, the Arlington was for years the largest Rochdale cooperative in America. But when it granted too much power to its manager, who began to muzzle members at meetings and was finally convicted of dishonesty, it soon collapsed.[9]

Almost all the nationalities had benefit associations and many had cooperatives. The Hibernian, Turner, Alsace, Saint Jean de Baptiste, Columbus, and Syrian societies were only a few of those providing insurance and relief. The German, French, Lithuanian, and Franco-Belgian cooperative stores were famous. Although most of the stores and benefit societies were started during the second decade after arrival in Lawrence, those formed by the post-1890 immigrants came much sooner. The relief groups paid up to $5.00 a week in sick benefits and $25-$100 at death, both ample sums. Monthly dues ranged from $.15 to $.50, a not inconsiderable amount in Lawrence at that time. With annual sales of $50,000 to $100,000, the stores were able to pay dividends ranging from 5 per cent to 11 per cent. Since Lithuanian and German cooperatives were scarce, the two in Lawrence were known throughout New England. Within the city, all the associations provided a substantial amount of security.[10]

Also in the second decade, immigrants began to demonstrate an interest in their former homes by commemorating patron saints and national heroes. The first observance of Saint Patrick's Day occurred in 1864, seventeen years after the first Irish migrations to Lawrence, and the parades were always colorful since the marchers wore green scarves and green carnations. Within five years, however, a debate began concerning the celebrations. Although some

9. *The Lawrence Sentinel,* June 25, Oct. 22, 1864, June 26, 1869; James Ford, *Co-operation in New England Urban and Rural* (New York, 1913), pp. 7, 69-70; *The Evening Tribune,* June 9, 1894, Dec. 30, 1903, Feb. 17, 1904.

10. Other benefit societies were Catholic Mutual Benefit Association, Alsace (German), Lafayette Court of Foresters, Jewish Benefit Lodge, Polish Young Men's Protective Association, and Russian National Benefit Society. *The Lawrence Sentinel,* June 25, Oct. 22, 1864, June 26, 1869, May 9, 30, July 4, 1874; *Lawrence Journal,* June 12, 1880, Jan. 8, 1881; *Sunday Telegram,* Sept. 4, 1887; Ford, *Co-operation,* pp. 35-40, 185f; *The Evening Tribune,* Oct. 9, 1897, May 19, 1898, Jan. 18, 1904; *Cour Lafayette,* No. 94, *Ordre des Forestiers d'Amérique, Statuts et Règlements* (Lawrence, 1911); *Sunday Sun,* Nov. 25, 1906, Oct. 20, 1907, June 30, 1912; *Al-Wafa,* Oct. 16, 1908. Other cooperatives included the British Equitable. *The Evening Tribune,* June 9, Dec. 10, 1894, Aug. 11, 1904; *Lawrence Journal,* May 30, 1885; Ford, *Co-operation,* pp. 69, 185f. For additional information, see dissertation copy, pp. 121-27.

felt that the money spent on the parades could better be devoted to charity, it was not until the depression of 1873 that they stopped. Even then one person maintained that unless they marched every two or three years, they would soon forget the day, and others stated that no one could be a true Irish patriot without keeping this Catholic holiday. Another, however, responded that patriotism had no connection with Catholicism or Saint Patrick's Day. From that point on the Irish paraded sporadically and held grand celebrations only in 1887 and 1897, when former Mayor Breen rode on a horse with green trappings. The history of Saint Patrick's Day in Lawrence reflects the basic conflict between those who would hold on to the old country and those who would break away. Those who needed it found security by holding on.

Other holidays were less controversial. The Scots banqueted in honor of Robert Burns every January. Although the Germans held frequent parades and celebrations on their own club anniversaries, they only occasionally feted a national hero or holiday. They paraded in 1869 to honor the centennial of the birth of the German statesman Friedrich H. A. Von Humboldt and in 1883 to observe Schiller's birthday and two centuries of German migrations to America, but there is no record of a parade celebrating victory in the Franco-Prussian War. While the English often marched on Saint George's Day, the Orangemen, with good reason, made less of the Battle of the Boyne, and the French Canadians only occasionally noted Saint Joseph's Day. Aside from the Columbus Day parade, the Italian festivities were always in honor of a church figure such as Saint Mary of Pompeii. The calendar of immigrant holidays was so full that it dominated the social schedule of the city.[11]

11. *The Lawrence Sentinel*, Mar. 12, 1864, Jan. 30, Mar. 20, 1869, Mar. 23, April 20, 1872; *Lawrence Journal*, Feb. 15, 1879, Mar. 19, 1887; *The Evening Tribune*, Mar. 5, 1897. From New Year's to Christmas ethnic groups marked these and other events:

JAN.	Robert Burns' Birthday		First Portuguese Immigration
FEB.	Chinese New Year	JUNE	St. Jean de Baptiste Day
MAR.	Robert Emmett's Birthday	JULY	Battle of the Boyne
APR.	Turnverein Exhibition		St. Joseph's Day
	St. George's Day		(Italian)
	Passover		Armenian Massacre
MAY	St. Michael's Day	AUG.	St. Anthony's Day
	(Portuguese)	SEPT.	Von Humboldt's Birthday

During the second decade the immigrants found another way to maintain ties with the old country: raising money for relief of the poor back home. The Irish were collecting funds as soon as they arrived in Lawrence; the English after only thirteen years. Later, during the Boer War, the Scots and English united to assist the "widowed orphans of Tommy Atkins." An Italian relief fund drive in 1910 raised close to $1,000 about twenty years after the first Italians reached the city. It was not difficult to reach the pocketbooks of Lawrence immigrants.[12]

Often the raising of money was to support some revolutionary movement in the old country. The Irish, of course, devoted much of their time and money to Fenianism and the home rule movement, and they were not alone in their trans-oceanic interests. Herr Fritsche, a member of the German Reichstag, addressed Germans at Matthes Hall to raise money for his party in Germany. When King Humbert I was assassinated in 1900, the Christopher Columbus Society sent a telegram of sympathy to the Italian royal house. The Armenian Hunchak party, which had a branch in Lawrence, wanted Armenian independence, as did a certain Mr. Galesian, who maintained that if the Armenians had the vote as the Jews and Irish did, there would be American gunboats off Turkey. While the United States and Britain wrangled over Venezuela, Lawrence Armenians petitioned the President to start cooperating with the British in order to help Eastern Christians against the Turks. "Young Syria," flourishing in Lawrence, wanted the United States to start a revolt to free Syria from the same Turks. Although a mass meeting protested against the abusive treatment of the Jews in Russia, the Lawrence Jews split in 1905 over the issue of the peace petition sent by the United States to the Czar.[13] These efforts and protests, vain as they usually were, did serve to unite strangers in a new land.

First German Immigration	St. Michael's Day
Atonement Day	(Italian)
Rosh Hashana	Columbus Day
Yom Kippur	NOV. Schiller's Birthday
OCT. Virgin of Pompeii	Polish Revolution.

12. *Lawrence American,* July 19, 1862, Jan. 17, 1863; *The Evening Tribune,* Mar. 21, 1900; *Sunday Sun,* Jan. 10, 1909; *The Lawrence Courier,* Feb. 27, 1847; *The Lawrence Sentinel,* Dec. 24, 1870; *Lawrence Journal,* April 24, 1880.

13. *Ibid.,* Mar. 12, 1881; *The Evening Tribune,* May 2, 7, 1896, April 24, 1899, Aug. 3, 1900; *The Lawrence Sun,* Nov. 20, Aug. 28, 1905.

Immigrants in their third decade in Lawrence were able to devote time to more intellectual activities. All the earlier groups except the Scots started a newspaper between their twenty-third and thirty-first year in the city. The *Lawrence Journal* was the organ of pro-labor English immigrants between 1872 and 1877 and then became the weapon of the Sweeney family. The French-Canadian and German forces brought out *Le Drapeau* in 1874 and the *Anzeiger und Post* in 1882. Later immigrants, who moved faster in all categories, established the Syrian *Al-Ikbal* in 1904 and *Al-Wafa* in 1906, nine years after the start of Syrian migration to Lawrence.

Meanwhile, other evidences of intellectual ferment began to appear. Between 1875 and 1882 the Irish started the Catholic Debating Society, the Sheridan Dramatic Club, and the Emmett Literary Society, as well as the *Journal*. The talks and readings of Katie O'Keefe also began about this time. The English started a Glee and Madrigal Club in 1873 and the Germans got a school underway the same year. German and French-Canadian dramatic societies opened in the early 1880's, and the Canadians quickly followed with a literary society and a school. As in other areas, the later immigrants moved more rapidly and were able to produce Italian and Syrian schools by 1910. A year later there was a Syrian play, "The Black Knight."[14]

Active participation in American politics came with the rise of the second- and third-generation Americans during the group's third and fourth decades in the city. There was a German Hayes Club in 1876, but the first overt British political organization had to await the Albion Club of 1886. The French Canadians held numerous naturalization meetings in the 1890's in order to strengthen their position in local politics. Aside from the Armenian Republican Club, the later immigrants had not organized politically by 1912. But even though each group did not have its own political club, the immigrants were soon identified with a party. This identification—the process of joining with their fellow-coun-

14. *Lawrence American,* Aug. 24, 1866; *Lawrence Journal,* Nov. 24, 1877, Feb. 7, 1880, Aug. 27, 1881, May 27, 1882, Jan. 12, 1884, Jan. 16, 1886; *The Essex Eagle,* Dec. 27, 1873, Jan. 16, 1875; *Al-Wafa,* Mar. 18, 1910; *The Evening Tribune,* Centennial Edition, 1953.

trymen in politics—brought additional security to the foreign-born.[15]

The Irish were such staunch Democrats that every effort to organize an Irish Republican Club "fizzled." Lists of campaign contributors, names of delegates, and nominees, as well as editorial comment, all reflected the well-known Irish-Democratic alliance. When John Breen was elected mayor in 1881, it marked the ascendancy of the Irish in the Democratic party. Right after the Civil War the Irish were deeply entrenched in Wards Three and Four and the Democrats won those wards in four of the five elections studied. After the gerrymandering of 1875 had concentrated many of the Irish in Ward Three, it went Democratic even more decidedly than before. During the period 1884-1912 the only two precincts to go Democratic in all the fifteen elections studied were the two in and about the "plains," marked 4 or (5) and 6 or (8) on the map, where the Irish population was the greatest. The parts that were Democratic least often were those with almost no Irish population: Prospect Hill, 1 or (1), Tower Hill 9 or (14) and 10 or (15), and South Lawrence outside the "shanty" district, 12 or (16).[16]

15. *The Essex Eagle,* July 22, 1876; *Lawrence Journal,* Dec. 19, 1885; *The Evening Tribune,* April 14, 15, 1890, Oct. 27, 1900.

16. Twenty-four of thirty-six newspaper references labeled the Irish Democrats. For documentation see Cole, "Lawrence," p. 186, n. 5. Almost all contributors to the Democratic city campaign fund in 1892 had Irish names. *The Evening Tribune,* Dec. 29, 1892; *Lawrence American,* Sept. 6, 1863, Sept. 30, Nov. 10, 1865; *The Lawrence Sentinel,* Dec. 31, 1870; *The Essex Eagle,* Oct. 22, Nov. 29, 1873; *Lawrence Journal,* Oct. 27, Nov. 3, 1877; *The Evening Tribune,* Nov. 16, 1891. See the adjoining map for a presentation of the different ward and precinct lines. At first the Irish were strongest in Wards Two and Three, but by 1865 they were strongest in Wards Three and Four. In 1865 the population of Wards Three and Four was 9,666 and the number of those born in Ireland was 3,397 or about 35 per cent. Oliver Warner, *Abstract of the Census of Massachusetts,—1865* . . . (Boston, 1867), p. 63. The total Irish population of the city in 1865 was 6,047. *Ibid.* Ward Six went Democratic twice; and Wards One and Two once each in 1865 and 1875. Thus out of thirty ward results in five elections the Democrats won only twelve, eight of them in Wards Three and Four, where the Irish were most numerous. Record of Elections, I, 181, 218, 253, 305, 343. In 1880 Ward Three had over 30 per cent Irish-born and many others with Irish parents. The population of Ward Three was 5,366 and the Irish numbered 2,568. Carroll D. Wright, *The Census of Massachusetts: 1880* . . . (Boston, 1883), p. 50. Record of Elections, I, 392, 440; II, 2, 29. Democratic vote in Ward Three averaged 672 in 1876, 1878, 1880, and 1882; Republican, 284. See Table XXII for an analysis of the ward and precinct voting records. Record of Elections, II, *passim.* For the actual figures see Cole, "Lawrence," Table XXXV, p. 427-33, and Record of Elections, II, *passim.*

Map V
PRECINCT BOUNDARIES

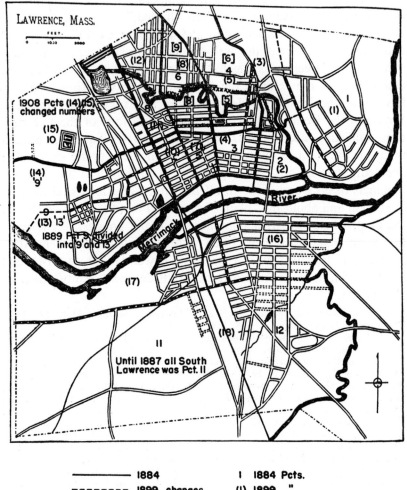

Minor changes at other times not indicated.

No less consistent was the English preference for the Republicans. Almost every newspaper article on the English in politics connected them with the Republican party. The Republican candidates in the 1890's included the Englishman Derbyshire in

Ward Five, the strongest English ward, and a number of men who were running for state representative. In the fifteen elections studied between 1854 and 1882, Ward Five went Republican thirteen times, and from 1884 to 1912 the precincts in Ward Five went Republican in thirty-six out of forty-two opportunities.[17]

Most Germans were also Republican, but some supported radical parties. Half of the newspaper statements tied the Germans with the Republican party, a third linked small groups of them with the radical movements, and a sixth connected them with the Democrats. There was always the debate as to whether the Republicans owed more to the Germans or to the English. Although the *Tribune* felt on one occasion that "the British-Americans did more to elect the Republican . . . than . . . the Germans," the party could not have agreed because after the election "the three Republican aldermen . . . gave the German element all it asked." Both the *American,* which supported the English point of view, and the *Anzeiger und Post* were Republican. The Republicans could not nominate Collins for mayor in 1891 after the Germans and British-Americans opposed him. Ward One, which had the greatest German population, went Republican in almost every election studied between 1858 and 1882. Then Precinct One, a German precinct in Ward One on Prospect Hill, voted Republican in thirteen of the fifteen elections analyzed between 1884 and 1912. This and the British Tower Hill sectors were the most consistently Republican areas in the city. When redistricting removed its German segments from Precinct Two in 1899, the Republican vote went down even though some other Republican areas had been added. When part of the German section was returned in 1906, the Republican total was restored.[18]

While the French Canadians occasionally strengthened the Republicans, they were never as reliable as the Germans or the Eng-

17. Thirteen newspaper articles out of seventeen called the English Republicans. For documentation see Cole, "Lawrence," p. 191, n. 12; *The Evening Tribune,* Nov. 24, 1891; Nov. 10, 1892; Oct. 14, 1893; Sept. 21, 1894. See Table XX. Record of Elections, I, II, *passim.*

18. Sixty-seven articles in all. Thirty called Germans Republicans; twenty-four, radicals; thirteen, Democrats. See Cole, "Lawrence," p. 192, n. 17; *The Evening Tribune,* April 18, Aug. 6, 1891, Nov. 7, 1892; *Anzeiger und Post,* Nov. 25, 1899. Precinct Two vote for Republican presidential candidate: 1896— 314; 1900—184; 1904—150; 1908—181. Record of Elections, I, II, *passim.*

lish. The French-Canadian press was basically Republican, but newspaper references showed that the Canadians themselves were as often Democrats as Republicans. Since the Canadians lived in wards that also had Irish or English residents, their voting record is not clear. When they were strongest in Precinct Seven, it went Republican and Democratic four times each. *Le Progrès* worried about the formation of both a French Republican Club and a French Democratic Club because it feared that neither party would feel obliged to give the Canadians favors or patronage. The *Tribune* reported in 1901 that the French-Canadian vote was still not going solidly for either party.[19]

With so many immigrants voting, both parties had to nominate them and a "balanced" ticket "embracing all elements" was an absolute necessity. In 1888 the *Journal* urged the Democrats to nominate one German, one French Canadian, and one Englishman for the Board of Aldermen. When neither an Englishman nor a German was nominated for any office in 1891, the *Tribune* soothingly referred to an "embarrassment of riches" that "nullified the intention" of selecting an Englishman and told the Germans unctuously that their candidate received "flattering support."[20] A typical government had an Irish or native mayor; one English, one German, and four native aldermen; and three Irish, one English, one German, and thirteen native councilmen.[21] In the years between 1873, when the first German was elected, and 1908, there were thirty-nine German councilmen and thirteen German aldermen. When they had no nominees in 1882, they were "indignant at the refusal of the 'stovepipe' element of the Republican Party, to nominate one of their element. . . ." The *Anzeiger und Post* always had German candidates to support, though rarely as many as in 1900 when it had thirteen for eight positions.[22]

19. Cole, "Lawrence," p. 199, n. 25. Record of Elections, II, *passim; The Evening Tribune,* Nov. 11, 20, Dec. 8, 1891, Nov. 23, 1892, Dec. 2, 1901; *Le Progrès,* Oct. 25, Nov. 2, 9, 16, 30, 1900, April 3, 1903.

20. *Lawrence Journal,* Nov. 3, 1883, Nov. 17, 1888; *The Evening Tribune,* Nov. 13, 16, Dec. 5, 1891, Oct. 21, 1893, Nov. 23, 1894, Nov. 20, 1896, Sept. 22, Nov. 19, Dec. 2, 1897, Oct. 6, 1898; *The Lawrence Sun,* Nov. 13, 1905.

21. *Lawrence American,* Jan. 9, 1864, Jan. 7, 1865, Jan. 5, 1866, Jan. 11, 1884, supplement; *The Evening Sentinel,* Dec. 7, 1867, Jan. 7, 1871, Jan. 6, 1872, Jan. 3, 1874; *The Essex Eagle,* Jan. 10, 1874, Jan. 2, 1875; *Lawrence Journal,* Jan. 12, Dec. 7, 1878, Dec. 31, 1881.

22. *Anzeiger und Post,* Dec. 1, 1900, Nov. 29, 1902, Feb. 8, 1908; *Campaign*

To appeal further to the immigrants a candidate would often teach himself a smattering of foreign languages so that he might speak to each group in its own particular tongue. The French Canadians were actually affronted when one poor candidate spoke to them in English. In listening to a candidate speak their own language, the immigrants found additional security in politics.

While part of the security that the immigrants derived from politics came from a sense of group solidarity and belonging, a more tangible form came from the jobs that they received. When the nativist *American* complained about the discharge of a native-born postman to make room for an Irishman, the *Sentinel* calmly replied, "Well, what of it?" and pointed out that Irish votes had elected the new mayor. Not all mayors felt that way, however, and in 1869 a Ward Five meeting of foreign-born citizens complained that they were "taxed without being represented." When the *Anzeiger* protested angrily at the failure of Adolph Vorholz to be made an assessor, the city government hastened to make him a clerk in the Street Department and to give editor Dick of the *Anzeiger* a job as registrar. *Le Progrès* continually complained that the Democratic donkey was kicking the Canadians by not giving them enough patronage.

In addition to appointments the immigrants wanted club liquor licenses. Feigning surprise that there was to be only "one license for ward five," the *Tribune* cried, "Sch-blood! The British-American element of Water Street will certainly take sweet revenge for this outrage." In 1904 the Germans abandoned the Republicans, who had refused to give them a license, in favor of Democratic Mayor Lynch, whom they called "liberal" for not "hunting down" their clubs. When he was re-elected, the *Anzeiger* trumpeted: "Lynch and License." This was one of the rewards that the immigrants won through politics.[23]

Only after a nationality had raised churches and clubs, founded

Budget, Dec. 4, 1882; *Lawrence Journal,* Dec. 3, 1881; *Le Progrès,* Oct. 25, Nov. 2, 9, 16, 1900, Nov. 21, 1902; *The Evening Tribune,* Nov. 24, Dec. 9, 1891, Oct. 6, Nov. 10, 23, 25, 1892, Jan. 5, Oct. 14, Nov. 10, 1893, Sept. 21, 1894, Nov. 18, 1895, Nov. 5, 1897.

23. *Municipal Records,* VI; *The Lawrence Sentinel,* Feb. 26, 1859, Jan. 23, 1869; *The Evening Tribune,* Jan. 7, 12, April 27, 1893, April 16, 1890; *Le Progrès,* June 29, July 6, 13, 20, Nov. 9, 1900, Jan. 11, 1901, Jan. 17, Feb. 21, 1902; *Anzeiger und Post,* Nov. 26, Dec. 3, 10, 1904.

schools and newspapers, and organized politically could it make Lawrence a center for its state-wide affairs. Not until the 1890's, for example, did the Irish hold a county meeting of the Hibernians in Lawrence. At about the same time the British-American Association, Daughters of Saint George, and the Scottish clans also held state conventions in Lawrence. When the Germans entertained the New England Turnfest in 1892 and a three-state Sangerfest in 1894, it was their first experience of this kind after more than four decades in the city. The *Anzeiger* stimulated the Germans' interest in state-wide matters by carrying news columns on a dozen communities with German population. Only the French Canadians were able to hold state meetings early in their stay in Lawrence. In 1881 they were hosts to French Canadians from all over New England. Since only the Armenians and Portuguese of the later immigrants held comparable gatherings before 1912, it appears that even the southeastern Europeans needed time before entering state activities.[24]

The formation of hyphenate associations followed the state conventions. Although the Irish set up an Irish-American Club in 1880, it disbanded and they had to reorganize at the end of the decade. The British formed the British-American Society at about the same time as the second Irish endeavor, but the French Canadians and Germans did not have hyphenate groups until the twentieth century.[25]

With the rise of hyphenate clubs the various phases of immigrant group activity came to a close. Although there were deviations, the nationalities in general formed their clubs according to a definite chronological order. This pattern provided the framework for the evolution of an immigrant society that was essentially the society of the whole city, and it provided the immigrants with varying types of security that changed as their needs changed. When immigrants were first in Lawrence and needed religious and financial help, they built churches and organized benefit societies.

24. *Lawrence Daily Eagle,* Oct. 1, 1902; *The Evening Tribune,* Feb. 9, 1891, June 11, 1892, June 20, Aug. 31, 1894, Feb. 22, 1899, April 30, 1900, Aug. 26, 1902; *Lawrence Journal,* Aug. 27, 1881.
25. *Ibid.,* Oct. 2, 1880, Jan. 28, July 14, 1888; *Sunday Sun,* Dec. 6, 1908; *The Lawrence Sun,* April 8, 1907.

Later when they had matured and felt the need of belonging, intellectual and political groups came into being. All immigrants preferred group activity to the individualism that some have attributed to nineteenth-century America. They also preferred to remain with their own people. There was no melting pot at work in Lawrence mixing the various nationalities. Group activity in Lawrence was part of the search for security. One found it first in his own church and later in a multitude of societies and less formal organizations. Since almost everyone in Lawrence was an immigrant, either a first-, second-, or third-generation American, and since Lawrence had no previous social structure, the immigrant organizations formed the society of the city. The close tie that all immigrants felt with the old country accounts for the large number of activities devoted to the affairs of Canada and Europe. From the very beginning when men and women gathered in boarding houses through the formation of churches and clubs and on to the strike of 1912, when men finally joined labor unions, the group dominated Lawrence.

NUMBER OF YEARS FROM THE TIME NATIONALITIES CAME TO LAWRENCE UNTIL THEY ESTABLISHED CERTAIN TYPES OF ORGANIZATIONS

	Early Immigrants					Later Immigrants			
	Irish	English	Scots	Germans	French Canadians	Italians	Portuguese	Jews	Syrians
Date at which 100 were in Lawrence	1847	1850	1855	1855	1855	1895	1895	1895	1895
Churches	6			17	14	5	11	6	11
Social Clubs	16	13	12	11	15	4	7	2	11
Benefit Associations or Cooperatives	16	16	25	19	15	0		0	16
Old Country Activities	0	24		26		17	16	7	
Old Country Celebrations	17	37	17	14	36	5			
Intellectual Groups	19	23		29	26	12			15
Newspapers	30	22		27	19				9
Political Organizations		35		21	35				
State Conventions	47	40	44	35	26		7		
Hyphenate Groups	33	38		53	52				

CHAPTER IX

Security in Americanism

At the end of the nineteenth century Lawrence was an "ardently American city," one in which native and immigrant shared a common faith in the United States. The members of the School Committee, mostly natives, showed it by adding another course in history to the curriculum, which it believed would kindle a "genuine patriotism" by "demonstrating the . . . superiority of our institutions." The immigrant clubs meanwhile were demonstrating their loyalty by a series of flag-raisings. The Irish started it when a division of the Hibernians raised a giant American flag, twelve feet by twenty-one feet. The Ladies Auxiliary of the German Freiheit Lodge soon after presented its men with a flag costing $300. During the Spanish-American War flag-raising became a mania with ceremonies at Turn Hall, the Saint Jean de Baptiste Society, and the Union Saint Joseph. Captain Joubert led ninety-one volunteers off to war and John Breen made a patriotic address as the Oakdale Club raised its flag. In this way immigrants, who gloried in retaining their own ethnic identity through a maze of societies, showed that they were just as American as the native-born. And just as the identification with the old country gave them security, so did this expression of Americanism.[1]

Nowhere did the immigrants demonstrate their Americanism more forcefully than in their newspapers. A comparison of the immigrant press with the native newspapers revealed great simi-

1. Public Schools of Lawrence, Mass., *Syllabus of Work in Geography* (Lawrence, 1895), p. 4; *The Evening Tribune*, June 6, 1890, Sept. 5, 1891, April 30, May 19-21, June 3, 7, 17, 1898, Mar. 6, April 20, 1899; *Sunday Sun*, Feb. 24, 1907. The Christopher Columbus Society and the English Social Club also dedicated flags.

larities, particularly in their devotion to certain American ideals. Like most Americans the native newspaper editors were proud of their country and, while they wanted some reforms, did not want to go too far.   The *Essex Eagle,* for example, saw no reason for a capital-labor struggle just because the one was "given the wealth of vast riches" and "brain" and the other "the wealth of muscle and sinew."   It blamed the fight on men who were "never satisfied" and who had "a disposition to overreach."   The *American,* however, urged capital to be more generous because it was so much stronger than labor.   The *Tribune,* which credited the workers instead of the entrepreneur for the success of Lawrence, attacked Cleveland for sending troops in the Pullman strike and criticized society for forcing women and children to work in mills.

But this was not radicalism.   The *Essex Eagle* "deprecated" strikes and implied that good Americans would go west when wages were not adequate instead of striking.   The *American* attributed the 1889 Fall River strike to professional agitators.   When McKinley was assassinated, the newspapers were filled with "fierce denunciations of the deed" and vigorous attacks on anarchism. That same year the *Tribune* condemned Emma Goldman and her "anarchistic friends," and a month before the great strike of 1912 the *Sunday Sun* called for the elimination of the "anarchistic element."   Consistent with this conservatism was the devotion of the press to the Horatio Alger ideal, and a fragment of this literature appeared in the *Essex Eagle* in 1868 when that paper enlarged on the glories of poverty.   A more complete expression, however, awaited the death of President Grant, who, according to a Lawrence eulogy, represented the "American idea that the humblest in origin may, under the fostering spirit of our institutions, become the most honored and noble."   Phrases such as "how to get rich," "boy to owner," and "successful business man" were common.[2]

The same phrases and the same beliefs appeared in the immigrant's newspapers.   The Irish *Journal* was never revolutionary even though it occasionally supported ideas then considered radical.

2. *The Essex Eagle,* July 18, 1868, Oct. 17, 1874, Feb. 20, 1875; *Lawrence American,* Feb. 19, 1886, Mar. 22, 1889; *The Evening Tribune,* Dec. 4, 1890, Feb. 3, 1891, July 7, 10, 1894, Sept. 16, 1895, May 13, 1897, April 26, Sept. 7, 14, 1901; *Sunday Sun,* July 30, 1905, Dec. 3, 1911; *Memorial Services, General U. S. Grant, Lawrence, Mass., August 8, 1885* (Lawrence, 1885).

It attacked monopolies because they interfered with a man's right to work as he pleased and because they gave the capitalists all the profit coming from the tariff. These same capitalists, it said, had bribed Republican senators into opposing reforms. The tariff, however, was perfectly legitimate because American business men, who paid twice as much for loans as the British, needed some compensation.

In supporting labor, the *Journal* came the closest to radicalism. Since it realized that lower wages meant less purchasing capacity and that reducing wages would kill "the goose that lays the golden eggs," it urged the Democratic party to support labor candidates. In 1887 the *Journal* dismissed the Socialist party as a "German product" with an "un-American" remedy and the Union Labor party as nothing but a group of old Greenbackers. But it praised the United Labor party for adopting the ideas of Henry George and repudiating socialism. This was as far as the Sweeneys would go. They ridiculed "Herr Most" when the German anarchist was pulled from under a bed after the Haymarket Riot. Fearing that the riot would harm the labor movement, they denied that the Knights of Labor were involved and blamed "misguided socialists and anarchists" instead. When asked by a member of the Knights whether or not to strike for higher wages, the *Journal* said no. Workers should be content to collect statistics and arouse public opinion. Meanwhile, "practice temperance and industry, and these reforms will come as fast as the people are ready to receive them, and in the meantime let us thank our stars that the American workingman is better clothed, better fed, better housed, and better paid than in any other country in the universe. Never strike. . . . Reason has replaced brute force in the world." Here was the perfect nineteenth-century faith in *laissez faire,* reason, and the inevitability of moderate reform. The *Journal* added: "The march of progress is ever upward and onward. . . ." The natives would not have disagreed.[3]

While the *Journal* was rarely self-conscious about its Irish origin, the French-Canadian *Progrès* was pathetically eager to show that its people were good Americans. It complained that natives

3. *Lawrence Journal,* Mar. 12, 1881, Feb. 10, 1883, Oct. 11, 1884, May 15, Sept. 18, 1886, Aug. 20, Oct. 29, Dec. 24, 1887, April 7, Aug. 18, Oct. 20, 1888.

laughed at them because they wrote and spoke wretched English. It found French Canadians apathetic and disloyal everywhere: they would not become naturalized; they did not join unions; they patronized the shops of other immigrants instead of their own; and in church they submitted to the "persecution of the Anglo-Irish language."

To remedy the church problem and to gain respect for the Canadians, *Le Progrès* led a fight to preserve the French language. The "elegant" French language, said the editors, was superior to the English, which was a brutal language of battle, and the German, which was too complicated. Unfortunately the Canadian children, ashamed of using French, grew up speaking English, which their parents could not understand.   And worse, many of the second generation changed their names to English equivalents.   Boulanger became Baker and Leblanc, White.   The French newspapers disdained also the "pidgin English-French" commonly used in the city.   Such mixtures as "avez-vous été au 'show'?" "hallo, Baptiste! comment ça feel?" "le rubber tire est busté" enfuriated *Le Progrès* and *Le Courrier*.   They implored French newspaper writers to avoid the use of English clichés in their articles, particularly such trite expressions as "high life," "last but not least," "the right man in the right place," and "leader."

Frightened and disillusioned by the unhappiness that had accompanied Canadian immigration to the United States, the French newspapers adopted a puritanical air in observing the changes. Drinking men and gum-chewing women, cigarette-smoking youths and blaspheming children were all anathema to *Le Progrès*, whose editors believed the younger generation wanted nothing but pleasure, was too blasé and uncontrolled.   Quite naturally it applauded the work of the Watch and Ward Society in suppressing books and slot machines and urged the society to investigate nudity in fine art.

To stop the assimilation of the French Canadians, *Le Progrès* put its hopes on the home, the church, and the school.   After parents had given their children a love of the old Canadian traditions, the French church and school would keep them good Frenchmen and good Catholics.   When a French Canadian married, he must marry a Catholic.   The French press looked scornfully upon the Irish, the Portuguese, and the Belgians, who willingly let them-

selves be absorbed. Many of them, said *Le Progrès,* had not suffered the crises the French had endured, while others, such as the
Irish, became intensely patriotic only to become popular. The
terms "Canayen," meaning half American and half Canadian, and
"Canuck" enraged *Le Progrès.*

But the Canadian newspapers were fighting in vain; the very
acts they despised attested to the Americanization that had already taken place. The Puritanism with which they attacked the
Canadian youth was in itself an important part of Americanism,
as was the concern for "success" which preoccupied *Le Progrès.*
Its very name—"Progress"—was also an important assumption in
the minds of most Americans. Even while warning its readers
against absorption, it denied wanting them to become a "band
apart." The maintenance of old traditions did not preclude loyalty
to America.

Politically *Le Progrès* was no more anxious than the *Journal*
to alter the American way. It constantly urged its readers to become naturalized and vote. Evil trusts should be eliminated, but
the government should help business with the protective tariff.
By supporting the tariff *Le Progrès* revealed the extent of its
Americanization because many Canadians opposed the tariff on
the grounds that it hurt Canadian exports to the United States.
Le Progrès would allow unions, but any government aid to labor
would be merely helping one class at the expense of another. The
"perverse doctrines" of anarchism and socialism were intolerable.
Somewhat more conservative than the *Journal, Le Progrès* was
consistently Republican. So, in spite of its desire to prevent assimilation, *Le Progrès* showed that it was far more American than
it would admit or could even suspect.[4]

From the insecure *Progrès* there was a marked change to the
resolute and self-righteous *Anzeiger und Post.* While *Le Progrès*

4. For fear of persecution see *Le Progrès,* May 12, June 9, 1899, June 23,
Sept. 7, 1900, April 25, 1902. For preservation of language see *ibid.,* Jan. 27,
June 2, 30, July 14, 1899, Feb. 2, Mar. 2, 1900, June 7, 1901, Feb. 7, 11, June
24, July 2, 1902, Sept. 22, 1903, Jan. 12, April 22, June 10, 1904, June 8, 1905,
April 16, 1908; *Le Courrier de Lawrence,* April 4, May 16, 30, 1912. For efforts
to prevent assimilation see *Le Progrès,* July 20, 1900, May 10, 1901, Feb. 7,
1902, May 8, 1903, Oct. 26, 1905. For political views see *ibid.,* Feb. 9, Aug. 3,
1900, July 12, Sept. 13, 1901, Aug. 12, 1902, May 1, 1903, Nov. 5, 1904, Oct.
25, 1906.

mourned the failure of Canadians to preserve their culture, the *Anzeiger* said Germans had no reason to "creep in the shadows" and proudly listed German influences on American life. Christmas, it said, was better celebrated the German way than in the old Puritan style. German music, art, idealism, love of beer, in short, the German ability to understand and enjoy life, were invaluable in America, where people were too intent on making money. The *Anzeiger* complained that in America, where material matters dominated the intellectual, the teacher had little influence and there was little regard for the law. Unlike *Le Progrès* the *Anzeiger* was sure enough of the German position in America to criticize American life and did not care if some Germans failed to retain their old customs. Enough of the German traditions would remain anyway. Thus while *Le Progrès* became Americanized because it was so afraid of America, the *Anzeiger* did so because it did not fear America. But both found security in their Americanism.

While the Irish *Journal* epitomized the late nineteenth-century cult of reason, moderation, and inevitable reform, and *Le Progrès* reverted to Puritan ideals, the *Anzeiger* represented the Progressive mentality. Coming three decades later than the *Journal,* the *Anzeiger* was unwilling to wait for *laissez faire* to improve American life and therefore supported measures that were in most Progressive platforms. These included a tariff for revenue only, the dissolution of all trusts, a ban on child labor, the initiative and referendum, and the direct election of senators. Puritanism with its opposition to intoxicants was obviously out of the question for the beer-drinking Germans, who rated the right to imbibe on a plane with freedom of speech and labeled prohibition "fanaticism."

Though the *Anzeiger* wanted reform and occasionally used radical terms, it was not a socialist paper and supported only the milder demands of socialism. This ambivalence stood out in its attitude toward labor issues. First it opposed the strikers of 1902 and urged them to go back to work. Then three years later it attacked certain millowners for using strikebreakers and said the owners were protected by the police, the militia, and the courts. But, it added, the workers had only themselves to blame because they elected men to office from the very class that was holding them in "economic slavery," men who "forged new weapons" for the capitalist over the laborer.   The *Anzeiger* came the closest to socialism when it suggested taking away the Supreme Court's right of judicial review in order to keep the will of the people from being thwarted and to protect labor.   It applauded the reforms pushed by the socialist Victor Berger but denounced state ownership and anarchism.   Like most Progressives—indeed, most Americans —the editors of the *Anzeiger* admired some of the socialists' ideas but did not care for socialism.[5]

To some, the *Anzeiger* and *Le Progrès* seemed most un-American in their attacks on imperialism.   *Le Progrès* feared a rise of militarism that would disgrace the United States in the future.   Comparing the United States with the Macedon of Alexander, the paper accused it of wanting Canada in order to "inundate" it with goods.   When the *Anzeiger* argued that a boiler explosion was probably responsible for the sinking of the *Maine,* it said that those not influenced by "highriding chauvinism" agreed. With the words "protect us from militarism" it ridiculed the concept that the United States had to have a great army and navy in order to "march at the peak of civilization."   The *Anzeiger* doubted that intervention in Nicaragua would make us more loved in Central America or even increase our trade.   As the World War approached, it blamed the yellow press for the arms race.   But this anti-imperialism was not really un-American for a large segment of the population deplored the actions of Theodore Roosevelt, Albert Beveridge, and Henry Cabot Lodge.   *Le Progrès* maintained that the end of imperialism would mean a return to the "past traditions" of the United States, and the *Anzeiger* compared resistance to imperialism in 1900 to the "spirit of '76."[6]

The best example of the immigrants' search for security in Americanism came between 1907 and 1910 in the Syrian *Al-Wafa* (Fidelity), which was actually the second newspaper published in

5. For German adjustment to American life see *Anzeiger und Post,* Mar. 25, Oct. 14, 1899, Sept. 15, 1900, July 16, 23, Aug. 6, Sept. 3, 24, 1904, Jan. 28, Feb. 11, Oct. 7, Dec. 30, 1905, June 16, 1906, May 2, 1908, Dec. 18, 1909. For political views see *ibid.,* Nov. 25, Dec. 30, 1899, Feb. 17, Mar. 3, April 14, Nov. 24, 1900, Nov. 9, Dec. 7, 14, 1907, Mar. 21, Oct. 3, 1908, May 27, 1911.

6. *Le Progrès,* Jan. 19, Mar. 30, 1900, June 6, 1902, April 1, Sept. 1, 1904, May 18, 1905; *Anzeiger und Post,* July 8, 1899, July 29, Sept. 16, 1905, April 6, Sept. 28, Nov. 30, 1907, April 24, May 29, June 5, 1909, June 4, 1910, July 29, 1911.

Arabic in Lawrence. The first, *Al-Ikbal* (Prosperity), lasted only briefly. *Al-Wafa* eagerly encouraged the Americanization of its readers. Instead of the self-conscious talk about retaining the mother tongue, *Al-Wafa* said simply: study English because it will help you earn money. It suggested that the Syrians use the United States as a college and take advantage of the great opportunity that was theirs. No immigrant should presume to improve American laws or to change the "magnificent constitution." The Syrian who did things the American way would get ahead much faster than the one who tried to retain the old customs. Rarely did *Al-Wafa* show the insecurity of *Le Progrès*. Once when the Syrians were accused of being Mongolians and therefore ineligible for citizenship, it did carry articles proving they were Caucasians and occasionally it supported the idea of separate Syrian schools and priests.

Such was the Americanization of *Al-Wafa* that it accepted Progressivism, wealth, and generosity as the great virtues of the United States. It was even enthusiastically in favor of American imperialism. Believing Japan a menace to the Philippines and Hawaii, *Al-Wafa* urged sending the Atlantic fleet to the Pacific. The Japanese fleet was a "wave approaching the United States," and America must build up its navy to prepare for the inevitable war. Seizing Panama and building a canal were perfectly proper because the United States was destined to expand from Colombia to the Arctic.[7]

The immigrant newspapers, then, shared many views, some critical of the United States. Of the four leading papers, all, even *Al-Wafa,* were opposed to monopoly. Two, the *Anzeiger* and *Le Progrès,* were anxious to preserve their old customs, though for different reasons. Of the four, only the *Anzeiger* was not conservative and its efforts at radicalism were occasional and hesitant. But while the *Journal* and *Anzeiger* wanted only moderate changes, they both used revolutionary terms, and this may explain why so many people linked the immigrant to the radical movement. Though only *Al-Wafa* supported imperialism, all four were patriotic.

7. *Al-Wafa,* April 30, Sept. 17, Nov. 15, 26, Dec. 13, 1907, Jan. 14, Mar. 17, April 14, 1908, Mar. 19, 1909. George Abdo of Salem, Mass., translated *Al-Wafa* from the Arabic for me.

More important than the criticisms of the adopted country were the many explicit and implicit acceptances. All were democratic in their opposition to monarchy, privilege, and oppression. And while all but *Al-Wafa* would modify certain features of American life, they agreed that they could best attain their ideals in the United States. They adopted the new country and its institutions almost without a murmur, even though they found much in America that was unfamiliar. Though unaccustomed to city life, the editors adjusted to it and their newspapers were an important part of the new urban environment. The newspapers made no attack on the two-party system, on the written constitution, on the quadrennial presidential elections, all institutions fundamental to the United States, and the one attack on the Supreme Court was not followed up. The freedom that America accorded women, as strange to most peasants as the urban scene, went unchallenged. Whether it was the Puritanism of *Le Progrès,* the naïve optimism of *Al-Wafa,* the moderate reforming instincts of the *Journal,* or the Progressivism of the *Anzeiger,* each of the newspapers adopted some theme of American political and social thought. But most basically American was their unanimous acceptance of the cult of success and faith in progress. Their very titles—"Progress," "Advertiser," "Prosperity," and "Fidelity"—were as American as baseball. There was little to distinguish the immigrant newspapers from the native.

The Lawrence clergy, whether native or immigrant, interpreted Americanism in the same manner as the journalists. Typical of the native ministers was William Lawrence, who started his career at Grace Episcopal Church in Lawrence and later became the famous Bishop of Massachusetts. His letters revealed that even though he was the grandson of Abbott Lawrence, he did not at first share his grandfather's concern for his fellow man. The funeral that he performed for the baby of an Irish couple in the tenement district showed his original reluctance to take much part in the society about him. After going through the service in the shabby home, Lawrence begged off from the trip to the cemetery because he had a cold, but the drunken father reacted so violently that Lawrence felt obliged to go. The picture of the sniffling young clergyman cowed by an intoxicated worker is not a pretty one. Within a few months Lawrence had other encounters with drunken workers, one whose wife ran away after their baby died and another whose wife threw herself out of a third story window. To such tragedies the young rector responded at first with a singular lack of feeling. When he went to the cemetery it was through fear, and he wrote about the incident only because he thought his father might enjoy the description of the tenement.

But the immigrant city changed William Lawrence. Within a year he was able to appreciate the devotion of workers who came to the church after eleven hours in the factories and who contributed generously to church drives, and the situation of an unemployed woman who said she was reduced to two crackers a day moved him. When the city heat sent him off to Bar Harbor, he remarked: "How the children up here in the tenements live through it I don't see." Lawrence soon came to believe that after preaching Christ the first duty of the rector was to help the poor. Not only did he oppose child labor and monthly wage payments, but he even blamed the 1882 strike on his uncle who was treasurer at the Pacific. There is no record, however, that William Lawrence actually did much to improve the condition of the poor.[8]

Equally hesitant about reform were the other Protestant clergymen. Reverend Talmage, for example, delivered a sermon against idleness saying: "I propose for . . . idlers: On the one side of them put some healthy work; on the other side put a rawhide, and let them take their choice." During the strike of 1894 the Protestant clergy took a stand considered unsympathetic to the workers. When told that the strikers wanted contributions to their benefit fund, Reverend Young of the Unitarian Church replied that the church should not take sides. Management, he said, was not anti-labor, nor had the owners ganged up against their employees. "Who is the capitalist?" continued Young, "Often he is from the ranks of the laborers;—a man who by superior energy, brain power, application, has secured more than the average." Reverend Kerr said that while the church was against covetousness and was not for

8. Letters from William R. Lawrence to his father, A. A. Lawrence, Collection of A. A. Lawrence Letters, MSS, Massachusetts Historical Society Library, XLV (1871-76); XLVI (1876-77); XLVII (1877); XLVIII (1877-78); William Lawrence, *The City Church* (Lawrence, 1896), pp. 21-27; William Lawrence, *Memories of a Happy Life* (Boston, 1926), pp. 48-53.

one particular class, it still wanted order. Reverend Keese opposed labor unions because they allowed passions to run wild, but he did support their emphasis on the brotherhood of man. Though these churchmen felt sorry for the workers, they would do little to upset the *status quo*.[9]

Spokesman for the immigrant Catholics in Lawrence was Father James T. O'Reilly, who as priest at Saint Mary's from 1886 to 1925, reflected or influenced what all the Irish were thinking. Saint Mary's calendar, which O'Reilly edited, revealed not only his views but those of his parish. During his regime Father O'Reilly concentrated almost all the English-speaking Catholic churches in Lawrence and Methuen under his control, and with ten assistants guided as many as 20,000 souls. As priest at Saint Mary's and prior of the Augustinian community he held the most important Augustinian post in America. Within three years of his coming he had paid off $100,000 or 50 per cent of the Augustinian debt. He carried on an extensive building program, started the parish calendar, and founded a number of societies. Working far beyond his own group, O'Reilly helped set up several immigrant churches, including Greek, Syrian, Portuguese, and Lithuanian parishes. He spearheaded the celebration of Columbus Day in 1892 in order to help the few Italians in Lawrence.

The man who did this constructive work was born in Lansingburgh, New York, of an Irish family, in 1851, and came to Lawrence in 1886 at the age of thirty-five. He may have become acquainted with Lawrence boys earlier when he attended Villanova College. He steadily increased his influence and popularity so that in 1895, when he left for a visit to Rome, his parishioners gave him $2,100 and on his return held a big parade in his honor. The *Tribune* said he had endeared himself to the people of Lawrence and, when he was elected to the Board of Library Trustees, declared that he would be a valuable member. He was also elected to the School Committee, started a cooperative bank, and led the anti-saloon movement. The 1899 celebration of the twenty-fifth anniversary of his ordination was an event in which the entire city participated.[10]

9. *The Evening Tribune,* April 20, 1891, Mar. 5, 1894, June 12, 1897.
10. *The American Foundation of the Sisters of Notre Dame de Namur . . .* (Philadelphia, 1928), p. 305; Alice L. Walsh, *A Sketch of the Life and Labors*

For O'Reilly the doctrines of Catholicism were universal and unchanging. In supporting Pope Leo's statement condemning "Americanisms" and all other compromises with liberalism, he called for a "fixed code of doctrine." He continually exhorted his parishioners to be better Catholics. All must attend church even when on a seaside vacation; young people were to read Catholic literature and marry Catholics; they must not read the works of authors such as Bulwer-Lytton; nor were they to get divorces. When he encouraged his flock to discuss religion, they had only to consult the parish calendar to discover what to say.

Whenever anti-Catholic prejudice threatened, O'Reilly was the first to object, whether it was attacking the Essex County Training School for its advertisement, "No Catholic Need Apply," or exerting pressure to get the G.A.R. to give a salute at Saint Mary's School on Decoration Day. He even accused the supposedly non-sectarian Young Men's Christian Association of proselytizing for the Protestant churches. When he openly denounced the public schools for not teaching religion, O'Reilly drew Protestant opposition. "Our public schools," he stated, "fail to supply the wholesome, life-giving draught [of knowledge]." While Reverend Young condemned this speech as "un-American," at least half of Lawrence was in sympathy with O'Reilly.[11]

If O'Reilly was un-American, so were his native Protestant critics because their views were almost identical to his. Even though he seemed to be strongly pro-labor at first, he gradually shifted until, in 1912, he was in the owners' camp. In 1894 O'Reilly criticized the mill owners for cutting wages just because the market was off. He sent $50.00 to the strike leaders "as an evidence," he said, "of my faith in the justice of your cause, and as a most emphatic protest against the inhumanity of those who would rather lose one hundred thousand dollars ($100,000) in defeating you than allow it to you as fair compensation for your

of the Reverend James T. O'Reilly, . . . (Lawrence, 1924), pp. 4, 44-45, 61-77, 89; Sunday Register, Feb. 19, 1899; Augustinian Fathers, Lawrence, Mass., Our Parish Calendar, III (1898-99), No. 12, p. 13; The Evening Tribune, July 1, Aug. 1, Dec. 23, 1895, April 29, 1897, July 1, 1898, Feb. 18, April 5, 1899.

11. Walsh, O'Reilly, pp. 10-14; Sunday Register, Feb. 26, Mar. 5, 1899; The Evening Tribune, Feb. 27, June 20, 26, 1899, Mar. 10, 1902; Notre Dame de Namur, p. 305; Parish Calendar, II (1897-98), No. 12, p. 15; XI (1906-7), No. 1, p. 1; XVI (1911-12), No. 1, p. 21; No. 3, p. 25.

labor." As the strike progressed, O'Reilly maintained that William Wood at the Washington Mill had asked him to get the strikers back to work, but Wood denied it. When, however, the strike seemed hopeless and the corporation offered to take the strikers back with promises of good pay, O'Reilly did encourage them to return. Shortly afterward he presided at the Boston meeting of the Massachusetts Total Abstinence Union and voted not to use Pullman cars because of the Pullman strike. For these 1894 actions he was called "a champion of labor" and "a tower of strength to the laboring element of Lawrence."

But James O'Reilly was by no means a radical. In 1896 he said naïvely that the mills should shut down that summer to give the workers a rest—without pay. He warned the owners of the trouble ahead before the strike of 1902 and later begged the workers to return. At the Gompers banquet in 1905 he asked capital and labor to see the best in each other and avoid class hatred. Socialism he attacked as anti-Catholic, impracticable, and dangerous. Since he believed strongly in personal independence, he opposed a bill that would have fed the children in the public schools. His ardent patriotism appeared at the 1892 Columbus Day celebration, when he organized a large group of girls into a marching flag formation. The meaning of America he summed up in an address at the death of President McKinley: "The spirit that threatens the destruction of our institutions is the spirit of materialism, and it is spreading rapidly everywhere. No God— no religion, no morality, no respect for law, no obedience to authority, the disintegration of the 'human family.' These are the weaknesses of our civilization that are producing this crop of anarchists. . . ."[12]

Here was an American priest of Irish background who was basically conservative and yet felt deeply the troubles of the workingman. Like the immigrant newspaper editors he accepted most

12. Walsh, *O'Reilly*, pp. 54-55, 103; *The Evening Tribune*, Mar. 23, April 27, July 25, 1894. *The Evening Tribune* said that O'Reilly's labor attitudes put the church in a better light. *The Evening Tribune*, Mar. 24, 1894; *Parish Calendar*, II (1897-98), No. 10, p. 20. For O'Reilly's basic conservatism: *ibid.*, I (1896-97), No. 3, p. 23; X (1905-6), No. 1, p. 19; No. 5, p. 9; XII (1907-8), No. 10, p. 17; XIII (1908-9), No. 2, p. 3; XV (1910-11), No. 1, p. 13; No. 2, p. 15; XVI (1911-12), No. 1, p. 11; No. 8, p. 15; *The Evening Tribune*, May 6, 1902; Walsh, *O'Reilly*, pp. 10-16.

of America and was moved to action only to rebuke sectarian attack or oppression of labor. That he was as much a child of nineteenth-century liberalism as the *Tribune* or the *Journal* or even William Lawrence was clear in his passionate love of individualism and independence. Had he been more concerned with the national scene he might have adopted the Progressivism of the *Anzeiger,* but since he saw only the flock about him, he was still deep in nineteenth-century Americanism when the strike of 1912 arrived.

The positions taken by the Lawrence clergy were then exactly those occupied by the immigrant newspapers. The same acceptance of America, advocacy of moderate reform, abhorrence of radicalism, belief in hard work, independence, and propriety, and faith in patriotism and success appeared in both. These ideas were not unusual because they were the same as those motivating the native press, native Lawrence citizens, and most Americans at the end of the nineteenth century. In the immigrant city of Lawrence the first- or second-generation American found security by speaking, writing, or listening to the same brand of Americanism as that expressed by the natives. This was security in Americanism.

Meanwhile the immigrants were proving their Americanism by becoming citizens and voting. The politicians, particularly the Democrats, were so anxious to naturalize the immigrants that they often paid the four-dollar naturalization fee. The Republican *Essex Eagle* said bitterly that the immigrant voted Democratic just because his friends did, but admitted that the Democratic party did help him become a citizen. So the Republicans went to work. While the French Naturalization Club was Democratic, the Republicans more than matched it with the Franco-American Independent Club and Le Club Lincoln. A giant French naturalization meeting took place at the Music Hall in the fall of 1902 with the clergy, naturalization clubs, press, and political parties participating. By 1910, 42 per cent of the foreign-born in Lawrence were naturalized or had first papers, evidence that the immigrant city was rapidly turning the immigrant into an American.[13]

13. *Lawrence American,* Oct. 29, 1864, Oct. 28, 1887; *The Lawrence Sentinel,* Oct. 30, 1869; *The Essex Eagle,* Oct. 26, 1872, Sept. 5, 1874; *The Evening Tribune,* Sept. 21, 1899, Sept. 7, 1900, April 19, 1901, July 18, Sept. 23, 1902. Foreign-born whites in Lawrence in 1910: total 17,414; naturalized 6,588; first papers 678; alien 9,608; unknown 540. United States Census Bureau, *Thirteenth*

This naturalization drive made many eligible to vote. The state census reports showed the following percentages of legal voters of all males of voting age:

Born in	1875	1885
Canada*	22%	20%
England**	47%	53%
Germany	41%	54%
Ireland	59%	64%
All Foreign-born	49%	55%

* French Canadians only in 1885
** All British in 1875

The ethnic groups that had been in Lawrence longest had the highest proportion of eligible voters, but the high Irish percentage may also be attributed to the naturalization activity of the Democratic party.

Though it is not possible to determine exactly how many of the immigrants actually voted, the figures for the city as a whole give a good approximation since such a large proportion of the residents were foreign-born. In 1875 and 1885 about 40 per cent of the males of voting age turned out to vote; the percentage rose to 60 per cent in 1900 but returned to 40 per cent in 1910. Such percentages were high: the figure for 1885, for example, meant that 55 per cent of the legal voters went to the polls, the second highest percentage in the state.[14] The voting records of the im-

Census of the United States . . . 1910. Abstract of the Census . . . with Supplement for Massachusetts . . . (Washington, 1913), p. 597. Of the total number of citizens in 1885, 45 per cent were naturalized. Carroll D. Wright, The Census of Massachusetts: 1885, I, Part 1 (Boston, 1887), 105. Lawrence was second of twenty-three Massachusetts cities. Bureau of Statistics of Labor, Nineteenth Annual Report . . . 1888, Mass. Pub. Doc. 15, pp. 196, 211.

14. Ibid., pp. 147, 196, 206; Bureau of Statistics of Labor, Thirteenth Annual Report . . . 1882, Mass. Pub. Doc. 15, p. 113; Immigration Commission, "Woolen and Worsted Goods in Representative Community A," Immigrants in Industries, Part 4: Woolen and Worsted Goods Manufacturing, II, Immigration Commission, Reports, X, 61 Congress, 2 Session, Doc. 633 (Washington, 1911), p. 788. The Commission report for 1909 showed 68 per cent of the Irish workers eligible and less than 15 per cent of the southeastern Europeans. Bureau of Statistics of Labor, Thirteenth Annual Report . . . 1882, pp. 170, 177; Bureau of Statistics of Labor, Nineteenth Annual Report . . . 1888, pp. 196, 223; Secretary of the Commonwealth [of Masachusetts], Number of Assessed Polls, Registered Voters, and Persons who Voted . . . 1890, Mass. Pub. Doc. 43, p. 23; ibid., 1900, p. 22; ibid., 1910, p. 23.

migrant precincts also showed that the foreign-born were exercising their political rights.

Percentage of Males of Voting Age Who Voted

1900

Lawrence	59	Precinct 10 (French	
Precinct 3 (German)	66	Canadian)	34
Precinct 5 (Irish)	71	Precinct 14 (English)	75

1910

Lawrence	39	Precinct 10 (French	
Precinct 3 (German)	49	Canadian)	18
Precinct 5 (Irish		Precinct 15 (English)	45
and Italian)	33	Precinct 2 (Italian)	15

The Irish and English were more active politically than the city taken as a whole; the French Canadians and Italians less.[15]

A summary for Lawrence in 1885 showed that: 45 per cent of the citizens were naturalized citizens (second in the state); 55 per cent of the foreign-born males of voting age were legal voters (first in the state); 39 per cent of the total males of voting age actually voted; 55 per cent of the legal voters actually voted (second in the state). Immigrant Lawrence had a better voting record than most cities in the state and its immigration participation was high. During the 1912 strike many asserted that immigrants did not take advantage of their political rights and were basically un-American. The Lawrence record tells another story. The foreign-born were eager to become Americans politically because in that way they found security.

Another idea expressed in 1912 was that most immigrants were anarchists or socialists and posed a great threat to the United States. Radicalism in Lawrence was predominantly a German affair. Shortly after their arrival the Germans were discussing socialism at Turn Hall, and in the late 1870's and early 1880's they supported Benjamin Butler because of his labor and Greenback views. The more violently radical Germans flirted with anarchism. When Johann Most, the German anarchist, spoke to 200 of them in 1886, he tried to unite the Knights of Labor, the

15. *Ibid., 1890,* pp. 22-23; *ibid., 1900,* p. 22; *ibid., 1910,* pp. 22-23.

Socialists, and the Communists of the city into a section of his International. A vigorous atheist, he declared that "wherever a priest or minister puts his feet, there no grass grows for ten years." Such statements as this and "a rifle in the house is better than a thousand ballots . . ." so frightened the Lawrence Germans that only six joined his movement and Most was never mentioned again in the Lawrence newspapers.

Meanwhile the German Socialist Labor party, which represented the views of many anarchists, was flourishing in Lawrence. Starting in 1874, ten years later it had 900 members parading and in 1886 its members hung flags from Turn Hall during the Haymarket Riot. In 1891 the *Tribune* reported that traditionally Republican Germans would strongly support the Socialist Labor candidate for the state legislature and thereby help the Democrats. The Socialist Laborites were the most violent of the German radicals. In 1897 their posters read: "Workingmen of the World Unite! You have Nothing to Lose but Your Chains and a World to Gain."

Most of the German Socialists, however, were only mildly radical, interested more, for example, in an income tax than in a revolution. A visiting Socialist speaking before a serious and respectable gathering of the most prominent Germans in Lawrence was careful to distinguish between socialism and anarchism. The *Anzeiger* maintained that socialism was not trying to spread free love and anarchism but was only striving for the good of mankind.[16]

Not all Lawrence radicals were Germans. The first non-German Socialist meeting occurred in 1891. Then in 1893 an Irishman, Maurice Hennessey, introduced a Socialist who declared that workers were "slaves not freemen," because "the law of wages" was "inexorable." The same speaker later roused the crowd by saying: "The laboring men have just enough to sustain them. They generally receive about $300 a year. . . . I heard of a dinner that cost $150 the other day in Boston." Herbert Casson, a

16. *Lawrence Journal*, Oct. 26, 1878, Sept. 30, Oct. 21, 1882, Nov. 3, 1883, Nov. 19, 1887; *Lawrence American*, April 9, 1886. There was a German Labor party in 1884. *Lawrence Morning News*, May 19, 1884; *Lawrence American*, Oct. 22, 1886; *The Evening Tribune*, Feb. 23, Sept. 26, Oct. 20, 1891, Nov. 3, 1893, Oct. 2, 1897, Jan. 2, 1899; *Anzeiger und Post*, Sept. 22, 1906, Jan. 16, 1911.

Socialist from Lynn, spoke in Armenian in 1894. John Ogilvie, who was either Scotch or English, was called "the original Socialist" of Lawrence. The *Anzeiger und Post* in 1900 commented on the strong Jewish support given an address by Job Harriman, the Socialist candidate for president. There was an Italian branch of the Socialist Labor party in 1906 and in 1910 the Italian anarchists organized a tiny Circolo di Studi Sociali.[17]

The Socialist parties did well in Lawrence in the 1890's and early twentieth century. In 1895 Lawrence ran behind only Boston and Holyoke in votes for the Socialist party candidate for governor. In 1899 the more revolutionary Socialist Labor party had serious hopes of electing a mayor. When the Socialists lost ground in the state election of 1903, Lawrence was one of the few cities to remain a Socialist center. Even there the movement encountered hostility. A crowd drove Socialist speakers from Appleton Street on a Sunday afternoon in 1903 and the next week bombarded others with rotten eggs.

The vote for the Socialist and Socialist Labor presidential candidates in Lawrence between 1896 and 1912 demonstrated that socialism in Lawrence was primarily German and mild. The Socialist Labor group was far more revolutionary and violent than the Socialist party, but it never did as well.

Redistricting between 1896 and 1900 added the German part of old Precinct Two to a section of old Precinct One and created a new Precinct Three, which was strongly German. Consequently the vote for the two Socialist parties in 1900 in Precinct Three went up and their vote in Precinct Two dropped. When the line separating Precincts Two and Three was altered in 1906, some of the Germans found themselves back in Precinct Two again. As a result the Socialist vote in Precinct Two went back up at the expense of Precinct Three. The formation of Precinct Six in 1906 took German sections away from Precinct Five with the result that Six began to show an interest in socialism and Five lost Socialist votes. In every case but one the Socialist areas coincided with German sectors, and every German center, furthermore, showed

17. *The Evening Tribune,* Feb. 23, 1891, Sept. 14, 1893. For Italian socialists and anarchists see *Il Proletario,* Nov. 11, 25, 1906, Feb. 23, 1908, and *L'Era Nuova,* Dec. 10, 1910, Sept. 9, 30, 1911, Sept. 21, 1912. Kindness of Professor Fenton.

VOTE FOR SOCIALIST LABOR AND SOCIALIST PRESIDENTIAL
CANDIDATES BY PRECINCTS

Party and Year	Precinct						Other	Total
	1	2	3	4	5	6		
1896								
Socialist Labor	37	30	9	25	4	15	19	139
1900								
Socialist Labor	7	6	9	5	8	*	74	109
Socialist	22	8	59	3	38	*	89	219
1904								
Socialist Labor	4	4	5	4	5	*	48	70
Socialist	45	5	79	9	34	*	165	337
1908								
Socialist Labor	2	2	0	2	0	4	9	19
Socialist	41	24	48	4	14	29	138	298
1912								
Socialist Labor	3	1	1	0	0	3	35	43
Socialist	107	24	93	10	26	47	213	520

Socialist strength. When the Socialist movement divided into the
militant Socialist Labor party and the milder Socialist party, Lawrence followed the lead of the Germans in choosing the less revolutionary party.[18]

The immigrant city did give some support to the radical movement and most of this support came from its immigrants. The
large majority of its immigrants, however, ignored socialism and
most of those who adopted it chose its mildest form. There was
never more than a handful of anarchists. Up to 1912 nothing in
Lawrence supported the thesis that most immigrants were vicious
un-American radicals. Throughout the United States there were
many people interested in socialism; almost a million voted for
Eugene Debs for president in 1912 and 30,000 more supported the
Socialist Labor candidate that year. So even the city's mild flirtation
with socialism was part of the way in which the immigrant city became American. Both native and immigrant thought and voted
alike in Lawrence. In the newspapers, in the churches, and at the
polls there was little to distinguish between the native and immigrant

18. *The Evening Tribune,* Nov. 11, 1895, Jan. 24, Oct. 7, 1899, Oct. 16,
1903; *Anzeiger und Post,* Oct. 10, Nov. 7, 1903; Record of Elections in the City
of Lawrence, MSS, City Clerk's Office, Lawrence, Mass., II (1880-1923), *passim.*

interpretation of Americanism. In short the immigrants had become Americans; they felt that they belonged to the new country; they had achieved the deepest form of security. But the 1912 strike lay just ahead, and since it was led by anarchists and socialists, it would deeply challenge the Americanism of the immigrants.

While the narrative of Lawrence seems to confirm the 1912 strike observers' opinion that Lawrence was a city of despair, the foregoing study of the immigrants' search for security shows that writers have never understood Lawrence. The twentieth-century despair was only superficial because the immigrant had always been able to find some kind of security through either his family, his job, his club, or simply in being an American. With such security the immigrants entered the strike year of 1912. Dissatisfied with their wages and their living conditions, they were willing to accept anarchist and Socialist leadership to gain a better life. But they knew that they would never be anarchists or Socialists and they knew that conditions would soon be better. Lacking such insight, those who described the strike could not comprehend it. We shall now see what happened and what it meant.

Part Three

Immigrant City to American City, 1912-1921

CHAPTER X

The Lawrence Strike, 1912

The year 1912 was to be the start of a new era for Lawrence, with a revised city charter and the publication of the depressing White Fund survey of living conditions in the city. The charter established a form of government that was typical of those set up throughout the United States during the Progressive period. A commission of five men, which replaced a cumbersome twenty-five-man body, was to run the city with the help of such new officials as a purchasing agent and a Commissioner of Public Health and Charities. Public contracts and the initiative, referendum, and recall were to make the government more democratic. The White Fund survey was to provide information on the basis of which the new government could act.

In spite of the sluggish year of 1911 there was optimism among the city's business men. The greatest worsted center in the world, with such large concerns as the American Woolen Company, the Arlington Mill, and the Pacific Mill, was expected to stage a come-back as it had after the depression years of 1857, 1873, and 1893. Management believed it had nothing to fear from unions and considered Lawrence a peaceful labor city. Unions in Lawrence had never been able to organize more than a tenth of the city's workers at any one time before 1912. The very absence of unionism was one of the reasons why William Wood, President of the American Woolen Company, built the Wood Mill in Lawrence in 1905.[1]

1. *An Act to Revise the Charter of the City of Lawrence, 1911*, Massachusetts Acts 1911, Ch. 621, pp. 9-22; *Le Progrès*, Jan. 11, 1906; Bureau of Statistics of Labor, *Thirty-ninth Annual Report . . . 1909*, Mass. Pub. Doc. 15, p. 191; Bureau of Statistics of Labor, *Forty-second Annual Report . . . 1912*, Mass. Pub. Doc. 15, p. 108; Charles P. Neill, *Report on Strike of Textile Workers*

Wood was one of the self-made industrial giants who made Horatio Alger's tales plausible. The son of an Azores seaman, he was born on Martha's Vineyard in 1858, but soon migrated to southern Massachusetts where he grew up in the textile mills. He came to Lawrence while still in his twenties to be assistant manager of the Washington Mills and later became treasurer. He was made treasurer of the American Woolen Company when it was organized in 1899; by 1912 he was its president. Next to John Breen and Father O'Reilly, Wood was probably the most important first- or second-generation American in Lawrence down to 1912.

From his meteoric rise to business success until his suicide, William Wood's career was continually bizarre. Although he owned a Commonwealth Avenue city residence in Boston and a North Shore estate, home for Billy Wood was the Elizabethan house with Victorian trimmings which adorned his eighty-acre Arden in Shawsheen Village, Andover. The village became the headquarters of the American Woolen Company, and scrutinizing every move from his mansion on the hill was Billy Wood, an eastern George Pullman and supposedly the "most important man in the woolen industry in the world." Wood found it difficult to remember that he was himself a second-generation American. Once he congratulated Judge Stone for a particularly harsh attack on some Armenian criminals. He was always a conservative Republican of the McKinley vintage. To get backing for the protective tariff he warned that foreign manufacturers were preparing to flood the American market with cheap goods. As a delegate to the Republican Convention of 1896 he wanted McKinley to speak out in favor of hard money. During the strike of 1902 he blamed Annie Herzog, one of the strike leaders, instead of the company for the suffering of the workers. When Roosevelt was ready to step down in 1908, Wood wanted Joe Cannon to be the next president as the spokesman for a businessmen's administration.[2]

---

in Lawrence, Mass. in 1912, 62 Congress, 2 Session, Senate Doc. 870 (Washington, 1912), p. 11; *The Strike at Lawrence, Mass. Hearings before the Committee on Rules of the House of Representatives . . . 1912,* 62 Congress, 2 Session, House Doc. 671 (Washington, 1912), p. 59.

2. Life of Wm. M. Wood, Typewritten MS at Baker Library, Harvard, pp. 1-7; *The Evening Tribune,* Feb. 26, 1894; *The Lawrence Sun,* Oct. 1, 1906;

The weather in January, 1912, was cold, damp, and dark. In the Merrimack Valley the first four months of the year were usually a period of endless rain, sleet, and snow, with only occasional glimpses of the sun. It was always a bad time of year in Lawrence: the Pemberton disaster, the typhoid fever epidemic of 1891, and all the strikes—1882, 1894, 1902—had occurred between the New Year and April. The strike of 1912 was to be no exception.

It started with a mass meeting on Wednesday evening, January 10, held by the Italian Branch of I.W.W. Local 20. Presiding over the meeting was Angelo Rocco, a twenty-five-year-old high school student who was one of the founders of the I.W.W. in Lawrence. When the union decided that all Italian textile operatives should strike because of a pay reduction, Rocco sent a telegram to Joseph Ettor, the professional I.W.W. strike organizer, asking him to come to Lawrence. There had been no actual lowering of the wage rate, but when the state put its new fifty-four-hour law into effect at the start of 1912, the mills not only reduced the hours but cut pay proportionately. Since the owners had previously kept wages at the same weekly level when reducing hours and since the loss of twenty or thirty cents a week meant a great deal to the workers, they were worried and angry. The absence of adequate advance notice made them even more ugly.

The outbreak came on Friday, January 12. During the morning immigrant workers in the Wood plant suddenly left their machines, picked up clubs and other weapons, and ran through the mill cutting belts, damaging machines, ordering all to quit, and threatening those who demurred. After repeating the process at the Washington, the mob rushed the police and received a few broken heads for its audacity. While nothing else happened that morning, the initial violence, the threats of blowing up the mill, and the prominence of the Italians, formed a picture the strike observers could not forget.

Although Saturday was quiet and it seemed as though the strike would collapse, Ettor was busy organizing the city. Joe

Sunday Sun, Dec. 17, 1910; American Woolen Company, *Shawsheen* (Providence, R.I., 1924); "Dynamite in the Lawrence Strike," *The Literary Digest,* XLV (1912), 407.

Ettor, a swarthy heavy-set man in his twenties, had been running strikes for several years. He knew how to arouse workers and how to keep them working in harmony. To arouse the Italians he made vicious attacks on the natives. The natives, he said, thought an Italian was "all right so long as he wants to live next door to a dog and work for $4.20 a week. But when they want a little more . . . they are foreigners, then Socialists, and anarchists. . . ." To get the strikers to work together he greatly expanded Local 20 and by so doing pushed the I.W.W. ahead of the A.F.L. He also established a strike committee and a relief organization with members from almost every nationality in the city. Aware that immigrants dominated the labor force in Lawrence, Ettor oriented his union, strike committee, and relief group along ethnic lines.[3]

Monday, January 15, was the key to the strike. It was fairly easy to get men out, but after a weekend to talk it over with their families and priests, they usually trooped back to work. But early this Monday morning in a bitterly cold snowstorm swirling about them, somewhere between 7,000 and 8,000 strikers formed picket lines around the gates of the Washington and Wood Mills and kept all others from entering. In a disorderly parade some 15,000 agitated workers then swarmed over to the Prospect Mill, where they threw stones at the windows, and on to the Atlantic and Pacific, where the militia, on hand to relieve the tired police, met them with fire hoses. Although the *New York Times* spoke of a "Bayonet Charge on Lawrence Strikers," there was no serious injury except the accidental stabbing of a Syrian boy, but thousands of immigrants never forgot the icy shock of the water from the hoses.[4]

3. Justus Ebert, *The Trial of a New Society* (Cleveland, 1913), pp. 33, 36, 49; *The Evening Tribune*, Jan. 1, 11, 12, 16, 1912. For a strike chronology see Table XXIII. Bureau of Statistics of Labor, *Forty-third Annual Report . . . 1912*, Pub. Doc. 15, p. 61. There had been a small announcement of the wage reduction on page 14 of *The Evening Tribune*, Jan. 1, 1912. *Strike at Lawrence*, p. 266; *Boston Evening Transcript*, Jan. 18, 1912; Interview with Angelo Rocco by Professor Edwin Fenton, kindness of Professor Fenton. Material in this chapter from *La Gazzetta del Massachusetts* [Boston], *L'Era Nuova*, *Il Proletario*, and *L'Araldo Italiano* also by kindness of Professor Fenton. Professor Fenton's doctoral dissertation at Harvard is on Italian immigrants in American labor organizations in northeastern United States.
4. *The New York Times*, Jan. 16, 1912, p. 1.

There were three great I.W.W. parades on Tuesday, Wednesday, and Thursday but surprisingly little violence. Ettor led the first on Union Street on Tuesday. On Wednesday 3,000 workers started toward the Common, where they picked up another 7,000 and then ran into the militia at the foot of Hampshire Street near the mills. Here the strikers threw ice and the militia officers used the backs of their swords. Farris Marad and the Syrian Drum Corps led the Thursday parade, when once again orderly troops kept several thousand strikers at bay in the mill district.

Then as parades were suspended for ten days, other events kept up the tempo of the strike. The committee met daily with representatives of each nationality bringing in reports on his fellow countrymen. On Friday, the day after Marad's parade, the police discovered a cache of dynamite in his dye shop after getting a tip from John Breen, son of the old party boss. Put on the defensive by this discovery, the strikers disclaimed responsibility and argued that Breen and the mill owners had planted it. The police found dynamite also in a cemetery lot and in a shoe store next to Colombo's printing office, where Ettor got his mail. The arrival of the poet Socialist Arturo Giovannitti and Big Bill Haywood also kept excitement high. A crowd of 10,000 listened to the Italian, Franco-Belgian, and German bands playing their national anthems as they waited at the railroad station to greet Haywood. A roster of radical agitators, including the "red flame" Elizabeth Gurley Flynn, got off the train with him. Management, meanwhile, was doing everything possible to quell the strike. Rumors of scabs and Pinkerton detectives filled the city.[5]

After the tactical lull and exactly two weeks after the start of the strike, the two main participants, Joe Ettor and Billy Wood, met in Boston, where the former demanded a 15 per cent raise for all operatives and the latter turned him down. The weekend passed and then on Monday, January 29, a fortnight after the first picketing, strikers attacked trolley cars on Broadway carrying people to

5. *The Evening Tribune,* Jan. 18-25, 1912; Ebert, *Trial,* pp. 62-63, 69, 75; *The Leader,* Jan. 28, 1912; "The Social Significance of Arturo Giovannitti," *Current Opinion,* LIV (1913), 24-26; *Boston Evening Transcript,* Jan. 24, 1912; Transcript of the Trial of *Commonwealth* vs. *Joseph Caruso, Joseph J. Ettor, Arturo Giovannitti, alias,* Superior Court, Essex County, Massachusetts, Sept.-Oct., 1912, p. 262.

work at about seven in the morning. Armed with stones and ice
500 strikers broke 188 trolley car windows in an effort to prevent
operatives from returning to work. On the same day a crowd
gathered on Union Street, where someone stabbed a policeman
named Benoit and a shot killed one of the strikers, Annie LoPezzi.
On that same day Bill Haywood gave his first speech in Lawrence.
No wonder the shocked *New York Times* returned the strike to
the front page, giving it the lead headline and announcing, "Real
Labor War Now in Lawrence."

Actually the strike was not unusually violent with only one
death in two weeks, but the city authorities were acting vigorously.
Foreigners with concealed weapons got terms in jail of one or two
years. Many immigrants were arrested on the vague charge of
intimidation or loitering. On Tuesday and Wednesday, January
30 and 31, immediately after the shooting, the police arrested
Joseph Caruso for the murder of Annie LoPezzi and arrested Ettor
and Giovannitti for inciting him. After a hearing the three
Italians were held for the grand jury and eventually indicted.
The imprisonment of Ettor was such a blow to the strikers that the
Transcript proclaimed: "The passing out of Ettor means [the]
ascendancy of the white-skinned races at Lawrence."

At the same time the police brought in John Breen for planting
the dynamite in Marad's shop. The case against Breen was so
clear that the police court bound him over to the grand jury without a hearing. Since the dynamite had been wrapped in a copy
of an undertaker's journal that was missing from only one funeral
parlor, Breen's, and since Breen had alerted the police to the
exact location of the dynamite, the judge was convinced of his
implication. The court meanwhile acquitted the persons in whose
homes the dynamite had been found.[6]

Lawrence, filled with rifles and rumors, reporters and reformers, had already become the notorious city of 1912 and the
strikers made it worse when they suddenly evacuated 300 of

6. *The New York Times,* Jan. 30, 1912; *Boston Evening Transcript,* Jan.
15, 19, Feb. 1, 1912; *The Evening Tribune,* Jan. 31, Feb. 1-3, 12, 21, 1912;
Citizens' Association of Lawrence, Mass., *Telling the Truth about the Ettor-
Giovannitti Case . . .* (Lawrence, 1912), p. 1; Samuel Gompers, "The Lawrence
Dynamite Conspiracy," *American Federationist,* XIX (1912), 815, 817.

their children in order, they said, to keep them from starving. Most of the children went to Socialists in New York City, but some ended up in Barre, Vermont, with the Socialist stone cutters. Since a gigantic parade greeted their arrival in New York, many felt that the Socialists were merely seeking publicity. Unwilling to let outsiders believe that it could not care for its children, the city government issued an order that no child could leave the city without its parents' written consent. When the strikers made two unsuccessful attempts to remove more of their children, the police would not let them go, and many women and children were jostled in the riots. Prejudiced sources, such as the I.W.W. publicist Justus Ebert and the Socialist *Call*, defended the exodus as the "humane" old French and Italian method of strike relief, but those on the other side accused the strikers of exploiting the children. The departure of the young people was certainly more than a relief measure, but the city was on shaky legal ground in stopping it.[7]

This was the final use of force during the strike. All events thereafter led to a settlement. On the day following the second railroad station riot most of the halls held meetings to discuss the rumor that the Italians were thinking of going back to work. When they failed to return, the mills began to offer concessions, and finally, two weeks later, the strike committee, backed by the cheers of a great outdoor mass meeting, voted to accept. Eight weeks after the first decision to go out, the strike was over. Within a few days almost everyone was back in the factories, with substantial wage increases all along the line. Workers formerly receiving $5.00 a week were to get more than $6.00; $8.00 operatives were raised to almost $8.75; and the higher paid craftsmen made substantial gains. Throughout New England wages went up so fast that 1912 became a banner year for the textile workers.[8] For these people Lawrence was a famous city, not a notorious one.

But while the operatives reveled in their new-found prosperity, bitterness continued in Lawrence during the remainder of the year.

7. *The Evening Tribune*, Feb. 10, 17, 22, 24, 1912; *The New York Call*, Feb. 13, 17, 19, Mar. 31, 1912; Ebert, *Trial*, p. 76; *Strike at Lawrence*, p. 368; Lorin F. Deland, "The Lawrence Strike: A Study," *The Atlantic Monthly*, CIX (1912), 696.

8. Robert A. Woods, "The Breadth and Depth of the Lawrence Outcome," *The Survey*, XXVIII (1912), 67-68.

The articles appearing in magazines and newspapers throughout the country and the testimony at the federal strike hearings placed the city in an extremely poor light. An anarchist May Day parade and the debate over the disposition of the strike relief funds ruffled the feelings of many. Two trials also kept the strike sentiments alive. In the dynamite affair Breen got off with just a fine and was not at first required to testify, quite probably to protect President Wood. In a mysterious and poorly documented series of events contractor Ernest Pittman, who had built the Wood Mill, supposedly confessed to Attorney General Pelletier on August 19 while drunk that he had provided the dynamite for Wood and Breen. Apparently horrified by his indiscretion, he committed suicide the next day. Pelletier eventually had Wood and two others indicted for conspiracy to plant dynamite, but even Pittman's confession and a corroboration from Breen were not enough to convict Wood. Late in September the Caruso-Giovannitti-Ettor trial began in Salem with the state trying to prove that Joseph Caruso killed Annie LoPezzi while incited by the other two. Though the trial ended in an acquittal, it led to an unauthorized sympathy strike in Lawrence and kept feelings high.[9]

Lawrence responded to the strike on the basis of nationality. The old-time natives disapproved of it as the work of immigrants. The earlier immigrants, particularly the Irish, were also opposed to the strike. The Irish had no representative on the strike committee and none of their organizations paraded with the I.W.W. on Memorial Day. There were many Irishmen among the city officials, most of whom were out of sympathy with the strikers. Judge Mahoney in the city court handed out stiff sentences to strikers; Assistant Marshal John J. Sullivan detained children at the railroad station; School Committee member John Breen hid dynamite; Mayor Scanlon supposedly brought in Sherman Agency detectives, many of them Irish. Father O'Reilly's parish calendar condemned the I.W.W. for misleading the newly arrived foreigners. The scurrilous *Leader* even insisted that O'Reilly opposed the strike because most of the striking Italians were Protestant. According

9. Gompers, "Conspiracy," pp. 817-18; Ebert, *Trial*, pp. 92-93, 95, 102; *The Leader*, Oct. 20, 1912; *The Evening Tribune*, May 19, 21, 24, June 7, 1913; Trial Transcript; *The Lawrence Sun*, Sept. 28, 1912; *Sunday Sun*, Sept. 19, 1912; *L'Era Nuova*, Oct. 5, 1912.

to the *Leader* the Protestant ministers begged the mill owners not to let O'Reilly settle the strike. While O'Reilly was humanely sympathetic toward the strikers, he took every opportunity to attack socialism and never actually sided with the workers.

In this attitude of wishing the strikers well, but disapproving of their radical leaders, the Irish and Father O'Reilly were consistent with the ideas they had held in the decade before 1912. Well established economically, politically, and socially, they had begun to think of themselves as natives and part of the process was to oppose the strike and the "foreigners" involved in it. They would not abandon the security that they had found in Americanism. While John Breen, the boss, had bitterly fought the corporations in 1882, his son, John Breen the undertaker, helped them in the dynamite plot against the strikers. Father O'Reilly had shifted from attacking the mill owners in 1894 to supporting them passively in 1912, and Mayor Scanlon, who had been with the owners during the strike, came out against tariff reduction when it was over. As the Irish made the transition, their nineteenth-century leaders began to die off. After the great boss John Breen, his work done, left in 1910, he was followed by Michael Carney and John Joyce, wealthy beverage dealers, Alderman John Tobin, and Katie O'Keefe. The story of Joyce, whom the *Tribune* called the "full typification of that great word—success," was similar to that of the others. Born in County Limerick in 1844, he was at work in the Washington Mill by the age of sixteen. After forming the Curran and Joyce soft drink company, he made a fortune and in his waning years retired to "Ledgemont," a large granite home in Andover. Such an immigrant could not support a strike.[10]

Those who arrived after the Civil War were almost as apathetic. A crowd of seven thousand strikers booed the French-Canadian priest who told them to go back to work and would have attacked

10. Trial Transcript, pp. 1081, 1609, 2172, 2194; *The Lawrence Sun,* May 31, 1912; *Strike at Lawrence,* p. 123; Ebert, *Trial,* pp. 39, 41, 54; *The Evening Tribune,* Jan. 12, Feb. 22, Mar. 4, 1912; *The Leader,* Mar. 10, 31, Nov. 24, 1912; Interview with Dr. Constant Calitri by Professor Edwin Fenton in 1951 through the kindness of Professor Fenton. Calitri said that few Irish struck and then only when absolutely necessary. Calitri was himself active in the strike. Augustinian Fathers, Lawrence, Mass., *Our Parish Calendar,* XIII (1908-9), No. 4, p. 7; XVI (1911-12), Nos. 10-12; XVII (1912-13), No. 6, p. 1; No. 7, p. 13; *The Evening Tribune,* April 8, 10, July 2, 1913, Jan. 27, 1917, Jan. 2, 1918.

his house if Ettor had not intervened. *Le Courrier* said the "capitalists" could pay higher wages, but it otherwise did not support the strikers. Ettor addressed a German mass meeting in its native tongue, and some of the Germans, principally the Socialists, left work, but not until half way through the strike did a majority of the Germans abandon their jobs. At the end only 400 enrolled in the I.W.W. Although the *Anzeiger und Post* was sympathetic with the "willing and peaceful" strikers, it strongly reproved the violence of the "rough criminal fellows." The operatives, it said, had struck because disgraceful conditions had exhausted their patience, but they had gone too far in exporting children. While the English had a branch of Local 20 and five representatives on the strike committee, including Socialist Thomas Holliday, they were far from unanimous in support of the strike. At the end of the first week many of them were still at work. Scabbing was common at the Arlington, where many Englishmen were employed and where the owners sent youths to break up an English strike meeting. Although the English, Canadians, and Germans did not oppose the strike as wholeheartedly as the Irish, they were far more against it than the later arrivals.[11]

The Italians, almost all of whom struck, were the backbone of the strike and provided part of its local leadership. Shortly before the strike, Angelo Rocco formed the Italian I.W.W. local which called in Ettor. When Ettor set up the multi-national strike committee, Rocco and three other English-speaking Italians were the leaders of the Italian sub-committee. The police arrested Rocco a few weeks later when he appeared at the head of an Italian mob outside the Prospect Mill gates. Although he maintained that he was only keeping the rioters from breaking down the doors of the factory, the police put him in jail. His arrest on the same day that Ettor and Giovannitti were jailed deprived the strikers, particularly the Italians, of much of their leadership.[12]

11. *Le Courrier de Lawrence*, Feb. 15, 22, 1912; *Boston Evening Transcript*, Jan. 31, 1912; *Solidarity*, Mar. 2, 1912. This reference to *Solidarity* and those that follow in this chapter are by the kindness of Professor Edwin Fenton. *Anzeiger und Post*, Jan. 20, Feb. 17, 24, Sept. 21, Oct. 5, 1912; *Strike at Lawrence*, p. 60; Trial Transcript, pp. 2259, 2280, 2338, 2352, 2382, 2395; Ebert, *Trial*, p. 41; Rocco Interview; *The Evening Tribune*, Jan. 19, Feb. 23, 1912.

12. Rocco Interview; *Strike at Lawrence*, p. 60; Trial Transcript, pp. 643, 2352, 2475; *La Gazzetta del Massachusetts*, Feb. 6, 1912.

The Italians were often turbulent and unruly during the strike. They ran through the mills and destroyed machinery the first day. One was quoted as saying: "We are going to fight them for more bread; we are going to get a pair of shoes for our barefoot children; we are going to get another set of underwear for them." Two weeks later the Italians threw chunks of ice at the trolley cars. The entire trial of Ettor and Giovannitti was an attempt to prove that they inflamed the Italians and were responsible for the murder of Annie LoPezzi. A circular in Italian, supposedly the work of Ettor, ended with the charge: "Throw them [those urging the strikers to go back to work] down the stairs. Break their bones; and leave them a remembrance for life." According to Clark Carter, the city missionary, there was real terror in the city. "The Italians are afraid the Syrians are going to blow them up or stab them, and the threats are so numerous . . . that many do not dare leave their houses. . . . They have gone from house to house at midnight . . . and said to them: 'Do not go to work, no work; work, kill you.'" When four Italians threatened to kill Paul Cassannanca if he went to work, he alerted the police, who followed him to an Italian meeting at Chabis Hall. He quickly walked over to the four, tipped his hat to the police, and watched the Italians marched off to jail. A Black Hand notice appeared one morning on the front door of the Loomfixers' Hall on Margin Street, but in the end the violence was mostly talk and murders did not occur.[13]

The Italian language was heard so often throughout Lawrence that observers came to believe that it was a purely Italian strike. Whether it was Ettor, Rocco, Giovannitti, or a lesser figure, someone was always addressing a mob of shivering strikers in Italian. And when the strikers marched, they shifted from the "Marseillaise" to Italian songs in the Italian quarter.

In spite of the common language, however, the Italian businessmen and priests split with the workers. Father Milanese supposedly received $50,000 from Wood for his efforts to get strikers back to work and for cautioning them against the use of force. This

13. *Strike at Lawrence,* pp. 37, 123, 372; Trial Transcript, pp. 1037, 1244, 1256, 1400-1, 2228, 2299, 2411, 2419, 2669; Calitri Interview; *The Lawrence Sun,* Jan. 15, 16, 18, 19, 1912; *Solidarity,* Jan. 15, 20, 1912; *The Evening Tribune,* Jan. 12, 1912. A Jewish worker also spoke of the Black Hand. *Boston Evening Transcript,* Jan. 20, 1912.

may not be true, but Milanese was never enthusiastic about the strike even though he supported it for the first two weeks and assisted ably in relief work. Italian businessmen formed a board of trade and appointed the Italian banker Jeremiah Campopiano, who was their president, to confer with the mill owners. Campopiano was accused of encouraging the Boston Italian journal *La Gazzetta* to oppose the strike. Doctor Constant Calitri, an Italian radical, said that the Italian storekeepers were against the strikers. But Fabrizio Pitocchelli, the well-known "Peter Kelley," who had been an Italian banker in Lawrence for fifteen years and who owned much real estate, provided the surety for Haywood's bond. In general, the Italian church and business groups were closer to the position of the Irish and French Canadians than to that of the Italian workers.[14]

Probably the second most important group of strikers were the Franco-Belgians. In the forefront of the radical labor movement ever since they arrived, they had provided several of the original Lawrence anarchists and "Wobblies." Cyrille Detollenaere, who was close to Ettor in the strike, was a member of the I.W.W. in 1905 and helped organize the Franco-Belgian branch of Local 20. As the strike got underway, the Franco-Belgians allowed the strikers to use their cooperative as headquarters. They were always among the most violent, even to the point of suggesting that all scabs be thrown in the river.[15]

In a lesser way the others contributed to the strike. The three Syrians on the strike committee were particularly important: Farris Marad, dyer, tailor, special policeman, and court interpreter; James Brox, grocer; and Doctor Hajjar. When interviewed years later, Marad denied that he was influential in the strike and said he had done little more than lead one of the parades. Even then he had turned the strikers away from the mills and avoided possible use of force. Brox had joined the I.W.W. in 1911 and during the strike invited Ettor to speak at one of the Syrian churches. Not

14. *Strike at Lawrence*, p. 311; Calitri Interview; *The New York Call*, Jan. 22, 1912; *The Lawrence Sun*, Jan. 18, Feb. 6, 1912; *La Gazzetta del Massachusetts*, Jan. 23, May 18, 1912; *The Evening Tribune*, Jan. 15, Mar. 1, 1912; Trial Transcript, pp. 2608, 2769-74.

15. *Solidarity*, July 22, 1911; *Strike at Lawrence*, p. 60; Rocco Interview; Ebert, *Trial*, p. 41; Trial Transcript, pp. 2209, 2264-66, 2466, 2475.

only did the Poles contribute Chabis Hall, but they also took part in the early rioting and threw ice at the soldiers. Polish bakeries gave free bread to strikers and Polish barbers would not shave scabs. The Portuguese allowed their hall to be used for some disorderly meetings but were themselves extremely cautious. Although they decided to strike, they also agreed to stay away from the other strikers so as to avoid unnecessary involvement. One group of Lithuanians supported the I.W.W., while another, mostly Lithuanian Catholics, repudiated it because of its link with the Marxist International. Some Lithuanians took part in demonstrations and some lost their jobs. For them, as for all immigrants, the decision to strike was a hard one.[16]

In its own way each ethnic group adjusted to the strike. The Irish city official naturally behaved differently from the Italian operative or the Franco-Belgian anarchist. The division of the city's immigration history into three periods makes considerable sense when applied to the strike. Those who came first, the Irish, joined the natives in opposing the strike. Among those who arrived after 1865 the Germans were interested in principle but not in action, the Canadians not even interested in principle. The late-arriving Italians, Franco-Belgians, and Poles made the strike a success. Within some groups, especially the Italian and Lithuanian, differences in occupation occasionally caused a schism, but otherwise the order of arrival, that is, the immigrant cycle, determined the way in which nationalities responded to the strike. Although all immigrants and their agencies, such as newspapers and churches, sympathized with the "just cause" of the strikers, most were reluctant to resort to violence. Only when moved to great rage did the immigrant worker become destructive and such

16. Though generally peaceful, the Syrians did help stop the machines at the Wood Mill. *The Lawrence Sun*, Jan. 13, 24, 1912; *Strike at Lawrence*, p. 301; Trial Transcript, p. 2228. Interview with Farris Marad, kindness of Professor Edwin Fenton. Trial Transcript, pp. 2195, 2590-91, 2598, 2601; Ebert, *Trial*, p. 46; *The Evening Tribune*, Jan. 17, 18, 23, 1912; *The Lawrence Sun*, Jan. 18, 1912. For Poles see Trial Transcript, pp. 2228, 2410, 2419, 2669; *The Lawrence Sun*, Jan. 17, Feb. 27, 1912; *Strike at Lawrence*, pp. 310-11; *The Evening Tribune*, Jan. 20, 1912. For Portuguese see *Strike at Lawrence*, p. 288; *The Lawrence Sun*, Jan. 18, 1912. For Lithuanians see *The Evening Tribune*, Jan. 18, Feb. 8, 23, 1912; *The Lawrence Sun*, Jan. 13, 24, 1912; Simas Suziedelis, *The Story of St. Francis Lithuanian Parish*, The Reverend A. Bruzas, tr. (Lawrence, 1953), pp. 86-90.

incidents were not common. When the immigrants found themselves caught in the strike, they reacted to it on the basis of their
immigrant status.

As the natives were trapped in the strike, they responded by
reviving their intolerance of immigrants. The strike of 1912 was
one of the last in a long line of nativist episodes starting with the
"Black House" riot of 1847. The new Citizens' Association,
formed during the strike to defend the city's name, said that nine
thousand of the strikers, including 90 per cent of the new members
of the I.W.W., were first-generation Americans, most of them
unable to speak English and all ignorant of the "real spirit of
America." While the militiamen, many of them Harvard boys,
sympathized with the strikers' demands, they were against all
"foreigners." Fearing that the immigrants would destroy property,
the city government would allow only English-speaking persons
to use the streets near the mills. Much of the feeling between
native and foreigner was actually between former immigrants like
the Irish, who now thought of themselves as natives, and recent
immigrants like the Italians. The year 1912 was, for these reasons,
a high point in the intolerance of the city and marked the peak as
well as the end of the decades of despair. The invasion of the
southeastern Europeans had led to a revival of prejudice that had
not been seen since the Know-Nothing days before the Civil War.
The 1912 strike, therefore, demonstrated clearly the influence of
the immigrant cycle on both labor disputes and ethnic friction and
provided a climax to the narrative of the city's history.[17]

As a corollary, the strike also brought to a climax the various
phases of the immigrant's search for security in Lawrence. During
the strike the family was more than ever the focal point of immigrant life. When immigrants went so far as to send their children
away, it proved how much the strike meant to them. Some, unable to stand the troubles of strike-torn Lawrence, escaped by
returning to their ancestral homes and families across the sea. A
crowd gathered early in February to see 126 Italians off for Boston,
where they would take the *Canopic* to Italy. Because of the strong
family ties between the old world and the new, European nations

17. Citizens' Association, *A Reign of Terror in an American City* (Lawrence,
1912); Walter Weyl, "The Strikers in Lawrence," *The Outlook*, C (1912), 310.

evidenced great concern over the strike and the trial that followed. For those who stayed in Lawrence the family unit with several members working was more than ever the only means of finding economic security. The Labor Commissioner's report on the strike analyzed about fifty families whose wage earners worked in the mills. The median family with both parents working had a weekly income of $12.00 to $14.00. When only the father worked, the median was barely $8.00. Wherever there were high-income families, there were always four or five working. The family provided security during the strike as never before.[18]

As a result of the strike the immigrant found greater security also in the mills. Pay for Lawrence textile workers, which hit a zenith of $8.75 a week in 1909, went down somewhat in the slow years of 1910 and 1911. The *Tribune's* survey of the poorer-paid textile workers set the median between $5.00 and $6.00 a week at the start of the strike and the eighteen youthful witnesses at the Washington hearings and the Salem trial had a median in the same range. Ettor always maintained that the average pay in the mills was $6.00 a week. Actually the average was probably as high as $7.50 or $8.00 because the *Tribune* study did not include any of the higher-paid operatives, the witnesses were all young and receiving low wages, and Ettor most certainly quoted a low figure; but it was still below the 1909 average, which was close to $9.00. The substantial increases after the strike then brought the pay back to the 1909 position and the immigrant was that much closer to the security for which he was looking.

There was still evidence that many immigrants had money. Campopiano said that each Italian leaving Lawrence in 1912 took with him savings of from $100 to $500, while the White Star Line agent said fifty of them alone took $12,000 out. The large sums raised for the relief funds and the Ettor trial indicated substantial savings. Immigrants were still poor, but enough had money to give the others hope.[19]

18. Two hundred left for Russian Poland. *The Lawrence Sun,* Feb. 10, 1912. One thousand Italians left early in February. *The Evening Tribune,* Feb. 5, 6, 1912. For French-Canadian departures see *ibid.* The Russians took such large quantities of clothing and furniture that it looked like a permanent departure. *The Lawrence Sun,* Feb. 10, 1912; Neill, *Report,* pp. 161-62; *Boston Evening Transcript,* Feb. 25, 1912.

19. *Sunday Sun,* June 5, 1910, Feb. 10, 1911; *The Lawrence Sun,* July 9,

The increased strength of the Lawrence labor unions resulting from the strike gave the immigrant the means of fighting for an even better life. Membership rose from four thousand to seventeen thousand within a year. While many did not remain permanent members, Lawrence was never again the anti-union city it had once been. To counter the gains of the I.W.W., John Golden had come to Lawrence shortly after the start of the strike. Following Ettor's lead, he put an Italian named D'Allesandro to work organizing his fellow countrymen for the A.F.L. Since the I.W.W. suspected that Golden and the A.F.L. opposed the strike, feeling was bitter. By midsummer the A.F.L. had made some inroads into the I.W.W. and to exploit its gain set up the *Union Label Monthly*. By printing it in Italian and Polish, as well as English, the A.F.L. acknowledged the importance of ethnos in the city.[20]

While labor was fighting internally, its leaders and its newspaper supporters were continuing the protests against the mill owners which had started far back in the nineteenth century. Many articles assumed that Wood had been systematically violating the contract labor law since the 1890's. One educated Italian said during the strike that he had been induced to come to America by Wood's posters, which showed a "well dressed, prosperous appearing workman emerging from the mills with bundles of money in his hands and on the opposite corner a bank building . . . with the workman entering to put away his savings." But as before evidence was lacking.

Other sources accused Wood of anti-labor tactics. They maintained that he used Fathers Milanese and O'Reilly and Mayor Scanlon to break the strike, and it does appear that these men were lukewarm toward the strikers. The dynamite plot was an owners' scheme to destroy the strike and the Ettor trial an attempt to prove that immigrants were radicals. But the corporations did

1910. The studies appeared in *The Evening Tribune,* Jan. 18, 20, 1912. Trial Transcript, p. 2141; *Strike at Lawrence,* pp. 32, 150, 152, 155-59, 165, 168, 169, 173, 237, 241; *Boston Evening Transcript,* Jan. 18, Feb. 25, 1912.

20. Lawrence was first in the state in 1913 in average number of members per union. Bureau of Statistics of Labor, *Forty-fourth Annual Report . . . 1913,* Mass. Pub. Doc. 15, Part III, pp. 43, 341, 377; *The Evening Tribune,* Jan. 16, Feb. 9, Mar. 6, 9, 1912; Mary K. O'Sullivan, "The Labor War at Lawrence," *The Survey,* XXVIII (1912), 72-74; *Sunday Sun,* July 7, 1912; *Union Label Monthly,* Sept. 30, 1912.

not follow the old practice of refusing to rehire strike leaders.[21]

The strike showed dramatically the importance of immigrant organizations in the life of the city. The meetings held at Chabis Hall, at the Portuguese center, at the Franco-Belgian Cooperative, and beneath the Syrian Church demonstrated the part played by national groups. So did the relief work of the immigrant societies, the presence of the Syrian band at the head of a parade, and the contributions of the Franco-Belgian Cooperative. Local 20, which started the strike, divided itself along ethnic lines as did the strike and relief committees. No one was really on his own; all depended upon some group. As the strikers discussed their problems, French, German, Italian, Polish, Hebrew, and other languages were used. The outcome of the strike, just as the whole history of the city before it, depended upon ethnic considerations.

The radical leaders of the strike made many believe that the city was filled with un-American anarchists and Socialists. Before the strike Lawrence had only a few Socialists and a handful of anarchists. There was one tiny anarchist cell, a Socialist Labor party with an Italian branch, a Socialist party with a German branch, and, of course, Local 20 of the I.W.W. with its Italian, Polish, and Franco-Belgian branches. That was all and during the strike the number of local radicals did not increase. One Italian anarchist, Ettore Giannini, was on the strike committee, and two others named Antonio Colombo and Walter Pollano promoted the strike with a newspaper called *Il Purgante*. Colombo ran the printing office where Ettor received his mail and next to which the police found the dynamite. The anarchists and Socialists who were so prominent—Ettor, Haywood, Flynn, and Giovannitti—all were outsiders. Aside from the I.W.W. none of the local radical organizations had anything to do with the strike. Several of the Lawrence workers who testified at the Washington hearings and at the Salem trial were regarded as troublemakers in the mills, but none uttered any Socialist or anarchist propaganda

21. *The Evening Tribune,* Jan. 30, Feb. 5, Mar. 18-19, 1912; *The Leader,* Jan. 21, Feb. 4, Mar. 10, 31, 1912; Dumont Goodyear, "The Lawrence Textile Strike," *The Independent,* LXXII (1912), 299; Deland, "Strike," p. 698; "The Lawrence Strike: A Review," *The Outlook,* C (1912), 533; *Anzeiger und Post,* Jan. 27, 1912; Calitri Interview; Rocco Interview; *Solidarity,* Jan. 20, 1912; *The Lawrence Sun,* April 21, 1912. A few Italians were not rehired, but this was not the general rule.

CHAPTER XI

American City, 1912-1921

To prove to the world what Lawrence already knew, the citizens of the immigrant city took steps to demonstrate their Americanism. Their efforts set the tone for the entire decade following the strike. To repudiate the city's notorious reputation the newly formed Citizens' Association published in 1912 a series of pamphlets. While one proclaimed: "Lawrence—Here She Stands: For God and Country!" a second wanted people to see "Lawrence As It Really Is, Not As Syndicalists, Anarchists, Socialists, Suffragists, Pseudo Philanthropists and Muckraking Yellow Journalists Have Painted it."[1]

But in the meantime the anarchists were undermining their work. One group met on the "plains" to hear speeches defending Ettor and Giovannitti on September 14, 1912. On September 30 a massive parade in honor of Annie LoPezzi, led by the famous anarchist Carlo Tresca, drew anarchists from Haverhill and Boston to Lawrence. Fifty red and black flags intermixed with 3,000 umbrellas gave the rainy day procession a weird appearance. The banners carrying the slogan "No God, No Country" particularly aroused the immigrant city.[2]

Responding to the challenge, Father O'Reilly planned a tremendous "God and Country" parade to be held by the entire city on October 12, just twenty years after the Columbus Day parade he had organized in 1892. On this Columbus Day, 1912, O'Reilly led 32,000 marchers through the main streets with banners reading

1. Citizens' Association of Lawrence, Mass., *Telling the Truth about the Ettor-Giovannitti Case* . . . (Lawrence, 1912); Citizens' Association, Lawrence, Mass., *Lawrence As It Really Is* . . . (Lawrence, 1912).
2. *L'Era Nuova*, Sept. 21, Oct. 5, 26, 1912; *Sunday Sun*, Sept. 29, 1912.

"For God and Country." The vast numbers participating in this all-city affair represented and united its immigrant groups. Immigrants who had come together in January to strike now joined to pledge their Americanism. The immigrant had been tested and was now demonstrating his loyalty. The Irish, who had been here the longest and were generally the most Americanized, led the parade. *Le Courrier,* representing the thoroughly Americanized French Canadians, called it a "grand and superb" performance that would show the rest of the country that Lawrence would "no longer tolerate parades of anarchists and manifestations of people without faith nor law. . . ." The Saint Mary's Calendar, which spoke for Catholics of all nationalities, bitterly condemned the "No God, No Country" banners of the anarchist parade. The question posed by the strike and the parade was answered. Lawrence followed the leadership of the I.W.W. instead of the A.F.L., but at the same time it adhered to the moderation that all groups immigrant or native had always supported. The patriotism nurtured in the nineteenth century burst forth full grown on Columbus Day, 1912.[3]

While the immigrant was pledging his devotion to America, efforts were being made to help him adjust to his new world. When the Men and Religion Forward movement made a survey of "Efforts to Americanize Immigrants," it found seven non-English-speaking Catholic churches, two synagogues, and seven immigrant Protestant churches already at work. The International Institute for Women was trying to speed the assimilation of immigrant women through a variety of classes, home visits, and social affairs. Other agencies were promoting naturalization by staging elaborate ceremonies when citizenship was granted. Since the immigrant was already an American in spirit when he arrived in Lawrence, these efforts promised to be successful.

Lawrence became so well known for Americanization that its School Committee was asked to help publish a book called "The American Plan for Education in Citizenship," which soon achieved a national reputation. Its aim was to help the schools "keep the

3. *The Evening Tribune,* Centennial Edition, 1953, "For God and Country" Section; *Le Courrier de Lawrence,* Oct. 10, 17, 1912; Augustinian Fathers, Lawrence, Mass., *Our Parish Calendar,* XVII (1912), No. 7, p. 13; *The Leader,* Oct. 13, 1912.

republic safe" and to "permeate every course of study with loyalty to American ideals." History was to teach "love and loyalty for America," civics to inculcate "devotion to the Community," and literature to arouse enthusiasm for the things "which the American spirit holds dear." The principles of the plan were first, "sacrifice for country"; second, belief in America as "the land of opportunity"; third, patriotism; fourth, faith in American democracy; fifth, obedience to law; and last, love of country. While the good American was tolerant of other "liberal" forms of government, "internationalism . . . [was to] supplement Americanism, not destroy it." It was fitting that an immigrant city, Lawrence, should have devised this forthright definition of Americanism. It was simply the way in which earlier immigrants told later ones how to be good Americans.[4]

The intense Americanization drive had an unfortunate counterpart in nativism. When a bill was proposed that all schools in the state teach English and that the State Board of Education control parochial schools, it aroused the Catholic clergy in Lawrence. So did the argument that the foreign schools had fomented the strike of 1912. Father O'Reilly took great pains to point out that Angelo Rocco was educated in the public schools and that the French Canadians, most of whom attended their own schools, had taken little part in the strike. The Guardians of Liberty, who had a secret handclasp and called themselves "Minute Men," began to issue anti-Catholic pamphlets such as *The Menace* and *Speak Kindly of Roman Catholics.* When the Knights of Columbus spoke out against the publications, the Chamber of Commerce, which was basically native, attacked the Knights for "their . . . malicious, unpatriotic, and un-American efforts . . . to stir up religious strife or bigotry." Among the Lithuanians a split arose between the Protestant majority and the Catholics.[5]

In the decade after the strike immigration declined. By 1915 the percentage of foreign-born had suffered its first important reduction, dropping from 48 per cent in 1910 to 46 per cent. By

4. *The Evening Tribune,* Mar. 2, 1912; John J. Mahoney and H. H. Chamberlin, *A Statement of Aims and Principles* (National Security League, *The Lawrence Plan for Education in Citizenship,* No. 1) (New York, 1918).

5. *The Evening Tribune,* Oct. 24, 1913, April 21, 22, Nov. 6, 1914, Feb. 18, Mar. 5, 19, 1915, Aug. 5, 1916, Feb. 27, 1917, Dec. 24, 1918, Jan. 2, 1919.

1920 it was only 42 per cent. The population barely increased during those ten years, a great change from the tremendous gains of the previous seven decades.[6] Immigration societies, nonetheless, continued to dominate the city. A new French Catholic church, additional Jewish, Polish, and Italian schools, and a new hall for the Saint Michael Polish Society demonstrated the vigor of both old and new immigrants. The semi-centennials of the Hibernians and the Saint Jean de Baptiste Society entertained the city. The Gaelic League brought the Irish a taste of the old country and the visits of General Andranike from Armenia and Garibaldi's daughter from Italy renewed the attachments of the later immigrants. Many of the nationalities raised money during and after the war to relieve suffering in Europe. The Jews started a Zionist drive and staged organized protests against the Polish pogroms and the Ukrainian massacres. The Syrians petitioned the State Department for information about their countrymen in Turkey.

The World War gave the immigrant further chances to prove his Americanism. First it touched off a series of flag-raisings similar to those about 1898. When recent arrivals flocked to volunteer for combat, they helped counteract the resentment felt because non-citizens were not required to go to war. Four Liberty Loan drives, each for about $4 million, went "over the top." The $16 million, said the *Tribune,* was another "vindication of 1912." To collect the money the city fell back upon its only sure organizational base, immigrant groups. The Italians, most criticized in 1912, were particularly generous and their mass meetings were the feature of every drive. As its heroes returned home each nationality held banquets in their honor and built memorials for the dead. The immigrants had proven that they were Americans by spending their money and their lives for their country.[7]

In its tolerant treatment of the German immigrants Lawrence attained its highest degree of Americanism. Although the city had enough Germans to be second in Massachusetts in number of German female aliens registered, the *Tribune* reported no attacks

6. *Ibid.,* Mar. 17, 1917; United States Census Bureau, *Fourteenth Census of the United States . . . 1920,* III (Washington, 1922), 464. See Table I.
7. *The Evening Tribune,* Mar. 18, May 20, 1913, April 1, 1914, Feb. 4, 1916, Feb. 26, Mar. 27, June 16, Oct. 24, 29, 1917, Feb. 9, May 2, 18, Oct. 1, 1918, April 29, 1920, Feb. 26, 1921.

and showed no prejudice itself. It did carry less German news, but this was partly because the German societies were less active during the war. Since they knew they had built up considerable respect in Lawrence, the Germans determined to retain it by being unobtrusive. They held one mass meeting in 1914 to raise relief money for Germany and to protest against the treatment of Germans in the American press. But they took part in neither the great Columbus Day Peace Parade of 1915, the victory celebration of 1918, nor the Britain's Day parade of the same year. The German societies did not contribute much to the Liberty Loan drives except the third, when Albert A. Schaake was particularly active and a big German meeting helped make it a success. The Germans strengthened their position in 1918 by holding a rally at which the speakers blamed the war on the "damnable Junker regime" in the old country. Lawrence was so tolerant that a Turner convention met there in 1917, and the same year W. F. Biederwolf, an evangelist, and Fritz Kreisler performed before enthusiastic crowds.[8]

The League of Nations debate gave the Irish a unique opportunity to demonstrate their loyalty and attack the public schools and the British at the same time. Father O'Reilly presided over a mass meeting that petitioned Wilson to fight for Irish self-determination at the Versailles Conference. The Friends of Irish Freedom protested against a pro-League speaker in the White Fund series because they considered the League only a scheme to strengthen Britain. They then demanded that the Irish-dominated City Council condemn the League Covenant as a "menace to the peace of the United States." Under such "a pagan document" the United States "would become the subject colony of the world government framed by President Wilson." Since they believed that article ten would force the United States to fight against Ireland if it rose in rebellion, the Irish were naturally against it and the entire Covenant. In general they felt that the League would give Great Britain control over the United States. While sympathetic, the City Council voted merely to endorse the stand taken by Senators Lodge and Walsh, who were for the League but with reservations.

8. *Ibid.*, Sept. 2, 1914, Mar. 20, July 31, Aug. 6, Oct. 11, 1915, Feb. 5, 17, Nov. 8, 1917, April 11, 24, May 2, 4, 18, Aug. 30, Oct. 19, Nov. 13, Dec. 7, 1918, Feb. 6, 1920.

Still undaunted, the Friends then carried the fight to the public schools, which they said were submerged in a sea of British propaganda. According to their version the teachers favored Great Britain in telling the Evangeline story. In addition they used a current events magazine that was pro-League and hired a speaker who defended the British position in Ireland. Even worse were the pro-British books used in school. Thompson and Bigwood's *Lest We Forget* included poems by that "anti-Catholic bigot Rudyard Kipling" and called England more democratic than the United States. A. B. Hart's *Short History of the United States* said that the Navigation Acts had not oppressed the American colonies. The Friends protested also against the history program set up in the schools by the National Security League, an organization that they believed was supporting Great Britain. Although the school superintendent refuted the charges and showed where the Friends had taken words out of context, the Irish had clearly established their position of defending the United States against Great Britain.[9]

The desperate efforts of the Lawrence immigrants to demonstrate their Americanism received a temporary setback in the textile strike of 1919. Started in the depths of the winter during a slack textile period as the direct result of an attempt to lower wages along with hours, led by confused radicals (called, variously, Communists, Socialists, and anarchists) most of whom were from outside Lawrence, opposed by the A.F.L. and the English-speaking workers, and carried on mainly by Russians and Italians, this strike was similar to its predecessor in 1912. When the American Woolen Company cut hours to forty-eight and reduced pay proportionately, Ime Kaplan, a twenty-five-year-old Russian, and Samuel Bramhall, another immigrant, led thousands of laborers away from their machines. Angelo Rocco was still in the forefront, this time as attorney for the strikers. The Irish-controlled city government once again hampered the strike by arresting the leaders for evading the draft and disturbing the peace, and by refusing the workers permission to parade or even hold outdoor meetings. As before, workers and police clashed on the picket lines. Children again left for out-of-town care. Comparable to the discovery of

9. *Ibid.*, Aug. 1, 1914, Dec. 13, 1918, Jan. 24, Feb. 2, April 17, July 15, 1920.

dynamite in 1912 was the bomb explosion that destroyed part of a trolley-car track in 1919. Supporting the owners were more private detectives, and defending the workers were outside journals such as the New York *Call*. When it was over on May 22, 1919, the workers had won another victory, but one less decisive than in 1912.[10]

While the strike revived the belief that immigrants were un-American, it gave those who refused to participate the chance to show their own loyalty by condemning the strike leaders as Communists. In addition to Kaplan and Bramhall, A. J. Muste, a Russian-born clergyman, a Reverend Long, Anthony Caprao, Nathan Klineman, and Joseph Salerno provided leadership which many called "Bolshevik." After Mayor White announced that there would be no bolshevism in Lawrence, the *Tribune* supported him with an attack on intellectuals called "No Liberty in Bolshevism." When Samuel Bramhall would not guarantee the singing of the *Star Spangled Banner* at a proposed meeting in 1921, the City Council refused to grant him the use of the Common. Public denunciations of communism were frequent. Stirred up by these charges and moved by the red scare sweeping the country, the United States government stepped in to arrest most of the strike leaders as aliens liable for deportation. The immigration officials, however, could not find enough evidence to send them back to Europe.[11]

Even those who took part in the strike managed to recover some of the prestige that they lost in it. In January of 1921 the Italian textile workers made a statement blaming outsiders for the strike. They attacked Muste, Long, Bramhall, and the others for their radicalism and spoke out against all efforts to "de-Americanize" the workers. Earlier the Lithuanians had denied statements that they would leave America if they lost the strike. In stilted phrases they proclaimed their Americanism: ". . . the Catholic Lithuanians of Lawrence, both strikers and non-strikers, do love this great city of Lawrence and this glorious country of America. . . ." Just as in the October 12 parade in 1912 the immigrants of Lawrence were revealing their true devotion to the

10. *Ibid.*, Jan. 14-June 9, 1919; *The New York Times*, Jan. 24-May 25, 1919.

11. *The Evening Tribune*, June 24, Oct. 1, Nov. 7, Dec. 10, 1919, Jan. 3, 7, 24, Feb. 2, 1920, April 18, 1921.

United States. They would follow alien leaders for better conditions but would never adopt un-American views.[12]

The reaction of Lawrence to the immigration restriction laws of 1917 and 1921, laws to which the 1912 strike had contributed, demonstrated how Americanized the city had become. Unlike the early days when Lawrence was wildly concerned about immigration laws, the city paid little attention to the new measures. The Syrians and Italians complained that the literacy test of 1917 would keep many of their families split, but there was no other opposition. The quota system of 1921 meant the end of three-quarters of a century of unlimited immigration to Lawrence, but it went unnoticed. Since it was now an American city, Lawrence did not seem to care if free immigration were ended.[13]

As Lawrence completed its shift from an immigrant city to an American city, signs of the coming of the twenties—none related to immigration—were frequent. In 1915 the Lenox Motor Car Company set up a plant in the city and the complications of the automobile age followed. The difficulty of enforcing the Volstead Act made the post-war crime wave in Lawrence even worse. Late in 1920 the stock market quotations began to find a place on the front page of the *Tribune* and the frenzied career of Charles Ponzi touched many in Lawrence. Hints of the wild twenties came in a city ordinance that prohibited darkening dance halls, a custom new to once Puritan Lawrence and one that Father O'Reilly and *Le Progrès* must have deplored. With the national makeup of the United States and Lawrence frozen, with all ethnic groups well established, and with the Americanism of the newcomers generally accepted, it is time to leave the story of Lawrence. Billy Wood anticipated the end of an era by announcing in 1920 his plans for a million-dollar plant and model village in nearby Shawsheen. Never again was he primarily interested in Lawrence.

By 1921 the meaning of Lawrence was clear. The simple picture of a notorious, poverty-stricken, un-American city that the strike observers had broadcast to the world in 1912 was false. The true story of the city was the one the immigrants knew. For almost seven decades between 1845 and 1912 a gigantic cycle of

12. *Ibid.*, Jan. 21, 1921, May 2, 1919.
13. *Ibid.*, Jan. 9, 14, 1913, Jan. 22, 1915, April 23, 1921.

immigration had shaped the history of Lawrence by dividing it into three periods. The Irish in 1850 were replaced by the French Canadians in 1865 and the Italians in 1890, and each group became more like the natives as their decades in the city accumulated. The very natives who liked to consider themselves superior to the foreign-born were themselves a generation or two removed from immigrant status and behaved as they did not because they were native-born but because of their particular position in the immigrant cycle. The fact that Lawrence was completely the child of immigration made the impact of the immigrant cycle that much greater.

The Lawrence experience was similar to that in many American cities. Like all immigrant centers it was closely tied to the old countries and also to the other immigrant cities of America. The group instinct of each nationality, therefore, remained strong and Lawrence experienced the same movements that were going on in Europe and in the United States. Like many cities Lawrence enjoyed a half-urban, half-rural situation which made the shift from farm life in Europe and Canada easier than in a city such as Boston, but more difficult than in parts of the American West. This environment also made Lawrence less a city of tragedy than it might have been by easing the hardships of the periodic depressions. By proving that the immigrants in Lawrence were neither hopelessly poor nor un-American, the story of the immigrant city suggests that immigrants all over the United States were better off and more easily assimilated than generations of writers would admit.

The Lawrence immigrants and those like them in hundreds of similar cities found security in their new country. The security came first from their families and clubs. Rugged individualism no more existed in Lawrence then than it does now. Whether for economic support, for social pleasure, for intellectual stimulation, for protection against prejudice, or for the expression of hatreds of their own, mutual activity was an essential feature of the immigrants' search for security. There was no "melting pot." The Italians did not marry Irishmen just as the natives did not marry foreigners. There was no such thing as an immigrant mind or an immigrant morality or an immigrant political party in Lawrence.

Each nationality differed in eating habits, in games, and in political preference.

The story of Lawrence gave some support to the view that immigrants in America led a tragic life suffering from crowding, filth, exploitation, and poverty. The immigrant quarters were certainly overloaded and dirty; the new arrival was overworked in the mills; he was poor and ill at ease. Yet the story of the city suggested many modifications to this picture of despair. The immigrant cycle moved the newcomer, or at least his children, up out of the squalor to better homes, better jobs, and higher pay. Though driven hard in the mills, most operatives believed themselves better off than in the old country and, when they learned to organize, began to do something about working conditions. Not all immigrants were desperately poor and even those that were found relief within their own ethnic groups and found hope from the example of those who had succeeded.

It was difficult to contrast immigrants with Americans in Lawrence because as soon as the immigrant arrived he became an American, and he was most American in his unwillingness to face reality. While he often talked in radical terms, enough to brand himself a dangerous revolutionary, he actually wanted only moderate reform. While he prated of individualism and independence, he desired most to be with his family or fellow-countrymen. Though he denounced all manifestations of discrimination when aimed at him, he himself soon exhibited the worst sort of prejudice. Even when he thought himself fighting against absorption, he showed through his belief in material progress and his tacit acceptance of city life that he was already assimilated. And, finally, in spite of his belief in independent progress, what he really craved was security. The most chauvinistic of patriots, the most optimistic of optimists, the immigrant was more American than the native-born. Those whom the Citizens' Association had called ignorant of the "real spirit of America" were themselves the makers of the spirit.[14]

This was the truth about Lawrence which the observers in 1912 were unable to detect. They did not realize that Lawrence,

14. Citizens' Association, Lawrence, Mass., *A Reign of Terror in an American City* (Lawrence, 1912).

designed as a model city, had gone through three periods of mass invasion in the process of becoming an immigrant city. During this time poor and frightened immigrants sought security and found it in their families, in their clubs, in the mills, and in desperate efforts to be Americans. The strike was a paradox. To the unseeing, it revealed an un-American city where security was utterly lacking. To those who knew, it marked the emergence of Lawrence as an American city with all the security that the term American implied.

Tables

Table I

NATIVITY OF LAWRENCE POPULATION, 1845-1920

Year	Total	Foreign-born	Ireland	England	Scotland	Canada	Germany	Russia	France	Italy	Turkey	Percentage of Total Foreign-born Population
1845	104											
1848	6,000	2,250	2,139									37.5%
1850	8,358											
1855	16,114	6,725	4,783	1,132	405	206	169					41.6%
1860	17,639											
1865	21,698	9,217	6,047	1,892	522	563	151					42.48%
1870	28,921	12,717	7,457	2,456	691	1,037	467					
1875	34,916	15,546	8,232	3,353	882	1,924	963					44.52%
1880	39,151	17,266	7,951	3,579	909	3,067	1,117					44.10%
1885	38,862	17,097	7,643	3,928	832	2,451	1,499	60		2		43.99%
1890	44,654	20,518	7,697	4,985	1,097	4,459	1,830	60		46	5	45.95%
1895	52,164	24,302	7,487	5,486	1,203	5,665	2,402	426	68	263	213	46.59%
1900	62,559	28,577	7,058	5,131	1,198	8,682	2,465	780	147	936	277	45.68%
1905	70,050	32,279	6,557	5,153	1,168	7,597	2,388	1297	435	2804	1332	46.08%
1910	85,892	41,319	5,943	5,659	1,336	9,498	2,301	4366	788	6693	2077	48.1%
1915	90,259											45.8%
1920	94,270	39,122										41.5%
1950	80,536											

This table is derived from statistics in Maurice B. Dorgan, *History of Lawrence, Mass., with War Records* (Cambridge, Mass., 1924), pp. 44, 174; Francis DeWitt, *Abstract of the Census of ... Massachusetts ... 1855* ... (Boston, 1857), pp. 105, 206; Oliver Warner, *Abstract of the Census of Massachusetts, 1860* ... (Boston, 1863); Oliver Warner, *Abstract of the Census of Massachusetts,—1865* ... (Boston, 1867), pp. 62-63; United States Census Office, *Ninth Census of the United States ... 1870*, I (Washington, 1872), 380-81; Carroll D. Wright, *Census of Massachusetts: 1875*, I (Boston, 1876), 44, 275, 288-311; Carroll D. Wright, *The Census of Massachusetts: 1880* ... (Boston, 1883), pp. 50, 127-28; Carroll D. Wright, *The Census of Massachusetts: 1885*, I, Part 1 (Boston, 1887), 507; United States Census Office, *Eleventh Census of the United States: 1890*, I (Washington, 1895), 670; Horace G. Wadlin, *Census of ... Massachusetts: 1895*, II (Boston, 1897), 607; United States Census Office, *Twelfth Census of the United States ... 1900*, II (Washington, 1902), 722, 796-97; Chief of the Bureau of Statistics of Labor, *Census of ... Massachusetts 1905*, I (Boston, 1909), 109, 678; United States Census Bureau, *Thirteenth Census of the United States ... 1910. Abstract of the Census ... with Supplement for Massachusetts* ... (Washington, 1913), pp. 596, 609; The Commonwealth of Massachusetts, *The Decennial Census 1945*, p. 13; The Commonwealth of Massachusetts, *The Population of Massachusetts ... 1950*, p. 18; *The Evening Tribune*, Mar. 17, 1917; United States Census Bureau, *Fourteenth Census of the United States ... 1920*, III (Washington, 1922), 464.

Table II
PERCENTAGE OF INCREASE IN TOTAL POPULATION OF LAWRENCE

1850-55	93	1870-75	21	1890-95	17	1910-15	5
1855-60	9	1875-80	12	1895-1900	20	1915-20	4
1860-65	23	1880-85	−1	1900-1905	12		
1865-70	33	1885-90	12	1905-10	23		

Derived from Table I.

Table III
PERCENTAGE OF CERTAIN ETHNIC GROUPS IN TOTAL POPULATION OF LAWRENCE, 1905

British-American	12.07 (11th of 33 cities in Massachusetts)
Irish	9.36 (7th)
British	9.11 (3rd)
Germanic	4.73 (3rd)
Russian	1.85 (6th)
Polish	1.13 (7th)
Greco-Latin	5.16 (3rd)
Asiatic	0.07 (8th)

Derived from *Census of Mass., 1905*, I, lxxvii.

Table IV
PERCENTAGE OF FOREIGN-BORN IN TOTAL POPULATION: RANK OF LAWRENCE IN STATE

1865	1. Holyoke	2. Lawrence	
1875	1. Fall River	2. Holyoke	3. Lawrence
1880	1. Holyoke	2. Fall River	3. Lawrence
1885	1. Holyoke	2. Fall River	3. Lawrence
1890	1. Fall River	2. Holyoke	3. Lawrence
1895	1. Fall River	2. Lawrence	3. Holyoke
1900	1. Fall River	2. Lawrence	3. Lowell
1905	1. Lawrence	2. Fall River	3. New Bedford

Derived from *Census of Mass., 1905*, I, xliii.

Table V
POPULATION BY WARDS AND PLACE OF BIRTH

	Lawrence	Ward I	Ward II	Ward III	Ward IV	Ward V	Ward VI
1855 Population	16,114	2679	3838	5581	1945	984	1069
Native-Born	9401	1761	2119	2799	1404	659	659
Foreign-Born	6729	936	1719	2782	541	325	410
1865 Population	21,698	3841	4737	5437	4229	2104	1350
Native-Born	12,481	2456	2904	2733	2250	1209	887
Foreign-Born	9217	1376	1824	2680	1979	895	463
Irish	6047	818	1217	2071	1326	235	380
English	1892	298	189	306	482	558	59
Scotch	522	125	196	50	68	68	15
Canadian	563	80	119	233	92	32	7
German	151	48	94	3	3	2	1
1870 Population	28,921	5183	5516	5849	6451	3630	2292
Native-Born	16,204	2999	3145	3025	3504	2051	1480
Foreign-Born	12,717	2184	2371	2824	2947	1579	812
1875 Population	34,916	6049	5874	5366	8404	5836	3387
Native-Born	19,370	3380	3406	2798	4410	3335	2041
Foreign-Born	15,546	2669	2468	2568	3994	2501	1346
Irish	8232	1171	1487	1815	2359	608	792
English	3353	492	320	193	686	1388	274
Scotch	882	198	190	71	142	234	47
Canadian	1924	250	119	415	755	230	155
German	963	511	328	39	13	9	63
1880 Population	39,151	6818	6086	8184	7214	6579	4270
Native-Born	21,885	3889	3463	4179	3860	3855	2639
Foreign-Born	17,266	2929	2623	4005	3354	2724	1631
Irish	7951	1046	1647	2538	1190	623	907
English	3579	539	339	414	564	1438	285
Scotch	909	190	151	90	118	263	97
Canadian	3067	309	116	829	1369	243	201
German	1117	700	258	16	20	24	99
1890 Population	44,654	6952	6338	8368	9147	7888	5961
Native-Born	24,136	3645	3470	4148	4457	4623	3784
Foreign-Born	20,518	3298	2862	4220	4690	3265	2177
1900 Population	62,559	9804	8537	10,159	11,722	11,821	10,516
Native-Born	33,982	5118	4667	4960	5803	6661	6773
Foreign-Born	28,577	4686	3870	5199	5919	5160	3743
1910 Population	85,892	14,186	13,571	14,236	13,581	16,180	14,138
Native-Born	44,252	6684	6390	6341	6643	9050	9144
Foreign-Born	41,319	7475	7168	7858	6848	6983	4971
Irish	5943	859	1007	1433	889	548	1207
English	5659	755	591	597	1158	1428	1130
Scotch	1336	188	138	122	164	322	402
Canadian, French	7698	99	112	715	2351	3240	1181
Canadian, Other	1800	340	260	169	264	405	416
German	2301	1489	380	133	152	41	106
Russian	4366	725	771	950	1346	448	126
Italian	6693	1721	3341	1374	75	26	156
French	788	178	117	124	32	248	89
Turkish	2077	85	183	1645	108	34	22
Austrian	1450	915	137	181	161	41	15

Derived from statistics listed in Table I.

Table VI
ANNUAL DEATH RATE IN LAWRENCE

1855	23.6 per 1,000 population
1860	32.9
1865	31.6
1856-1865	23.7
1870	17.2
1875	26.0
1880	21.7
1885	19.9
1890	26.5
1895	20.3
1900	20.4
1905	19.8
1910	17.9

Report . . . Relating to the Registry and Return of Births, Marriages, and Deaths . . ., Mass. Pub. Doc. 1, XIV (1855), 45; XIX (1860), xlvi; XXIV (1865), xlvi; XLIX (1890), 373; LIV (1895), 130; LIX (1900), 140; LXIV (1905), 195; LXIX (1910), 8.

Table VII
PERCENTAGES OF TOTAL DEATHS AT VARIOUS AGES IN LAWRENCE

	1847-1849	1857-1859	1867-1869	1877-1879	1887-1889	1899-1901	1907-1909
0	25	24	31	28	27	32	34
1	15	14	10	8	5	6	7
2	5	6	3	5	3	2	3
3	2	3	2	4	2	1	1
4	2	3	1	2	2	1	1
5-9	5	3	3	5	4	3	2
10-14	2	2	2	2	2	1	2
15-19	4	5	5	4	5	2	2
20-24	9	6	6	5	6	4	3
25-29	9	6	6	5	6	4	3
30-34	6	5	5	4	4	4	3
35-39	3	4	4	4	3	4	4
40-44	2	3	4	3	4	4	4
45-49	2	3	3	3	4	4	4
50-54	2	3	3	2	4	4	3
55-59	0.5	3	3	3	4	5	4
60-64	1	2	3	3	4	5	5
65-69	1	1	3	3	4	5	5
70-74	0.5	1	2	2	3	3	4
75-79	1	1	1	2	1	3	3
80-84	0.3		1	1	1	2	2
85-89			0.5	1	1	1	1
90-94					1		
95—							
Unknown	0.5				1		

Derived from *Report of Births, Marriages, and Deaths*, XVI (1857), 46-47; XVII (1858), xlvi-xlvii; XVIII (1859), xlvi-xlvii; XXVI (1867), xliv-xlv; XXVII (1868), xliv-xlv; XXVIII (1869), xliv-xlv; XXXVI (1877), xliv-xlv; XXXVII (1878), xliv-xlv; XXXVIII (1879), xliv-xlv; XLVI (1887), 52-53; XLVII (1888), 58-59; XLVIII (1889), 58-59; LVIII (1899), 36-37; LIX (1900), 36-37; LX (1901), 36-37; LXVI (1907), 36-37; LXVII (1908), 36-37; XLVIII (1909), 36-37; Essex Institute, *Vital Records of Lawrence Massachusetts to the End of the Year 1849* (Salem, Mass., 1926), pp. 103-25.

Table VIII

ARRESTS IN LAWRENCE, 1874-1881, BY NATIVITY OF FATHER

Year	Native-born	Foreign-born	Scotch	Irish	English	German	French	Canadian	Total
1874	264	1504(85)	40	1287	137	6	24	9	2096*
1875	228	1847(89)	33	1628	112	17	37	15	2075
1876	451	1553(76)	42	1358	137	18	23	12	2054
1877	350	1399(80)	19	1264	56	12	40	4	1750†
1878	277	1878(87)	12	1725	68	17	51	—	2155
1879	580	1557(73)	6	1341	89	10	94	—	2137
1880	390	1938(83)	20	1704	102	26	82	—	2328
1881	351	1603(82)	18	1364	90	22	83	21	1954
1874-1881	2893(18)	13,329(82)	190(1)	11,671(72)	791(5)	128(1)	434(3)	61	16,549‡

* 326 not listed as native or foreign.
† 1 not listed as native or foreign.
‡ 327 not listed as native or foreign.
Number in parentheses to right of figure indicates percentage of total arrests. Bureau of Statistics of Labor, "Fall River, Lowell, and Lawrence," *Thirteenth Annual Report . . .1882*, Mass. Pub. Doc. 15, p. 258.

Table IX

LITERACY OF FOREIGN-BORN EMPLOYEES IN LAWRENCE, 1909

General nativity	Number reporting complete data			Per cent who read			Per cent who read and write		
	Male	Fe-male	Total	Male	Fe-male	Total	Male	Fe-male	Total
Native-born of native father, white	688	543	1,231	99.7	100.0	99.8	99.7	100.0	99.8
Native-born of foreign father, by country of birth of father:									
Canada	215	339	554	98.6	98.5	98.6	98.6	98.5	98.6
England	407	354	761	100.0	100.0	100.0	100.0	100.0	100.0
Germany	245	267	512	100.0	100.0	100.0	100.0	100.0	100.0
Ireland	614	812	1,426	99.8	99.5	99.6	99.7	99.4	99.5
Scotland	72	67	139	100.0	100.0	100.0	100.0	100.0	100.0
Foreign-born by place of birth:									
Armenian	127	3	130	89.8	(a)	89.2	89.0	(a)	88.5
Canadian, French	373	591	964	90.3	95.6	93.6	86.3	95.1	91.7
Canadian, Other	69	193	262	98.6	96.4	96.9	97.1	95.3	95.8
English	1,682	777	2,459	99.6	98.6	99.3	99.5	98.1	99.1
French	261	184	445	95.4	91.8	93.9	95.0	91.3	93.5
German	556	229	785	99.8	99.1	99.6	99.8	99.1	99.6
Hebrew, Russian	92	75	167	96.7	88.0	92.8	96.7	88.0	92.8
Irish	564	511	1,075	95.4	97.3	96.3	94.1	95.9	95.0
Italian, North	597	341	938	73.2	48.7	64.3	72.7	48.1	63.8
Italian, South	1,540	1,011	2,551	63.7	39.7	54.2	63.1	39.2	53.6
Lithuanian	557	276	833	69.3	47.1	61.9	64.3	34.8	54.5
Polish	383	187	570	78.9	69.0	75.6	73.4	59.4	68.8
Portuguese	56	69	125	48.2	43.5	45.6	48.2	43.5	45.6
Russian	174	141	315	79.3	69.5	74.9	75.9	61.0	69.2
Scotch	202	120	322	100.0	100.0	100.0	99.5	100.0	99.7
Syrian	368	318	686	74.2	36.8	56.9	73.9	34.6	55.7
Grand total	10,109	7,646	17,755	87.5	81.8	85.1	86.5	80.4	83.9
Total native-born of foreign father	1,607	1,911	3,518	99.8	99.4	99.6	99.7	99.4	99.5
Total native-born	2,295	2,459	4,754	99.7	99.6	99.6	99.7	99.5	99.6
Total foreign-born	7,814	5,187	13,001	84.0	73.3	79.7	82.7	71.3	78.1

a Not computed, owing to small number involved.
This table includes only nationalities with 80 or more persons reporting. The totals,'however, are for all nationalities.
Immigration Commission, "Woolen and Worsted Goods in Representative Community A," *Immigrants in Industries, Part 4: Woolen and Worsted Goods Manufacturing,* II, Immigration Commission, *Reports,* X, 61 Congress, 2 Session, Doc. 633 (Washington, 1911), p. 775.

Table X
ANALYSIS OF A.P.A. LECTURES IN LAWRENCE 1893, 1894

Topics	1893 Nov. 27	1894 May 14	May 21	May 28	June 4	June 11	June 18	Sept. 6	Sept. 19	Oct. 4	Oct. 18	Nov. 1	Total
Political Influence of Catholic Church													21
Church in Politics	1	2	1	2	2	1		1	2	1			13
Divided Allegiance		1	1	1	1				1	2			7
Educational Qualification for Vote Needed								1					1
Influence of Church on Education													14
No Public Money for Parochial Schools		1		1			2	1			1	1	7
No Catholics on School Boards	1					1	1	1					4
Support Public Schools		1						1					2
Inspect Schools (Parochial)		1											1
Other Dangers from Church													17
Jesuits and Convents		2				1							3
Should Tax Church		1				1		1					3
Make United States Catholic									1				1
Hierarchy		1							2		1	1	5
Danger to Institutions						1	1			1			3
Other Dangers			2										2
Dangers of Immigration													14
Should Restrict it	1	1	1					1	1			1	6
Swamp New England		1											1
Should Keep Out Worst Only				1				1					2
Radical Labor Influence or Anarchism								1		1		1	3
Danger to Institutions								1					1
Other			1										1
Americanism													17
Institutions		1		1		1		1		1			5
Be An American		1	1	1	2						1	1	7
Flag	1			1	1							1	4
Patriotism			1										1
Tolerance Desirable													12
Catholic Church Not under A.P.A. Attack	1	1		1		1	2	1		1			8
Church Necessary to Help Irish		1											1
Irish in Civil War		1		1									2
Do Not Molest Immigrants				1									1
Grand Total													95

The Evening Tribune, Nov. 27, 1893, May 14, 21, 28, June 4, 11, 18, Sept. 6, 19, Oct. 4, 18, Nov. 1, 1894.

Table XI
LAWRENCE MARRIAGE RATE
(Annual Rate per 1,000 Population)

1856-65	13.3
1865-70	13.0
1875-80	11.05
1865	14.88
1870	13.3 (5th of 28 in state)
1875	10.9 (3rd)
1880	11.2 (5th)
1885	9.3 (12th)
1890	10.61 (9th)
1895	11.77
1900	10.55
1905	11.04
1910	12.75

Report of Births, Marriages, and Deaths, XXIV (1865), cxxvi-cxxvii; XXIX (1870); XXXIX (1880); XLIII (1884), 31; XLIX (1890), 215, 372-373; LIV (1895), 130; LIX (1900), 140; LXIV (1905), 195; LXIX (1910), 6-7.

Table XII
PERCENTAGE OF FOREIGN-BORN OF TOTAL MARRYING IN LAWRENCE

Year	Marriages	Total Parti-cipat-ing*	Both Native-Born	Both For-eign-Born	Native Male, Foreign Female	Foreign Male, Native Female	Foreign-Born Partici-pating
1850	188	362	98	83	—	—	166
1853-55	Avg. 313	620	127	162	12	9	345
1855	328	656	120	185	15	8	(60) 393
1860	291	578	133	137	11	8	(51) 293
1865	323	642	121	164	14	22	(57) 364
1870	384	768	143	186	22	33	(54) 427
1875	380	760	152	173	19	36	(53) 401
1880	439	878	192	155	54	38	(48) 402
1885	361	722	115	176	40	30	(58) 422
1890	474	946	122	237	68	46	(62) 588
1895	614	1228	165	287	76	86	(60) 736
1900	660	1320	161	350	76	73	(64) 849
1905	799	1598	205	414	93	87	(63)1008
1910	1095	2190	267	662	82	84	(68)1490

* The Total Participating does not include those whose nativity was unknown. The latter was a very small number. Number in parentheses to left of Total Foreign-Born Participating is the percentage of the total known participants.
Report of Births, Marriages, and Deaths, IX (1850), 5; XIV (1855), 121; XIX (1860), vii; XXIV (1865), vii; XXIX (1870), vii; XXIV (1875), vii; XXXIX (1880), vii; XLIV (1885), vii; XLIX (1890), 7; LIV (1895), 7; LIX (1900), 7; LXIV (1905), 7; LXIX (1910), 7.

Table XIII
NATIVE AND FOREIGN-BORN ENDOGAMOUS MARRIAGES IN LAWRENCE

Husband	Wife	
	Native-Born	Foreign-Born
1855		
Native-Born	120(89)	15(11)
Foreign-Born	8(4)	185(96)
1860		
Native-Born	133(92)	11(8)
Foreign-Born	8(6)	137(94)
1865		
Native-Born	121(90)	14(10)
Foreign-Born	22(12)	164(88)
1870		
Native-Born	143(87)	22(13)
Foreign-Born	33(15)	186(85)
1875		
Native-Born	152(89)	19(11)
Foreign-Born	36(17)	173(83)
1880		
Native-Born	192(78)	54(22)
Foreign-Born	38(20)	155(80)
1885		
Native-Born	115(74)	40(26)
Foreign-Born	30(15)	176(85)
1890		
Native-Born	122(65)	68(35)
Foreign-Born	46(16)	237(84)
1895		
Native-Born	165(68)	76(32)
Foreign-Born	86(23)	287(77)
1900		
Native-Born	161(68)	76(32)
Foreign-Born	73(17)	350(83)
1905		
Native-Born	205(69)	93(31)
Foreign-Born	87(17)	414(83)
1910		
Native-Born	267(77)	82(23)
Foreign-Born	84(11)	662(83)

Number in parentheses indicates the percentage of the total marriages for each group.
Derived from *Report of Births, Marriages, and Deaths*, XIV (1855), vii; XIX (1860), vii; XXIV (1865), vii; XXIX (1870), vii; XXXIV (1875), vii; XXXIX (1880), vii; XLIV (1885), vii; XLIX (1890), 7; LIV (1895), 7; LIX (1900), 7; LXIV (1905), 7; LXIX (1910), 7.

218

Table XIV
INTER- AND INTRA-MARRIAGE IN LAWRENCE

Birthplace of Husband	Total	Birthplace of Wife			
		United States	North-western Europe	Ireland	Canada
1847-49					
United States	5			1	4
Northwestern Europe	27	3(11)	20(74)	4(15)	
Ireland	215	4(4)		207(96)	
Canada	5	3			2
Southeastern Europe					
Asia					
TOTAL	252				
1854					
United States	154	142(92)	2(1)	5(3)	5(3)
Northwestern Europe	27	6(22)	18(67)	3(11)	
Ireland	122	1	1	119(98)	1
Canada	1	1			
Southeastern Europe	1			1	
Asia					
TOTAL	305				
1865					
United States	155	139(90)	4(3)	6(4)	6(4)
Northwestern Europe	65	10(15)	47(72)	6(9)	2(3)
Ireland	112	8(7)	5(4)	97(88)	2(2)
Canada	16	4(25)	2(13)	3(19)	7(44)
Southeastern Europe					
Asia					
TOTAL	348				
1875					
United States	173	147(85)	11(6)	6(4)	9(5)
Northwestern Europe	91	28(31)	49(54)	13(14)	1(1)
Ireland	99	12(12)	12(12)	74(74)	1(1)
Canada	32	9(28)	1(3)	3(9)	19(59)
Southeastern Europe	3	1	1		1
Asia					
TOTAL	398				
1882					
United States	260	195(75)	19(7)	21(8)	25(10)
Northwestern Europe	117	19(16)	89(76)	6(5)	2(2) 1(1)*
Ireland	89	19(21)	7(8)	62(70)	1(1)
Canada	42	8(19)	3(7)	1(2)	30(71)
Southeastern Europe	5		1(20)		4(80)**
Asia					
TOTAL	513				

Table XIV (Continued)

Birthplace of Husband	Total	United States	North-western Europe	Ireland	Canada	South-eastern Europe	Asia
1894							
United States	257	183(71)	28(11)	23(9)	21(8)	1	1
Northwestern Europe	137	23(17)	96(70)	9(7)	9(7)		
Ireland	78	20(26)	9(12)	47(60)	2(3)		
Canada	79	17(22)	3(4)	4(5)	55(70)		
Southeastern Europe	15	2(13)	1(7)	1(7)		11(73)	
Asia	3		1		1		1
TOTAL	570						
1902							
United States	335	212(63)	43(13)	33(10)	47(14)		
Northwestern Europe	136	49(36)	70(51)	8(6)	9(7)		
Ireland	65	13(20)	3(5)	48(74)	1(2)		
Canada	163	40(25)	6(4)	7(4)	110(67)		
Southeastern Europe	169	5(3)	2(1)		1(1)	161(95)	
Asia	26	1(4)					25(96)
TOTAL	896						
1912							
United States	388	282(73)	28(7)	23(6)	51(13)	4(1)	
Northwestern Europe	166	48(29)	106(64)	7(4)	5(3)		
Ireland	43	9(21)	5(12)	28(65)	1(2)		
Canada	115	54(47)	4(3)	2(2)	55(48)		
Southeastern Europe	434	15(4)	1		1	417(96)	
Asia	38	2(5)					36(95)
TOTAL	1184						

* Wife born in Asia.
** Wife born in southeastern Europe.
The totals for 1894 and 1902 do not check because they include three husbands from an area not listed.
Northwestern Europe includes England, Scotland, France, Germany.
Canada includes also Newfoundland, Nova Scotia, Prince Edward Island.
Southeastern Europe includes Italy, Azores, Portugal, Greece, Russia, Poland, Austria-Hungary.
Asia includes Syria, Armenia, Turkey, China.
The numbers in parentheses are the percentages of the marriages by husbands of one group. Derived from Record of Marriages City of Lawrence, MSS, City Clerk's Office, Lawrence, Mass., I (1850-59), 88-110, 114-15; II (1860-66), 87-109; IV (1872-77), 69-95; V (1878-82), 115-38; VI (1882-86), 1-11; VIII (1891-95), 96-126; XI (1902), 1-50; XVI (1912-13), 1-93. Essex Institute, *Vital Records*.

Table XV

AGGREGATE OF INTER- AND INTRA-MARRIAGES IN LAWRENCE FOR THE YEARS 1847-1849, 1854, 1865, 1875, 1882, 1894, 1902, 1912

Birthplace of Husband	Total	Birthplace of Wife					
		United States	North-western Europe	Ireland	Canada	South-eastern Europe	Asia
United States	1727	1300	135	118	168	5	1
Northwestern Europe	766	186	495	56	28	—	1
Ireland	819	86	42	682	9	—	—
Canada	451	136	19	20	276	—	—
Southeastern Europe	626	23	6	2	2	593	—
Asia	77	3	—	1	1	—	72
TOTAL	4466						

Derived from same sources as above.

Table XVI

ANNUAL BIRTH RATE IN LAWRENCE
(Births per 1,000 population)

1856-65	32.9
1865-69	34.6
1870	25.4
1875	28.8
1880	25.6
1885	25.4
1890	28.9
1895	25.1
1900	33.6
1905	29.8
1910	36.6

Report of Births, Marriages, and Deaths, XXIV (1865), cxxvi; XXVIII (1869), cxx; XLIX (1890), 372; LIV (1895), 130; LIX (1900), 140; LXIV (1905), 195; LXIX (1910), 6.

Table XVII
DENSITY OF POPULATION IN LAWRENCE BY ETHNIC GROUPS, 1912

AVERAGE NUMBER OF PERSONS PER APARTMENT AND PER ROOM, BY
NATIONALITY OF HEAD OF HOUSEHOLD

Nationality of head of household	Households	Average number of persons per—	
		Apartment	Room
Canadian, French	5	6.60	1.57
English	1	4.00	1.00
French	4	5.25	1.05
German	3	6.33	1.36
Hebrew	9	7.22	1.44
Irish	1	7.00	1.75
Italian	123	6.78	1.48
Lithuanian	12	8.00	1.66
Polish	13	9.00	2.02
Portuguese	4	6.50	1.30
Russian	1	7.00	1.75
Syrian	12	6.67	1.54
Total	188	6.96	1.52

AVERAGE NUMBER OF PERSONS PER ROOM AND NUMBER OF HOUSEHOLDS
HAVING TWO OR MORE PERSONS PER ROOM, BY NATIONALITY OF
HEAD OF HOUSEHOLD

Nationality of head of household	Households	Average number of persons per room	Households having two or more persons per room
Canadian, French	5	1.57	2
English	1	1.00	—
French	4	1.05	—
German	3	1.36	—
Hebrew	9	1.44	2
Irish	1	1.75	—
Italian	123	1.48	26
Lithuanian	12	1.66	3
Polish	13	2.02	9
Portuguese	4	1.30	—
Russian	1	1.75	—
Syrian	12	1.54	1
Total	188	1.52	43

Table XVII (Continued)

NUMBER OF HOUSEHOLDS OCCUPYING APARTMENTS OF EACH SPECIFIED
NUMBER OF ROOMS, BY NATIONALITY OF HEAD OF HOUSEHOLD

Nationality of head of household	House-holds	Number of households occupying apartments of—						
		2 rooms	3 rooms	4 rooms	5 rooms	6 rooms	7 rooms	10 rooms
Canadian, French	5	—	1	3	—	1	—	—
English	1	—	—	1	—	—	—	—
French	4	—	—	1	2	1	—	—
German	3	—	—	1	2	—	—	—
Hebrew	9	—	—	—	9	—	—	—
Irish	1	—	—	1	—	—	—	—
Italian	123	1	7	44	67	2	1	1
Lithuanian	12	—	1	—	11	—	—	—
Polish	13	—	—	8	4	1	—	—
Portuguese	4	—	—	1	2	1	—	—
Russian	1	—	—	1	—	—	—	—
Syrian	12	—	3	4	3	2	—	—
Total	188	1	12	65	100	8	1	1

HOUSEHOLDS OCCUPYING APARTMENTS OF EACH SPECIFIED NUMBER OF ROOMS,
BY NUMBER OF PERSONS PER HOUSEHOLD

Number of persons in household	House-holds	Number of households occupying apartments of—						
		2 rooms	3 rooms	4 rooms	5 rooms	6 rooms	7 rooms	10 rooms
Two persons	6	1	—	4	1	—	—	—
Three persons	7	—	3	1	3	—	—	—
Four persons	26	—	4	9	11	1	—	1
Five persons	22	—	4	9	9	—	—	—
Six persons	31	—	—	17	13	—	1	—
Seven persons	26	—	—	10	13	3	—	—
Eight persons	24	—	1	8	15	—	—	—
Nine persons	17	—	—	5	11	1	—	—
Ten persons	9	—	—	—	9	—	—	—
Eleven persons	5	—	—	1	4	—	—	—
Twelve persons	7	—	—	1	5	1	—	—
Thirteen persons	1	—	—	—	1	—	—	—
Fourteen persons	2	—	—	—	2	—	—	—
Fifteen persons	2	—	—	—	1	1	—	—
Sixteen persons	2	—	—	—	1	1	—	—
Seventeen persons	1	—	—	—	1	—	—	—
Total	188	1	12	65	100	8	1	1

Table XVII (Continued)

HOUSEHOLDS OF EACH SPECIFIED NUMBER OF PERSONS, BY NATIONALITY OF
HEAD OF HOUSEHOLD

Nationality of head of household	Households	Average number of persons per household	Households of each specified number of persons															
			2	3	4	5	6	7	8	9	10	11	12	13	14	15	16	17
Canadian, French	5	6.60	—	—	3	—	—	—	—	1	—	—	1	—	—	—	—	—
English	1	4.00	—	—	1	—	—	—	—	—	—	—	—	—	—	—	—	—
French	4	5.25	1	—	1	—	1	—	—	1	—	—	—	—	—	—	—	—
German	3	6.33	—	—	—	1	1	—	1	—	—	—	—	—	—	—	—	—
Hebrew	9	7.22	—	1	1	1	1	1	1	1	—	1	1	—	—	—	—	—
Irish	1	7.00	—	—	—	—	—	1	—	—	—	—	—	—	—	—	—	—
Italian	123	6.78	4	6	18	14	25	15	12	9	8	2	5	1	2	1	1	—
Lithuanian	12	8.00	—	—	1	1	—	3	4	1	1	—	—	—	—	1	—	—
Polish	13	9.00	1	—	—	1	1	1	3	2	—	2	—	—	—	—	1	1
Portuguese	4	6.50	—	—	—	1	1	1	1	—	—	—	—	—	—	—	—	—
Russian	1	7.00	—	—	—	—	—	1	—	—	—	—	—	—	—	—	—	—
Syrian	12	6.67	—	—	1	3	1	3	2	2	—	—	—	—	—	—	—	—
Total	188	6.96	6	7	26	22	31	26	24	17	9	5	7	1	2	2	2	1

Charles P. Neill, *Report on Strike of Textile Workers in Lawrence, Mass. in 1912*, 62 Congress, 2 Session, Senate Doc. 870 (Washington, 1912), pp. 156-58.

Table XVIII
EARNINGS OF EMPLOYEES IN LAWRENCE, 1909
PER CENT OF MALE EMPLOYEES 18 YEARS OF AGE OR OVER EARNING EACH
SPECIFIED AMOUNT PER WEEK, BY GENERAL NATIVITY

General nativity	Number reporting complete data	Average earnings per week	Per cent earning each specified amount per week					
			$5 or over	$7.50 or over	$10 or over	$12.50 or over	$15 or over	$20 or over
Native-born of native father, white	540	$11.03	100.0	91.5	58.1	33.3	12.0	2.2
Native-born of foreign father, by country of birth of father:								
Canada	126	10.78	100.0	88.9	61.1	31.0	10.3	.0
England	286	11.39	99.7	94.4	64.3	37.8	8.4	1.4
Germany	150	11.53	100.0	96.0	70.7	34.0	16.0	.7
Ireland	494	10.54	99.8	91.9	50.8	28.7	7.5	.2
Foreign-born, by place of birth:								
Armenian	123	7.46	99.2	46.3	10.6	.0	.0	.0
Canadian, French	331	10.80	100.0	93.4	58.0	27.5	10.0	.0
English	1,563	11.39	99.9	95.8	64.0	37.3	13.2	.6
French	234	11.07	100.0	96.6	75.6	20.9	4.7	.4
German	538	11.17	100.0	95.0	69.7	29.6	13.0	.2
Hebrew, Russian	84	9.07	100.0	81.0	34.5	2.4	.0	.0
Irish	551	10.21	99.8	94.9	45.9	22.5	6.0	.2
Italian, North	563	7.35	100.0	51.9	2.5	.4	.0	.0
Italian, South	1,371	6.84	100.0	27.9	1.1	.5	.1	.0
Lithuanian	550	7.82	99.6	58.2	8.4	2.4	.0	.0
Polish	375	8.01	100.0	50.7	15.5	3.7	.8	.0
Russian	170	8.59	100.0	77.1	20.0	4.7	.0	.0
Scotch	189	11.42	100.0	94.7	66.7	39.2	12.7	.5
Syrian	334	7.33	100.0	31.1	7.5	1.8	.3	.0
Grand total	8,973	9.55	99.9	73.4	38.9	19.4	6.4	.4
Total native-born of foreign father	1,135	10.96	99.8	92.4	58.9	32.4	9.3	.7
Total native-born	1,675	10.98	99.9	92.1	58.6	32.7	10.2	1.2
Total foreign-born	7,298	9.23	99.9	69.1	34.4	16.3	5.5	.2

Table XVIII (Continued)

PER CENT OF FEMALE EMPLOYEES 18 YEARS OF AGE OR OVER EARNING EACH
SPECIFIED AMOUNT PER WEEK, BY GENERAL NATIVITY

General nativity	Number reporting complete data	Average earnings per week	Per cent earning each specified amount per week				
			$5 or over	$7.50 or over	$10 or over	$12.50 or over	$15 or over
Native-born of native father, white	414	$8.03	98.8	53.4	15.2	0.5	0.2
Native-born of foreign father, by country of birth of father:							
Canada	217	8.06	97.2	63.1	18.0	1.8	.0
England	223	7.89	99.1	49.8	14.3	1.8	.0
Germany	168	8.94	98.8	74.4	34.5	3.6	.0
Ireland	658	8.13	99.2	55.0	16.9	1.2	.0
Foreign-born, by place of birth:							
Canadian, French	523	8.64	99.6	72.5	26.2	4.4	.0
Canadian, Other	170	8.52	99.4	59.4	27.6	2.9	.6
English	687	8.39	99.7	57.1	22.6	4.1	.1
French	165	9.32	100.0	67.9	42.4	4.8	.0
German	211	9.53	99.5	82.0	45.5	7.6	.9
Irish	495	8.24	99.8	52.7	21.6	1.4	.0
Italian, North	301	6.77	100.0	23.9	1.0	.0	.0
Italian, South	902	6.39	99.9	6.9	.0	.0	.0
Lithuanian	263	7.14	100.0	31.6	6.5	2.7	.0
Polish	182	7.10	100.0	29.1	4.4	1.1	.0
Russian	123	7.24	100.0	25.2	7.3	.0	.0
Scotch	115	9.06	99.1	70.4	37.4	7.0	.0
Syrian	282	6.73	100.0	14.2	1.8	.0	.0
Grand total	6,467	7.85	99.5	45.8	16.3	2.0	.1
Total native-born of foreign father	1,355	8.18	99.8	57.9	18.9	1.7	.0
Total native-born	1,771	8.14	98.8	56.7	18.0	1.5	.1
Total foreign-born	4,696	7.74	99.8	41.7	15.6	2.3	.1

This table includes only races with 80 or more reporting. The totals, however, are for all races.
The table shows wages or earnings for the period indicated, but no account is taken of voluntary lost time or lost time from shutdowns or other causes. In the various tables in this report showing annual earnings allowance is made for time lost during the year.
Immigration Commission, "Community A," pp. 757-58.

Table XIX
OCCUPATIONS, LAWRENCE, 1880

Selected Occupations	Total	Nativity				
		United States	Ireland	Germany	Great Britain	Canada
All occupations	19,153	8729	4799	637	2805	2044
Agriculture	142	89	25	1	12	15
Professional and personal service	2425	984	970	24	130	284
Boarding-house keepers	55	38	8	1	—	7
Domestic servants	556	235	217	2	17	78
Hotel employees	74	42	15	—	4	11
Laborers	1029	171	641	6	64	143
Launderers	65	28	21	2	2	6
Government employees	88	68	11	3	5	1
Physicians	52	39	2	1	4	6
Teachers	140	116	10	—	2	12
Trade, transportation	1746	1101	343	38	148	106
Clerks	497	374	36	5	36	41
Peddlers	82	31	25	6	19	1
Saloon keepers	112	22	63	8	14	5
Traders, dealers	555	323	128	13	58	30
Draymen, teamsters	163	109	36	1	4	13
Railroad officials, employees	193	135	39	1	5	12
Manufacturing, mechanical pursuits	14,840	6555	3461	574	2515	1639
Blacksmiths	121	53	38	—	13	16
Boot, shoe makers	89	23	26	10	15	14
Masons, stone cutters	181	93	53	4	11	18
Carpenters	492	300	54	11	59	67
Cigar makers	79	40	10	—	26	3
Textile mill workers	10,395	4111	2626	448	1865	1272
Workers in other manufacturing establishments	104	75	14	—	9	5
Engineers, firemen	93	44	21	2	22	3
Iron, steel workers	92	44	26	—	16	4
Machinists	528	302	55	9	106	54
Factory operatives (other)	227	91	36	24	65	10
Painters	198	134	19	6	27	10
Paper mill workers	384	162	150	6	30	35
Tailors, dressmakers	568	375	83	7	46	54

Derived from *Tenth Census . . . 1880*, I, 882.

Table XX
OCCUPATIONS, LAWRENCE, 1900

| Selected Occupations | Total | Native White | | Foreign White | Parentage | | | | |
		Native Parentage	Foreign Parentage		Ireland	Great Britain	Germany	Canada	Italy, Poland, Russia
MALES	20,111	3074	4919	12,031	5582	3413	1494	3797	1029
Agricultural pursuits	196	27	38	131	53	16	7	70	9
Professional service	525	214	161	149	124	73	32	44	3
Personal service	2352	238	478	1559	1001	213	80	495	129
Laborers	1463	89	240	1132	695	98	26	387	113
Servants	133	12	20	89	48	16	8	19	3
Watchmen, policemen	198	61	41	96	67	33	9	21	1
Trade, transportation	3649	1041	1053	1552	1056	445	188	613	152
Bookkeepers, clerks	517	191	218	108	130	94	32	45	1
Draymen, teamsters	560	93	141	326	220	47	21	153	—
Merchants	752	174	173	404	183	94	55	115	88
Salesmen	626	160	249	217	157	79	44	134	17
Steam railroad employees	417	158	73	185	145	31	3	70	—
Manufacturing and mechanical pursuits	13,389	1554	3189	8640	3348	2666	1187	2575	736
Bleachery, dye workers	463	40	132	290	195	113	9	35	28
Carpenters	988	239	166	583	132	128	78	359	1
Machinists	715	172	207	336	150	231	32	84	5
Masons	324	32	64	228	144	21	21	85	5
Painters	415	99	134	182	111	67	21	91	—
Paper mill workers	266	27	64	175	121	31	4	42	30
Plumbers	237	32	120	85	101	50	19	21	—
Tailors	101	5	18	74	23	21	15	11	9
Textile mill workers	866	45	238	583	211	231	97	195	17
Woolen mill workers	3152	142	628	2382	632	675	463	266	424
Worsted mill workers	667	38	146	488	206	167	106	41	49
FEMALES	10,143	1242	3427	5442	3615	1405	538	2178	324
Professional service	357	147	160	50	121	46	8	27	—
Personal service	1349	246	194	882	588	149	47	205	8
Servants	821	104	125	573	407	79	21	136	3
Trade, transportation	765	215	332	218	222	134	34	100	14
Manufacturing and mechanical pursuits	7671	634	2741	4291	2684	1076	449	1845	302
Cotton mill workers	2682	159	871	1652	920	310	99	908	76
Dressmakers	450	95	156	198	137	55	12	123	3
Textile mill workers	746	63	289	394	254	129	28	187	17
Woolen mill workers	2654	147	924	1583	924	382	242	474	184
Worsted mill workers	707	52	307	348	316	137	61	74	19

Derived from *Twelfth Census . . . 1900, Occupations*, 588-91.

Table XXI
WINNING PARTY IN LAWRENCE ELECTION RESULTS, 1850-1922

	President	Governor	Mayor
1850		W	
1851		W	
1852		W	
1853		W	D
1854		K-N	K-N
1855		K-N	K-N
1856	R	K-N	R
1857		R	R
1858		R	R
1859		R	D
1860	R	R	R
1861		R	R
1862		R	R
1863		R	R
1864	R	R	R
1865		R	R
1866		R	D
1867		R	D
1868	R	R	R
1869		D	D
1870		D	R
1871		D	R
1872	R	R	D
1873		D	D
1874		D	R
1875		D	D
1876	R	D	D
1877		D	R
1878		D	R
1879		D	R
1880	R	D	R
1881		R	D
1882		D	D
1883		D	D
1884	R	R	R
1885		D	D
1886		D	D
1887		D	R
1888	D	D	R
1889		D	D
1890		D	R
1891		D	D
1892	D	D	R
1893		D	D
1894		D	D
1895		R	R

Table XXI (Continued)

	President	Governor	Mayor
1896	R	R	R
1897		R	R
1898		D	R
1899		D	D
1900	D	R	D
1901		D	D
1902		D	D
1903		D	D
1904	R	D	D
1905		D	D
1906		R	D
1907		R	D
1908	R	D	R
1909		D	R
1910		D	D
1911		D	
1912	D	D	
1913		D	
1914		D	
1915		D	
1916	D	D	
1917		D	
1918		D	
1919		D	
1920	R	R	
1921		—	
1922		D	

R—Republican.   D—Democratic.   W—Whig.   K-N—Know-Nothing.
Record of Elections in the City of Lawrence, I, II, MSS City Clerk's Office, Lawrence, Mass. This covers the elections from 1853 on. For the 1850-52 results see *The Lawrence Courier*, Nov. 16, 1850, Nov. 15, 1851, Nov. 9, 1852.

Table XXII
SUMMARY OF WARD AND PRECINCT VOTING RECORDS

15 State Elections on Even-numbered Years, 1854-1882 Number of years went Democratic*	15 State Elections on Even-numbered Years, 1884-1912 Number of years went Democratic* 1884-98 (1899-)	
Ward One: 2	Precinct I (I) II (II) (III)	2 13 1 (out of 7)
Ward Two: 4	Precinct III (IV) IV (V) (VI)	1 15 3 (out of 4)
Ward Three: 9	Precinct V (VII) VI (VIII) (IX)	12 15 4 (out of 4)
Ward Four: 7	Precinct VII (X) VIII (XI) (XII)	11 5 (out of 7) 7 (out of 7)
Ward Five: 2	Precinct IX IX** (XIV) (XV) X (XV) (XIV) XIII** (XIII)	1 (out of 3) 1 (out of 12) 2 2 (out of 12)
Ward Six: 8	Precinct XI (XI) (XVII) XII** (XVI, XVIII)	1 (out of 12) 12 (out of 13) 5 (out of 13)

* Unless otherwise stated the number is out of 15 years.
** Precincts 1889-
For a picture of the various ward and precinct boundaries, see Map V, p. 148.
Until 1884 Lawrence had only six wards and no precincts. In 1884 eleven precincts were established, I-X north of the river and XI south. In 1889 Pct. XI was divided into Pcts. XI and XII, and Pct. IX (southern part of Tower Hill) was subdivided into Pcts. IX and XIII. There were a few boundary adjustments in the precincts in Wards II, III, IV in 1889 also. In 1899 there was a complete renumbering of the precincts, done in such a way that each ward was eventually to have three precincts instead of the original two. In the chart above, the precincts are listed opposite the wards within which they were located. The first row of precinct numbers are those in effect 1884-98. The precinct numbers in parentheses are those in effect after 1898 and they are placed next to their approximate equivalent in the first system. Precincts VI and IX in the new system were not so numbered until 1905.
The precincts in 1884 to 1912 that were most consistently Democratic were as follows:

("The Plains" Area)	Pct. IV(V)	15 out of 15 elections
("The Plains" Area)	Pct. VI(VIII)	15 out of 15
(The Shanty Area)	Pct. XI(XVII)	13 out of 15
	Pct. II(II)	13 out of 15
	Pct. V(VII)	12 out of 15
	Pct. VII(X)	11 out of 15
	Pct. VIII(XI)	10 out of 15

Those that went Democratic least often were:

Pct. III(IV)	1 out of 15
(Prospect Hill) Pct. I	2 out of 15
(Tower Hill) Pct. IX(XIV)(XV)	2 out of 15
(Tower Hill) Pct. X(XV)(XIV)	2 out of 15
Outskirts of So. Lawrence	
Pct. XII(XVI)	5 out of 13

Record of Elections, I, 19, 43, 68, 98, 127, 152, 181, 218, 253, 305, 343, 392, 440; II, 2, 29, 57, 79, 107, 128, 151, 168, 192, 212, 232, 259, 286, 305, 323, 339, 370.

Table XXIII

CHRONOLOGY OF THE STRIKE OF 1912

Mon.	Jan.	1	New government installed.
Wed.	Jan.	10	Italian meeting; Rocco telegraphed Ettor.
Thurs.	Jan.	11	All Italians decided to strike.
Fri.	Jan.	12	Start of strike; violence at Wood and Washington Mills.
Sat.	Jan.	13	Quiet; meeting led by Ettor at City Hall.
Mon.	Jan.	15	Snow storm; picketing; 15,000 paraded; militia arrived; Syrian stabbed.
Tues.	Jan.	16	Parade; Golden arrived.
Wed.	Jan.	17	10,000 paraded from Common to mills; stopped by militia.
Thurs.	Jan.	18	Parade led by Syrian Band and Marad.
Fri.	Jan.	19	Some scabs reported at work; dynamite found.
Sat.	Jan.	20	Giovannitti arrived.
Wed.	Jan.	24	Haywood arrived; Thomson and Flynn also.
Thurs.	Jan.	25	Pinkertons reported.
Fri.	Jan.	26	Ettor and Wood met in Boston.
Mon.	Jan.	29	Street cars attacked on Broadway—ice and stones; policeman stabbed; Annie LoPezzi shot and killed.
Tues.	Jan.	30	Ettor and Giovannitti arrested.
Wed.	Jan.	31	Ettor in court; Breen arrested.
Thurs.	Feb.	1	Ettor in jail.
Fri.	Feb.	2	Dynamite defenders acquitted; Breen tried in police court.
Sat.	Feb.	3	Breen held over for grand jury.
Mon.	Feb.	5	Peaceful.
Tues.	Feb.	6	Berger resolution in Congress.
Thurs.	Feb.	8	Mass. legislative committee to Lawrence; resolutions in Congress.
Sat.	Feb.	10	150 children to New York.
Mon.	Feb.	12	Ettor-Giovannitti hearings.
Tues.	Feb.	13	Immigrants leaving Lawrence for Europe.
Sat.	Feb.	17	150 more children left for New York; parade in New York to greet them.
Wed.	Feb.	21	Ettor and Giovannitti held for grand jury.
Thurs.	Feb.	22	Children prevented from leaving city; more scabbing reported.
Sat.	Feb.	24	More children stopped.
Sun.	Feb.	25	Meetings held in all halls.
Mon.	Feb.	26	Rumor that Italians were going back to work.
Fri.	Mar.	1	Wage concessions by Wood; workers left to testify in Washington.
Wed.	Mar.	6	Haywood to Washington to testify.
Wed.	Mar.	13	Committee decided to accept wage increase offered.
Thurs.	Mar.	14	Mass meeting on the Common supported decision of strike committee.
Mon.	Mar.	18	Strike over; a few Italians not taken back.
Sat.	Mar.	30	All children reported back in Lawrence.

Sources all indicated in Chapter X.

Selected Bibliography

I. PRIMARY MATERIAL

A. MASSACHUSETTS CENSUS REPORTS

Chief of the Bureau of Statistics of Labor. *Census of . . . Massachusetts 1905,* I. Boston, 1909.

DeWitt, Francis. *Abstract of the Census of . . . Massachusetts . . . 1855. . . .* Boston, 1857.

Wadlin, Horace G. *Census of . . . Massachusetts: 1895,* I, II, VII. Boston, 1896-1900.

Warner, Oliver. *Abstract of the Census of Massachusetts, 1860. . . .* Boston, 1863.

Warner, Oliver. *Abstract of the Census of Massachusetts,— 1865. . . .* Boston, 1867.

Wright, Carroll D. *Census of Massachusetts: 1875,* I, II. Boston, 1876-77.

Wright, Carroll D. *The Census of Massachusetts: 1880. . . .* Boston, 1883.

Wright, Carroll D. *The Census of Massachusetts: 1885,* I. Boston, 1887-88.

B. UNITED STATES CENSUS REPORTS

United States Census Office. *Ninth Census of the United States . . . 1870,* I. Washington, 1872.

United States Census Office. *Tenth Census of the United States . . . 1880,* I, XII, XVIII. Washington, 1883, 1886.

United States Census Office. *Eleventh Census of the United States: 1890,* I, II, XVII, XXIII. Washington, 1895-97.

United States Census Office. *Eleventh Census of the United States: 1890, Report on the Social Statistics of Cities. . . .* Washington, 1895.

United States Census Office. *Twelfth Census of the United States . . . 1900,* I, II, III. Washington, 1901-1902.

United States Census Bureau. *Twelfth Census of the United States, Special Reports, Occupations.* Washington, 1904.

United States Census Bureau. *Thirteenth Census . . . 1910. Abstract of the Census . . . with Supplement for Massachusetts. . . .* Boston, 1913.

United States Census Bureau. *Fourteenth Census of the United States . . . 1920,* III. Washington, 1922.

C. LAWRENCE GOVERNMENT DOCUMENTS

Assessors' Street Lists of Polls . . . 1884, 1894, 1902, 1912. Lawrence, 1884, 1894, 1902, 1912.

City Charter, City of Lawrence Adopted State Election November 7th, 1911. N.p., n.d.

City of Lawrence. Deaths, MSS, City Clerk's Office, Lawrence, Mass., XII (1911-13).

Lawrence Board of Health. *Report.* 1879-1912.

Lawrence City Documents, 1872-1912.

Librarian of the Free Public Library of the City of Lawrence. *Report,* 1873-1912.

Record of Elections in the City of Lawrence, MSS, City Clerk's Office, Lawrence, Mass., I (1853-80), II (1880-1923).

Record of Marriages City of Lawrence, MSS, City Clerk's Office, Lawrence, Mass. I (1850-59), II (1860-66), IV (1872-77), V (1878-82), VI (1882-86), VIII (1891-95), XI (1902), XVI (1912-13).

School Committee of . . . Lawrence. *Annual Report,* 1847-1912.

D. MASSACHUSETTS, ESSEX COUNTY, AND BOSTON GOVERNMENT DOCUMENTS

"An Act to Incorporate the Town of Lawrence," MS, Massachusetts Archives, Acts 1847, Ch. 190, House Doc. 136, passed by House, April 9, 1847; and Senate April 15, 1847.

An Act to Revise the Charter of the City of Lawrence, 1911. Massachusetts Acts 1911, Ch. 621.

Bureau of Statistics of Labor [of Massachusetts]. *Annual Report,* 1870-1913.

Bureau of Statistics of Labor. "Fall River, Lowell, and Lawrence," *Thirteenth Annual Report . . . 1882,* Mass. Pub. Doc. 31, pp. 193-415.

Massachusetts Board of Health. *Annual Report,* 1870-1912, Mass. Pub. Doc. 34.

Petition to Establish the Town of Lawrence, MS, Massachusetts Archives, Acts 1847, Ch. 190.

Public Documents of Massachusetts, 1857-1912.

Report . . . Relating to the Registry and Return of Births, Marriages, and Deaths . . . , 1850-1912, Mass. Pub. Doc. 1.

[Shattuck, Lemuel]. *Sanitary Survey of the Town of Lawrence.* Boston, 1850.

Transcript of the Trial of *Commonwealth* vs. *Joseph Caruso, Joseph J. Ettor, Arturo Giovannitti, alias.* Superior Court, Essex County, Massachusetts, September-October, 1912. 6 vols. Typewritten MSS of first four volumes in possession of Charles Mahoney, Lawrence, Mass.

E. UNITED STATES GOVERNMENT DOCUMENTS

Board of Trade of London. *Cost of Living in American Towns,* 62 Congress, 1 Session, Senate Doc. 22. Washington, 1911.

Immigration Commission. "Woolen and Worsted Goods in Representative Community A," *Immigrants in Industries, Part 4: Woolen and Worsted Goods Manufacturing,* II, Immigration Commission, *Reports,* X, 61 Congress, 2 Session, Doc. 633. Washington, 1911.

Neill, Charles P. *Report on Strike of Textile Workers in Lawrence, Mass. in 1912,* 62 Congress, 2 Session, Senate Doc. 870. Washington, 1912.

The Strike at Lawrence, Mass. Hearings before the Committee on Rules of the House of Representatives . . . 1912, 62 Congress, 2 Session, House Doc. 671. Washington, 1912.

F. NEWSPAPERS (Lawrence, Mass., unless followed by *)

Al-Wafa, April 16, 1907-May 10, 1910.

Anzeiger und Post, 1899-1912.

*Boston Evening Transcript,** Jan.-Mar., 1912.

Le Courrier de Lawrence, June, 1911-Dec., 1912.

The Essex Eagle, 1867-76.

The Evening Tribune, 1890-1921; Centennial Edition, 1953.

Lawrence American, 1862-66, 1877-89, Jan. 3-June 27, 1890.

The Lawrence Courier, 1847-61.

Lawrence Journal, 1877-88.

The Lawrence Sentinel, 1861-76.

The Lawrence Sun, 1905-12.

The Merrimack Courier, 1846-47.

Municipal Records and Memoranda, 1856-1859, 6 vols. Scrapbooks of clippings from *The Lawrence Courier, Lawrence American,* and *The Lawrence Sentinel.*

*The New York Call,** Jan.-Feb., 1912, Sunday edition Jan.-Mar., 1912.

*The New York Times,** Mar.-April, 1882; Jan.-Mar., 1912; Jan. 24-May 25, 1919.

Le Progrès, Dec. 30, 1898-July 30, 1908.

Shapleigh, Elizabeth. "Occupational Disease in the Textile Industry," *The New York Call,** Dec. 29, 1912, p. 13.

Solidarity,* Sept.-Dec., 1910, 1911, Jan.-April, Sept.-Oct., 1912.

Sunday Sun, 1905-12.

The Weekly People* (New York), Dec. 16, 1905, Jan.-Mar., 1912.

G. MAGAZINE ARTICLES TO 1913

Child, Richard W. "The Industrial Revolt at Lawrence," *Collier's Weekly,* XLVIII (1911-12), 13-15.

Deland, Lorin F. "The Lawrence Strike: A Study," *Atlantic Monthly,* CIX (1912), 694-705.

"The Exoneration of William M. Wood," *The Outlook,* CIV (1913), 351-52.

Gompers, Samuel. "The Lawrence Dynamite Conspiracy," *American Federationist,* XIX (1912), 815-23.

Lauck, W. Jett. "The Significance of the Situation at Lawrence: The Condition of the New England Woolen Mill Operative," *The Survey,* XXVII (1911-12), 1772-74.

"The Lawrence Strike: A Review," *The Outlook,* C (1912), 531-36.

"The Lawrence Strike from Various Angles," *The Survey,* XXVIII (1912), 65-82.

McPherson, John B. *The Lawrence Strike of 1912.* Reprinted from *Bulletin of the National Association of Wool Manufacturers.* Boston, Sept., 1912.

Pratt, Walter M. "The Lawrence Revolution," *New England Magazine,* XLVI (1912), 7-16.

Weyl, Walter E. "The Strikers in Lawrence," *The Outlook,* C (1912), 309-12.

Woods, Robert. "The Breadth and Depth of the Lawrence Outcome," *The Survey,* XXVIII (1912), 67-68.

Young, George H. "The City of Lawrence, Massachusetts," *New England Magazine,* New Series, XVII (1897-98), 581-97.

H. SOCIAL AND ECONOMIC SOURCES

An Authentic History of the Lawrence Calamity. . . . Boston, 1860.

The Essex Institute. *Vital Records of Lawrence Massachusetts to the End of the Year 1849.* Salem, Mass., 1926.

Ladies Union Charitable Society. *Report . . . of the Lawrence General Hospital . . . ,* I (1876), XI-XXXII (1886-1907), XXXIV-XXXVII (1909-12).

Lawrence City Mission. *Annual Report,* III (1862), VI-LIII (1865-1912).
The Lawrence Directory, 1848, 1853, 1857, 1859, 1912.
Life of Wm. M. Wood, Typewritten MS, Baker Library, Harvard.
O'Connor, Alice W. "A Study of the Immigration Problem in Lawrence, Massachusetts" (unpublished social worker's thesis, Lawrence, 1914).
Pacific Mills. *General Regulations.* N.p., n.d.
Todd, Robert E., and Frank B. Sanborn. *The Report of the Lawrence Survey.* Lawrence, 1912.

I. IDEOLOGICAL AND RELIGIOUS SOURCES

Augustinian Fathers, Lawrence, Mass. *Our Parish Calendar,* I-II (1896-98), IV (1899-1900), X-XVII (1905-13).
Citizens' Association, Lawrence, Mass. Five Pamphlets. Lawrence, 1912-1913.
Lawrence, William. *Memories of a Happy Life.* Boston, 1926.
Letters from William R. Lawrence to his father, A. A. Lawrence, Collection of A. A. Lawrence Letters, MSS, Massachusetts Historical Society Library, XLV-XLVIII.
Mahoney, John J. and H. H. Chamberlin. *A Statement of Aims and Principles* (National Security League, *The Lawrence Plan for Education in Citizenship, No. 1).* New York, 1918.
O'Keefe, Katherine A. *Sketch of Catholicity in Lawrence and Vicinity.* Lawrence, 1882.
Paroisse Sainte-Anne, Lawrence, Mass., *Congrégation des Daes de Ste. Anne.* Salem, Mass., 1908, 1912-13, 1916-17.
Paroisse Sainte-Anne, Lawrence, Mass., *Congrégation des Enfants de Marie.* Lawrence, 1909-12.
Sainte Anne's Church. *Bulletin Paroissial.* Lawrence, 1909-13.

J. INTERVIEWS

Interview with Angelo Rocco by Professor Edwin Fenton, 1951.
Interview with Dr. Constant Calitri by Professor Edwin Fenton, 1951.
Interview with Farris Marad by Professor Edwin Fenton, 1951.

K. MISCELLANEOUS SOURCES

Ebert, Justus. *The Trial of a New Society.* Cleveland, 1913.
The Industrial Workers of the World. *Ettor and Giovannitti before the Jury . . . 1912.* Chicago, 1912.

L. MAPS AND ATLASES

Barker, James K. *Map of the City of Lawrence, Mass.* Boston, 1853.

Hopkins and Co., G. M., pub. *City Atlas of Lawrence, Massachusetts, 1875.* Philadelphia, 1875.

Map of Lawrence 1880 from United States Census Office, *Tenth Census of the United States 1880, Report of the Social Statistics of Cities,* Part I, 228. Washington, 1886.

Sampson, Murdock, and Co. *Map of the City of Lawrence.* Boston, 1900.

II. SECONDARY MATERIAL

A. HISTORIES

Dorgan, Maurice B. *History of Lawrence, Mass. with War Records.* Cambridge, Mass., 1924.

Hayes, Jonathan F. C. *History of the City of Lawrence, Mass.* Lawrence, 1868.

Paradise, Scott H., and Claude M. Fuess. *The Story of Essex County.* 4 vols. New York, 1935.

Wadsworth, Horace A., comp. *History of Lawrence, Mass. . . .* Lawrence, 1879.

B. OTHER SECONDARY WORKS

Berthoff, Rowland Tappan. *British Immigrants in Industrial America, 1790-1950.* Cambridge, Mass., 1953.

Copeland, Melvin. *The Cotton Manufacturing Industry in the United States.* Cambridge, Mass., 1912.

Ford, James. *Co-operation in New England Urban and Rural.* New York, 1913.

Handlin, Oscar. *Boston's Immigrants.* Cambridge, Mass., 1941.

Smith, F. Morton. *The Essex Company on the Merrimack at Lawrence.* New York, 1947.

Solomon, Barbara M. *Ancestors and Immigrants.* Cambridge, Mass., 1956.

Walsh, Alice L. *A Sketch of the Life and Labors of the Rev. James T. O'Reilly. . . .* Lawrence, 1924.

Ware, Caroline. *The Early New England Cotton Manufactures.* Cambridge, Mass., 1931.

Index